ROLAND PARKER

Serverless Architecture with JavaScrip

Building Scalable Applications with AWS Lambda, Google Cloud Functions, and Azure Functions

Copyright © 2024 by ROLAND PARKER

All rights reserved. No part of this publication may be reproduced, stored or transmitted in any form or by any means, electronic, mechanical, photocopying, recording, scanning, or otherwise without written permission from the publisher. It is illegal to copy this book, post it to a website, or distribute it by any other means without permission.

First edition

This book was professionally typeset on Reedsy.
Find out more at reedsy.com

Contents

INTRODUCTION	1
CHAPTER 1: UNDERSTANDING SERVERLESS ARCHITECTURE	9
CHAPTER 2: SETTING UP YOUR SERVERLESS ENVIRONMENT	37
CHAPTER 3: AWS LAMBDA FUNDAMENTALS	66
4.1 Introduction to Google Cloud Functions	94
4.1.1 What Are Google Cloud Functions?	95
4.1.2 Core Features of Google Cloud Functions	96
4.1.3 Use Cases for Google Cloud Functions	98
Summary	99
4.2 Creating and Deploying Google Cloud Functions with...	100
4.2.1 Setting Up Your Environment	101
4.2.2 Creating Your First Google Cloud Function	102
4.2.3 Deploying Your Google Cloud Function	104
4.2.4 Testing Your Cloud Function	106
4.2.5 Updating and Managing Your Function	107
Summary	108
4.3 Integrating Google Cloud Functions with Other Google...	109
4.3.1 Integrating with Cloud Pub/Sub	110
4.3.2 Integrating with Cloud Storage	112
4.3.3 Integrating with Firestore	114
4.3.4 Additional Integrations	116
Summary	117
4.4 Securing Google Cloud Functions with IAM Roles	118
4.4.1 Understanding IAM Roles and Permissions	119
4.4.2 Securing HTTP Triggered Functions	120
4.4.3 Securing Functions Triggered by Cloud Events	122

4.4.4 Best Practices for Securing Google Cloud Functions	123
Summary	124
4.5 Monitoring and Debugging Google Cloud Functions	125
4.5.1 Monitoring with Google Cloud Monitoring	126
4.5.2 Logging with Google Cloud Logging	128
4.5.3 Debugging Google Cloud Functions	130
Summary	131
4.6 Google Cloud Functions vs. AWS Lambda: Key Differences	132
4.6.1 Language Support	133
4.6.2 Triggering Mechanisms	134
4.6.3 Deployment and Management Tools	135
4.6.4 Pricing Models	136
4.6.5 Cold Start Performance	137
4.6.6 Ecosystem and Integration	138
Summary	139
4.7 Best Practices for Google Cloud Functions	140
4.7.1 Keep Functions Small and Focused	141
4.7.2 Optimize Function Performance	142
4.7.3 Leverage Environment Variables	143
4.7.4 Implement Proper Error Handling	144
4.7.5 Monitor and Log Effectively	145
4.7.6 Secure Your Functions	146
Conclusion	147
CHAPTER 5: SERVERLESS STORAGE SOLUTIONS	148
5.1 Storing Data with AWS S3 in Serverless Applications	149
5.1.1 Key Features of AWS S3	150
5.1.2 Using AWS S3 with Serverless Applications	151
5.1.3 Best Practices for Using AWS S3	153
Summary	154
5.2 Using Google Cloud Storage with Serverless Architecture	155
5.2.1 Key Features of Google Cloud Storage	156
5.2.2 Setting Up Google Cloud Storage	157
5.2.3 Best Practices for Using Google Cloud Storage	159

Summary	160
5.3 Integrating AWS DynamoDB with Lambda Functions	161
5.3.1 Key Features of DynamoDB	162
5.3.2 Setting Up DynamoDB	163
5.3.3 Best Practices for Using DynamoDB with Lambda	166
Summary	167
5.4 Google Cloud Firestore and Serverless Integration	168
5.4.1 Key Features of Google Cloud Firestore	169
5.4.2 Setting Up Google Cloud Firestore	170
5.4.3 Best Practices for Using Firestore with Serverless...	173
Summary	174
5.5 Choosing Between SQL and NoSQL in Serverless...	175
5.5.1 Understanding SQL Databases	176
5.5.2 Understanding NoSQL Databases	177
5.5.3 Factors to Consider When Choosing	178
Summary	180
5.6 Handling Large Datasets and File Uploads in Serverless...	181
5.6.1 Strategies for Handling Large Datasets	182
5.6.2 Handling File Uploads	184
Conclusion	186
CHAPTER 6: API DEVELOPMENT IN A SERVERLESS ENVIRONMENT	187
6.1.1 Overview of RESTful APIs	188
6.1.2 Setting Up AWS Lambda for API Development	189
6.1.3 Creating API Endpoints	191
6.1.4 Testing the API	192
6.1.5 Integrating with Other AWS Services	193
6.1.6 Security Best Practices for APIs	195
Summary	196
6.2 Creating Serverless APIs with Google Cloud Functions and...	197
6.2.1 Overview of Google Cloud Functions	198
6.2.2 Setting Up Google API Gateway for Cloud Functions	199
6.2.3 Creating a Simple Google Cloud Function	200

6.2.4 Integrating Google API Gateway with Cloud Functions	201
6.2.5 Managing Authentication and Permissions	203
6.2.6 Monitoring and Logging Google Cloud Functions	204
6.2.7 Handling Errors and Retries in Cloud Functions	205
Summary	206
6.3 Securing APIs with OAuth and JWT in Serverless...	207
6.3.1 Overview of OAuth 2.0 for Serverless Applications	208
OAuth Flow for Serverless APIs:	209
6.3.2 Implementing OAuth 2.0 in AWS Lambda	210
6.3.3 Implementing OAuth 2.0 in Google Cloud Functions	212
6.3.4 Introduction to JSON Web Tokens (JWT)	214
6.3.5 Securing Serverless APIs with JWT	215
Steps for JWT Authentication:	216
6.3.6 Securing API Endpoints with Role-Based Access Control...	219
Summary	221
6.4 Rate Limiting and Throttling in Serverless APIs	222
6.4.1 Understanding Rate Limiting and Throttling	223
6.4.2 Importance of Rate Limiting and Throttling in...	224
6.4.3 Implementing Rate Limiting in AWS Lambda	225
Example:	227
6.4.4 Implementing Throttling in Google Cloud Functions	228
6.4.5 Best Practices for Implementing Rate Limiting and...	230
Summary	231
6.5 Handling CORS Issues in Serverless APIs	232
6.5.1 Understanding CORS	233
6.5.2 Importance of CORS in Serverless APIs	234
6.5.3 Implementing CORS in AWS Lambda	235
6.5.4 Implementing CORS in Google Cloud Functions	237
6.5.5 Best Practices for CORS Configuration	239
Summary	240
6.6 Building GraphQL APIs in a Serverless Environment	241
6.6.1 Understanding GraphQL Basics	242
6.6.2 Setting Up a GraphQL API with AWS Lambda	243

6.6.3 Building a GraphQL API with Google Cloud Functions	245
6.6.4 Benefits of Using GraphQL in Serverless Architecture	247
Conclusion	248
7.1 Connecting AWS Lambda to AWS RDS and Aurora	249
7.1.1 Overview of Amazon RDS and Aurora	250
7.1.2 Setting Up Amazon RDS or Aurora	251
7.1.3 Connecting Lambda Functions to RDS/Aurora	252
7.2 Using Amazon DynamoDB with AWS Lambda	254
7.2.1 Overview of Amazon DynamoDB	255
7.2.2 Setting Up DynamoDB	256
7.2.3 Connecting Lambda Functions to DynamoDB	257
7.3 Integrating Google Cloud Functions with Cloud SQL	259
7.3.1 Overview of Cloud SQL	260
7.3.2 Setting Up Cloud SQL	261
7.3.3 Connecting Cloud Functions to Cloud SQL	262
7.4 Best Practices for Database Management in Serverless...	264
Summary	265
7.2 Google Cloud Functions with Cloud SQL and Cloud...	266
7.2.1 Connecting Google Cloud Functions to Cloud SQL	267
7.2.2 Using Cloud Firestore with Google Cloud Functions	270
7.2.3 Best Practices for Using Cloud SQL and Firestore in...	273
Summary	275
7.3 Implementing Database Transactions in a Serverless...	276
7.3.1 Understanding Transactions	277
7.3.2 Implementing Transactions in AWS Lambda with DynamoDB	278
7.3.3 Implementing Transactions in Google Cloud Functions...	280
7.3.4 Best Practices for Transactions in Serverless...	282
Summary	283
7.4 Serverless Database Design Considerations	284
7.4.1 Scalability	285
7.4.2 Data Access Patterns	286
7.4.3 Latency and Performance	287
7.4.4 Cost Management	288

7.4.5 Security and Access Control	289
7.4.6 Backup and Recovery	290
Summary	291
7.5 Real-Time Data with Serverless Databases	292
7.5.1 Understanding Real-Time Data Requirements	293
7.5.2 Utilizing WebSockets for Real-Time Communication	294
7.5.3 Leveraging Change Data Capture (CDC)	295
7.5.4 Using Serverless Pub/Sub Messaging Systems	296
7.5.5 Implementing Real-Time Data with Serverless Databases	297
Summary	298
7.6 Migrating Databases for Serverless Architectures	299
7.6.1 Assessing Current Database Systems	300
7.6.2 Choosing the Right Serverless Database	301
7.6.3 Planning the Migration Process	302
7.6.4 Executing the Migration	303
7.6.5 Post-Migration Monitoring and Optimization	304
Conclusion	305
CHAPTER 8: EVENT-DRIVEN ARCHITECTURES IN SERVERLESS	306
CHAPTER 9: AUTHENTICATION AND AUTHORIZATION IN SERVERLESS...	328
CHAPTER 10: SERVERLESS MICROSERVICES ARCHITECTURE	357
CHAPTER 11: DEVOPS AND CI/CD FOR SERVERLESS APPLICATIONS	379
CHAPTER 12: MONITORING AND DEBUGGING SERVERLESS APPLICATIONS	397
CHAPTER 13: SCALING SERVERLESS APPLICATIONS	419
CHAPTER 14: SECURITY IN SERVERLESS ARCHITECTURE	435
CHAPTER 15: SERVERLESS ON OTHER CLOUD PLATFORMS	452
16.1 Building Serverless E-commerce Applications	468
16.2 Serverless Chatbots and Voice Assistants	471
16.3 Real-Time Data Processing with Serverless	474
Key Components of Real-Time Data Processing in Serverless...	475
Benefits of Serverless Real-Time Data Processing	477

Real-World Example	478
16.4 Implementing IoT with Serverless Computing	479
Key Components of Serverless IoT Architecture	480
Benefits of Using Serverless for IoT Applications	482
Real-World Example	483
16.5 Serverless Machine Learning Workflows	484
Key Components of Serverless Machine Learning Workflows	485
Benefits of Using Serverless for Machine Learning Workflows	487
Real-World Example	488
16.6 Case Studies: Companies Using Serverless at Scale	489
1. Coca-Cola	490
2. Spotify	491
3. iRobot	492
4. The BBC	493
5. Nordstrom	494
Conclusion	495
17.1 The Growing Popularity of Serverless	496
17.2 Serverless AI and Machine Learning	499
17.3 Edge Computing and the Future of Serverless	502
1. Improved Latency and Performance	503
2. Scalability at the Edge	504
3. Cost Efficiency	505
4. Enhanced Security and Privacy	506
5. Real-Time Data Processing for IoT	507
6. Flexibility and Agility	508
7. Integration with 5G Technology	509
Summary	510
17.4 Innovations in Serverless Databases	511
1. On-Demand Scaling	512
2. Consumption-Based Pricing Models	513
3. Automated Management and Maintenance	514
4. Global Distribution and Low Latency	515
5. Event-Driven Architecture	516

6. Enhanced Security Features	517
7. Integration with Serverless Frameworks	518
8. Support for Multiple Data Models	519
Summary	520
17.5 The Role of Containers in Serverless	521
1. Consistency Across Environments	522
2. Enhanced Portability	523
3. Improved Cold Start Times	524
4. Support for Stateful Applications	525
5. Seamless Integration with Microservices	526
6. Flexibility in Runtime Environments	527
7. Simplified Deployment and CI/CD	528
8. Resource Optimization	529
Summary	530
17.6 Final Thoughts: What's Next for Serverless...	531
1. Increased Adoption Across Industries	532
2. Enhanced Tooling and Ecosystem Maturity	533
3. Integration with AI and Machine Learning	534
4. Emphasis on Security and Compliance	535
5. Edge Computing and Serverless	536
6. Support for Hybrid and Multi-Cloud Architectures	537
7. Focus on Observability and Monitoring	538
8. Community and Knowledge Sharing	539
Conclusion for the Book	540
Appendix A: Glossary of Serverless Terminology	541
Appendix B: JavaScript and Node.js Cheat Sheet	543
Appendix C: AWS Lambda Pricing Model	545
Appendix D: Google Cloud Functions Pricing Model	546
Appendix E: Additional Resources and Reading List	547

INTRODUCTION

Overview of Serverless Computing

In today's digital landscape, serverless computing is rapidly becoming one of the most innovative and cost-effective approaches to application development. It offers a paradigm shift from traditional server-based infrastructures to cloud-based, event-driven systems that allow developers to focus solely on writing code without worrying about server management.

At its core, **serverless computing** enables you to run applications without the need to provision, scale, or manage any servers. Although the term "serverless" can be misleading—since servers are still involved in processing the tasks—the cloud provider handles the underlying infrastructure, such as scaling, maintenance, and patching, allowing you to concentrate on building the application itself.

Key cloud service providers such as **AWS Lambda, Google Cloud Functions**, and **Azure Functions** offer these serverless platforms, which execute your code in response to events, whether it's an HTTP request, file upload, database change, or a message in a queue. In return, developers are charged based on the execution time and the resources consumed by the functions, rather than paying for always-on infrastructure.

Some of the **main advantages** of serverless computing include:

- **Cost Efficiency**: You only pay for the exact compute time used, eliminating costs associated with idle server resources.
- **Automatic Scalability**: Serverless architectures automatically scale

based on demand, handling everything from a few requests per day to millions of events without any manual intervention.
- **Reduced Operational Complexity**: Developers no longer need to manage servers, operating systems, or runtime environments. The cloud provider takes care of all the underlying infrastructure.
- **Faster Time to Market**: Serverless frameworks enable rapid deployment and iteration of features, allowing businesses to roll out new updates more frequently and with fewer risks.

Why JavaScript for Serverless Applications?

JavaScript is a dominant language in the world of web development, known for its versatility and ease of use. It's also perfectly suited for serverless architectures due to its lightweight nature, event-driven model, and broad support across platforms.

Here's why JavaScript is an excellent choice for serverless applications:

1. **Universal Language**: JavaScript can be used both on the client-side (in browsers) and server-side (through platforms like Node.js). This makes it easier to write isomorphic code, where parts of the same application share code between the frontend and backend.
2. **Asynchronous and Event-Driven**: Serverless functions respond to events (like HTTP requests or database updates), and JavaScript's asynchronous nature aligns perfectly with the event-driven model of serverless architecture. Node.js, which is JavaScript's runtime on the server side, handles asynchronous tasks efficiently, making it ideal for cloud functions that deal with multiple concurrent events.
3. **Vast Ecosystem**: JavaScript has an extensive ecosystem of libraries and frameworks, making it easy to integrate with third-party APIs and services. For example, you can easily connect AWS Lambda functions to popular JavaScript packages using npm (Node Package Manager).
4. **Support by Major Cloud Providers**: Cloud service providers such as AWS and Google Cloud support JavaScript/Node.js as one of the

primary languages for serverless functions. This makes it easier for JavaScript developers to transition into serverless architecture without learning a new language or framework.

In the world of serverless, JavaScript's flexibility and scalability make it a top choice for building highly responsive and efficient applications.

Getting Started with Node.js

To build serverless applications with JavaScript, you'll need to be familiar with **Node.js**, a JavaScript runtime that enables server-side scripting. Node.js is crucial because most serverless platforms like AWS Lambda and Google Cloud Functions use Node.js for executing JavaScript code in the backend.

What is Node.js?

Node.js is an open-source, cross-platform runtime environment built on Chrome's V8 JavaScript engine. It allows developers to run JavaScript code outside of the browser, making it possible to build full-stack applications using JavaScript for both the front-end and back-end.

Key Features of Node.js:

- **Asynchronous and Event-Driven**: Node.js processes many operations asynchronously, which is essential for serverless functions that need to respond to multiple events simultaneously.
- **Single-Threaded but Scalable**: Node.js uses a single-threaded model, but its non-blocking nature allows it to handle many concurrent operations, which is important for scaling serverless applications.
- **Rich Ecosystem**: Node.js has a vast library of modules and packages available via npm, allowing you to easily extend the functionality of your serverless functions.

Setting Up Node.js:

To begin using Node.js for serverless development, you'll first need to install it on your machine. Node.js can be downloaded from its official website. Once installed, you can verify the installation by running node -v and npm -v in your terminal, which will return the current versions of Node.js and npm, respectively.

How to Use This Book

This book is designed to guide you through the world of serverless architecture, with a focus on leveraging JavaScript to build scalable, event-driven applications. Each chapter covers a specific area of serverless development, gradually taking you from the fundamentals to advanced topics.

- **Part 1** of the book introduces the basics of serverless architecture, cloud platforms, and the role of JavaScript and Node.js in serverless development.
- **Part 2** delves into creating and managing serverless applications using two of the most popular cloud providers: AWS Lambda and Google Cloud Functions.
- **Part 3** explores advanced topics such as managing databases, building APIs, event-driven architectures, and securing serverless applications.
- **Part 4** rounds out the book by covering practical use cases, serverless frameworks, and future trends in serverless computing.

Each chapter contains **practical examples** and **step-by-step tutorials** to help you build your own serverless applications, ensuring that by the end of the book, you'll have a solid understanding of how to use serverless architecture in real-world scenarios.

This book assumes a basic knowledge of JavaScript, but it will provide a refresher when necessary. It is designed to be approachable for beginners but also offers deeper insights for those looking to expand their expertise.

With this foundation, you are now ready to dive into the exciting world of **serverless architecture with JavaScript**. Let's begin!

A Quick Introduction to Cloud Platforms (AWS, Google Cloud, Azure)

As we step into the world of **serverless architecture**, it's important to understand the key cloud platforms that provide the infrastructure for deploying and running serverless applications. Cloud providers like **AWS (Amazon Web Services)**, **Google Cloud**, and **Microsoft Azure** offer a wide range of services that make serverless computing possible. Each of

INTRODUCTION

these platforms provides its own serverless functions, along with a variety of additional services that you can use to build, scale, and manage applications in the cloud.

AWS (Amazon Web Services)

Amazon Web Services (AWS) is one of the largest and most widely used cloud platforms in the world. AWS offers a comprehensive suite of cloud computing services that range from infrastructure (compute, storage, networking) to higher-level services such as machine learning, analytics, and serverless computing.

AWS was the pioneer of serverless computing with the introduction of **AWS Lambda** in 2014. Lambda allows you to run your JavaScript (or other supported languages) code in response to events, without the need to manage any servers. AWS Lambda integrates with many other AWS services, making it an incredibly versatile tool for building event-driven applications.

Key Services for Serverless on AWS:

- **AWS Lambda**: The core serverless function service that executes your code in response to events. It automatically scales and only charges for the time your code is running.
- **Amazon API Gateway**: A fully managed service that allows you to create and deploy APIs that can trigger Lambda functions.
- **Amazon S3 (Simple Storage Service)**: A scalable object storage service that can trigger Lambda functions when files are uploaded, modified, or deleted.
- **Amazon DynamoDB**: A NoSQL database service that is often used with Lambda functions for serverless data storage.
- **Amazon EventBridge**: A serverless event bus that helps manage and route events between AWS services and Lambda.

Advantages of AWS for Serverless:

- **Mature Ecosystem**: AWS offers a broad range of services that integrate seamlessly with Lambda, making it the most feature-rich platform for

serverless architectures.
- **Global Availability**: AWS has data centers across the globe, allowing you to deploy applications close to your users, improving performance and reducing latency.
- **Comprehensive Security**: AWS provides a strong security model with built-in features such as encryption, IAM (Identity and Access Management), and VPC integration.

Google Cloud

Google Cloud Platform (GCP) is another leading cloud provider that offers a strong set of serverless computing services. With its deep expertise in AI, machine learning, and data analytics, Google Cloud is a popular choice for developers looking to integrate serverless architectures with advanced data processing.

Google Cloud's serverless function service is known as **Google Cloud Functions**, which, like AWS Lambda, allows you to run your JavaScript code in response to events without managing servers. GCP is particularly well-suited for applications that need to take advantage of Google's AI and data analytics capabilities.

Key Services for Serverless on Google Cloud:

- **Google Cloud Functions**: The serverless function service that runs code in response to HTTP requests, database changes, and other events.
- **Google Cloud Pub/Sub**: A messaging service that helps you build event-driven systems by decoupling services and triggering Cloud Functions based on messages.
- **Firebase**: A popular backend-as-a-service platform that integrates seamlessly with Google Cloud Functions, allowing you to build real-time apps with serverless backends.
- **Google Cloud Storage**: A scalable object storage service that can trigger Cloud Functions when files are modified or uploaded.
- **Firestore**: A serverless NoSQL database that integrates well with Google Cloud Functions.

INTRODUCTION

Advantages of Google Cloud for Serverless:

- **AI and Machine Learning Integration**: Google Cloud's strength lies in its AI and machine learning services, which can easily be integrated into serverless applications.
- **Strong Developer Tools**: Google Cloud provides an extensive set of tools for developers, including Firebase, Stackdriver for monitoring, and Cloud Build for continuous integration.
- **Global Infrastructure**: Like AWS, Google Cloud has a global infrastructure, ensuring low latency and high availability for your applications.

Microsoft Azure

Microsoft Azure is a comprehensive cloud computing platform that is known for its strong integration with enterprise tools and services. Azure provides a wide range of services, including infrastructure-as-a-service (IaaS), platform-as-a-service (PaaS), and software-as-a-service (SaaS), making it a versatile platform for various use cases.

In the world of serverless computing, Azure offers **Azure Functions**, which are similar to AWS Lambda and Google Cloud Functions. Azure Functions allows you to run JavaScript (or other supported languages) code in response to events, and like the other platforms, it handles scaling automatically.

Key Services for Serverless on Azure:

- **Azure Functions**: The core serverless compute service that runs code on-demand in response to events such as HTTP requests, queue messages, or timers.
- **Azure Event Grid**: A service that routes events between applications and services, triggering Azure Functions based on these events.
- **Azure Logic Apps**: A service for automating workflows and integrating services with minimal code, which can call Azure Functions as part of the workflow.
- **Azure Cosmos DB**: A globally distributed, multi-model database that integrates with Azure Functions for serverless data storage.

- **Azure Blob Storage**: A scalable object storage service that can trigger Azure Functions when files are added or modified.

Advantages of Azure for Serverless:

- **Enterprise Integration**: Azure is a great choice for enterprises that already use Microsoft tools and services like Office 365, Active Directory, or Windows Server.
- **Strong Support for Multiple Languages**: Azure Functions support a wide range of programming languages, including JavaScript, C#, Python, and more.
- **Hybrid Cloud Capabilities**: Azure offers strong support for hybrid cloud environments, allowing you to integrate on-premise infrastructure with cloud services.

Choosing the Right Platform

Each of the cloud platforms—AWS, Google Cloud, and Azure—has its own strengths and unique features. Your choice of platform will depend on the specific needs of your application, such as the services you plan to use, your familiarity with the ecosystem, and the pricing model.

- **AWS** is ideal for those looking for a mature, feature-rich platform with a broad range of integrations.
- **Google Cloud** is a strong contender for applications that need advanced data processing or machine learning capabilities.
- **Azure** is a great choice for enterprises already invested in the Microsoft ecosystem or those needing hybrid cloud solutions.

In the following chapters, we will explore how to build serverless applications using both **AWS Lambda** and **Google Cloud Functions**, giving you practical experience with these platforms and helping you make an informed decision based on your project's needs.

CHAPTER 1: UNDERSTANDING SERVERLESS ARCHITECTURE

1.1 What is Serverless Architecture?

Serverless architecture is a cloud computing execution model in which the cloud provider dynamically manages the allocation of machine resources. Unlike traditional server-based architectures, where developers need to provision, manage, and scale the infrastructure, serverless removes the responsibility of server management. This enables developers to focus entirely on writing code and building the logic of applications.

At its core, serverless architecture enables you to run code in response to events, without needing to worry about server setup or ongoing server management tasks. Instead, you define the business logic in small, independent units of code known as **functions**. These functions are executed in response to triggers, such as HTTP requests, file uploads, database changes, or message queue events.

Key Characteristics of Serverless Architecture:

1. **No Server Management**:

- In serverless computing, the cloud provider takes care of server provisioning and management. You do not need to worry about hardware, virtual machines, or operating systems. This frees up developers from infrastructure-related responsibilities.

1. **Automatic Scalability**:

- Serverless architectures scale automatically in response to traffic or demand. The cloud provider ensures that the necessary resources are available to handle the load, whether there are thousands of requests per second or just a few.

1. **Pay-per-Use Billing Model**:

- One of the major advantages of serverless is the pay-per-use billing model. You are only charged for the actual execution time of your code. This is in contrast to traditional cloud infrastructure where you pay for server uptime, regardless of actual usage.

1. **Event-Driven Execution**:

- Serverless functions are typically executed in response to events. This could be an HTTP request, a message in a queue, a file upload, or other events. This event-driven approach allows for highly decoupled and modular systems.

1. **Short-Lived Execution**:

- Serverless functions are usually stateless and short-lived. They are executed when triggered, perform a task, and then terminate. The serverless function lifecycle is based on the concept of stateless computation.

1. **Managed Security and Maintenance**:

- The cloud provider ensures that the infrastructure is up-to-date with security patches, and handles aspects like load balancing, monitoring, and fault tolerance. This reduces the operational overhead and risk of security vulnerabilities.

CHAPTER 1: UNDERSTANDING SERVERLESS ARCHITECTURE

Benefits of Serverless Architecture:

1. **Focus on Business Logic**:

- Developers can focus on writing application logic and building features, rather than managing infrastructure or worrying about scaling issues.

1. **Cost Efficiency**:

- Since you are only charged for the actual execution time of your functions, serverless architecture can result in significant cost savings, especially for applications with unpredictable or variable usage patterns.

1. **Quick Time to Market**:

- Serverless allows developers to quickly build and deploy applications because infrastructure concerns are abstracted away. This leads to faster development cycles and quicker time to market.

1. **Built-In Fault Tolerance**:

- Serverless architectures are inherently fault-tolerant because cloud providers automatically distribute the execution of functions across multiple servers and locations, ensuring high availability.

1. **Effortless Scalability**:

- Applications built with serverless architecture automatically scale based on the demand. You don't need to manually add or remove servers as your application traffic fluctuates.

Challenges of Serverless Architecture:

1. **Cold Start Latency:**

- Serverless functions, especially in some platforms, may experience a slight delay (cold start) when they are first invoked after a period of inactivity. This can affect the performance of real-time applications.

1. **Limited Execution Time:**

- Serverless functions typically have a maximum execution time imposed by the cloud provider. This limits the use of serverless for long-running processes.

1. **Debugging and Monitoring:**

- Since serverless abstracts away the infrastructure, it can sometimes be challenging to debug and monitor distributed functions across multiple services. Advanced monitoring tools are required to track performance and troubleshoot issues.

1. **Vendor Lock-In:**

- Serverless architectures are often closely tied to specific cloud providers (such as AWS Lambda or Google Cloud Functions). Migrating from one provider to another can be complex and time-consuming, leading to potential vendor lock-in.

1. **Stateless Nature:**

- Serverless functions are stateless by design, meaning that they do not retain any memory or data between executions. This requires developers to design applications that store state externally, often in databases or caches.

CHAPTER 1: UNDERSTANDING SERVERLESS ARCHITECTURE

Serverless vs Traditional Architectures:

In summary, serverless architecture presents a paradigm shift in how we build, deploy, and manage applications. By abstracting away infrastructure management and allowing developers to focus on business logic, it opens up new possibilities for scalable, cost-efficient, and rapidly developed applications.

1.2 How Serverless Differs from Traditional Architectures

To fully grasp the significance of serverless architecture, it's important to understand how it differs from traditional server-based architectures. In this section, we'll break down the major distinctions between serverless and conventional approaches to building applications, focusing on key operational and technical differences.

1.2.1 Traditional Architectures

In traditional server-based architectures, the application runs on dedicated physical or virtual servers. These servers are provisioned, maintained, and scaled manually by system administrators or DevOps teams. The infrastructure is typically more rigid and requires careful planning, with developers and administrators responsible for provisioning hardware, operating system updates, server scaling, load balancing, and security.

Characteristics of Traditional Server-Based Architectures:

1. **Infrastructure Management**:

- Developers or IT teams must manage the underlying servers, including their configuration, updates, and security patches. They also must plan for peak loads by provisioning enough servers to handle the maximum expected demand.

1. **Scaling**:

- Scaling in traditional architectures is often manual or semi-automated. You need to configure scaling rules or manually add or remove servers as demand fluctuates. This process is resource-intensive and requires ongoing monitoring.

1. **Persistent Servers**:

- Traditional applications run on persistent servers that remain active and ready to serve requests at all times. These servers are constantly running, regardless of whether they are handling requests or sitting idle, leading to potential resource wastage.

1. **Upfront Costs**:

- Organizations typically incur high upfront costs for purchasing and provisioning hardware, with ongoing costs for server maintenance, including electricity, cooling, and IT personnel to manage the infrastructure.

1. **State Management**:

- In traditional architectures, applications can maintain in-memory state across requests and sessions. This makes it easier to manage user sessions or temporary data without needing external data stores for every operation.

1. **Monolithic Applications**:

- Traditional applications often follow a monolithic architecture, where all components (frontend, backend, database) are tightly coupled and run on the same server. Scaling such architectures requires scaling the entire application, even if only one part experiences high demand.

1. **Continuous Server Costs**:

- Since servers run continuously, organizations must pay for server uptime, whether or not the server is actively handling requests.

CHAPTER 1: UNDERSTANDING SERVERLESS ARCHITECTURE

1.2.2 Serverless Architecture

Serverless architecture takes a completely different approach. Instead of provisioning dedicated servers, applications are divided into small, independent units of code called functions. These functions are executed in response to events and automatically scaled based on demand. The cloud provider handles all the infrastructure, scaling, security, and maintenance, leaving developers free to focus on writing code.

Key Differences of Serverless Architecture:

1. **No Server Management**:

- One of the fundamental shifts with serverless architecture is that developers no longer need to worry about server provisioning, configuration, or maintenance. The cloud provider handles the underlying infrastructure entirely.

1. **Event-Driven Execution**:

- Serverless applications are typically event-driven, meaning that functions are executed only in response to specific events, such as HTTP requests, file uploads, or database triggers. This contrasts with traditional architectures, where servers are always running, waiting to handle requests.

1. **Automatic Scaling**:

- Serverless functions automatically scale up or down in response to the number of requests. This means that developers don't have to predict traffic patterns or manually provision extra servers during peak times.

1. **Stateless Functions**:

- Serverless functions are stateless by design. Each function execution is isolated from the previous one, and any necessary data is stored in external storage (databases, caches, etc.). This statelessness makes serverless functions lightweight and allows them to scale horizontally easily.

1. **Pay-per-Use Billing**:

- Serverless functions follow a pay-per-use model, meaning you only pay for the actual execution time of your functions. If your function isn't running, you're not incurring any costs. This is in contrast to traditional servers, which incur costs for the entire duration they are running, even when idle.

1. **Microservices-Oriented**:

- Serverless applications naturally fit into a microservices architecture, where different parts of the application (authentication, payments, notifications) are built as separate, independent services. Each function performs a specific task and can be scaled independently of other parts of the application.

1. **Ephemeral Resources**:

- Serverless functions are short-lived, existing only for the duration of their execution. This makes them highly scalable and disposable, as each invocation of a function is independent of others.

1. **Lower Operational Overhead**:

- Since infrastructure management, scaling, and security are handled by the cloud provider, organizations adopting serverless architecture significantly reduce their operational overhead. Developers focus purely on coding, while the provider takes care of the infrastructure.

CHAPTER 1: UNDERSTANDING SERVERLESS ARCHITECTURE

1. **Cold Starts**:

- One potential drawback of serverless is the concept of cold starts. Since serverless functions are stateless and don't maintain persistent instances, they may take longer to start if they haven't been used for a while. Cold starts add a small amount of latency to the first execution of a function after inactivity.

1.2.3 Comparing Serverless and Traditional Architectures:
1.2.4 Use Cases for Serverless vs Traditional Architectures
When to Use Traditional Architecture:

- **Long-Running Processes**:
- If your application has long-running processes (such as background jobs or data processing tasks that take hours), traditional servers may be a better fit since serverless functions have execution time limits.
- **Complex Applications**:
- Applications with complex stateful logic or that require a persistent connection (such as WebSocket servers) may be better suited to traditional architectures.
- **Full Control Over Infrastructure**:
- If you need full control over the underlying infrastructure (for compliance, security, or performance reasons), traditional architecture gives you more direct control.

When to Use Serverless Architecture:

- **Event-Driven Applications**:
- Applications where functions are triggered by external events, such as user actions, database updates, or message queue events, are ideal candidates for serverless architectures.
- **APIs and Microservices**:
- Serverless architectures are well-suited for APIs and microservices where

different parts of the application are independent and can scale separately.
- **High Traffic or Unpredictable Loads**:
- Serverless is perfect for applications with unpredictable traffic patterns or seasonal spikes in demand since it scales automatically based on usage.
- **Short-Lived Tasks**:
- Serverless is highly efficient for short-lived tasks such as processing HTTP requests, handling file uploads, or executing scheduled jobs.

Summary:

Serverless architecture represents a fundamental shift in how modern applications are built and managed. While traditional architectures still have their place for complex, long-running, or stateful applications, serverless offers a flexible, scalable, and cost-efficient alternative for event-driven and microservices-based applications.

1.3 Benefits of Serverless: Cost, Scalability, and Flexibility

Serverless architecture has gained significant traction due to the unique advantages it offers, particularly in terms of cost savings, scalability, and operational flexibility. In this section, we will explore these benefits in detail, examining how serverless can transform application development, deployment, and maintenance.

1.3.1 Cost Efficiency: Pay-per-Use Model

One of the most attractive aspects of serverless architecture is the cost model. Traditional infrastructure requires a continuous investment in server uptime, whether the application is actively being used or not. Serverless flips this paradigm by offering a *pay-per-use* billing model, which means you are only charged for the actual time your functions are executing.

Key Cost Benefits:

1. **No Idle Resource Costs**:

- In traditional architectures, you pay for the server resources even when they're idle, meaning you're charged for uptime, not actual usage. With serverless, you are only billed when your code is executed.

CHAPTER 1: UNDERSTANDING SERVERLESS ARCHITECTURE

- This makes serverless ideal for applications with variable traffic, where demand fluctuates significantly throughout the day or year.

1. **No Upfront Costs**:

- With serverless, there's no need for large upfront investments in hardware or long-term cloud infrastructure commitments. This pay-as-you-go approach minimizes financial risk and allows businesses to scale up their spending as their application usage grows.

1. **Fine-Grained Cost Control**:

- Since you are billed per execution (down to milliseconds of compute time), it's easier to optimize and control costs at a very granular level. This allows you to allocate your budget more effectively and avoid unexpected spikes in infrastructure costs.

1. **Reduced Operational Costs**:

- Serverless removes the need for dedicated system administrators or DevOps teams to manage and maintain servers, reducing operational overhead. The cloud provider handles server maintenance, updates, and scaling, further lowering costs.

Example:

For a typical web application using a traditional architecture, you might provision servers capable of handling peak load, even though that load only occurs 10% of the time. With serverless, you would pay only for the actual requests and processing time, saving potentially thousands of dollars in server uptime costs.

1.3.2 Scalability: Automatic and Seamless

Scalability is one of the most powerful advantages of serverless architecture. In traditional systems, scaling requires manual intervention or custom-built automation rules to provision or de-provision servers based on demand. Serverless architecture provides automatic scaling, where the underlying infrastructure dynamically adjusts based on real-time traffic.

Key Scalability Benefits:

1. **Automatic Scaling**:

- Serverless functions scale automatically based on incoming requests. When demand spikes, the cloud provider instantly provisions more instances of your function to handle the load. Conversely, when demand decreases, the number of function instances automatically scales down to zero.
- This dynamic scaling ensures that your application can handle any traffic load, from a few requests per day to millions of requests per second.

1. **No Need for Capacity Planning**:

- In traditional systems, developers and administrators must estimate the peak traffic and provision enough resources to handle it, which often leads to either over-provisioning (wasting resources) or under-provisioning (causing performance bottlenecks). With serverless, there's no need to predict future traffic patterns or manually adjust capacity.

1. **Effortless Global Scale**:

- Serverless platforms like AWS Lambda or Google Cloud Functions are globally distributed, which means your application can scale across multiple regions with minimal configuration. This makes it easier to serve users from different geographic locations with low latency.

1. **Event-Driven Scaling**:

- Serverless is particularly well-suited for event-driven applications. Each time an event occurs (such as an HTTP request, database update, or file upload), a new instance of the function is spun up to handle that event. This ensures that your application can handle multiple concurrent events without delay or manual intervention.

Example:

An e-commerce website running on a traditional architecture would need to be scaled manually during high-traffic events like Black Friday sales. With serverless, this scaling happens automatically, so you don't need to worry about provisioning additional servers or optimizing for peak performance.

1.3.3 Flexibility: Focus on Code, Not Infrastructure

With serverless, developers are empowered to focus on writing and deploying code rather than managing the underlying infrastructure. This shift leads to faster development cycles, simplified deployment pipelines, and more flexible application architecture.

Key Flexibility Benefits:

1. **No Server Management**:

- Since the cloud provider handles server provisioning, patching, and scaling, developers can dedicate their time entirely to building application features. This results in faster development cycles and less operational overhead.

1. **Agility in Development and Deployment**:

- Serverless architectures promote rapid development through the use of modular, event-driven functions. These functions can be developed, tested, and deployed independently, allowing teams to iterate quickly and roll out updates without impacting the entire application.

1. **Microservices and Modular Architecture**:

- Serverless functions naturally align with microservices architecture. Each function is responsible for a single piece of business logic, making it easier to isolate, test, and update specific features or services without affecting the entire application.
- This modular approach also simplifies collaboration between development teams, as each team can work on independent functions without stepping on each other's toes.

1. **Support for Multiple Languages**:

- Most serverless platforms support a variety of programming languages. For example, AWS Lambda supports JavaScript (Node.js), Python, Java, Ruby, and Go, giving teams the flexibility to choose the best language for each part of their application.

1. **Integration with Cloud Services**:

- Serverless applications can easily integrate with other cloud services like storage (e.g., AWS S3), databases (e.g., AWS DynamoDB), and messaging systems (e.g., AWS SQS). These integrations enable powerful workflows and automation without the need for complex infrastructure setup.

1. **Improved DevOps Workflow**:

- With serverless, the continuous integration and continuous delivery (CI/CD) pipeline is greatly simplified. Functions can be deployed individually, without redeploying the entire application, which leads to faster deployment cycles and reduced risk of downtime.

Example:
A startup building a real-time notification system can deploy a serverless architecture with AWS Lambda functions handling user notifications, easily integrating with Amazon SNS (Simple Notification Service) for real-time

message delivery. This reduces infrastructure management and accelerates the development process.

1.3.4 Environmental Benefits

By scaling only when necessary and paying only for what is used, serverless architectures promote efficient use of computing resources. This not only reduces operational costs but also has environmental benefits.

Key Environmental Benefits:

1. **Energy Efficiency**:

- Serverless applications reduce energy consumption by minimizing the number of active servers. With no need for constantly running servers, organizations can significantly reduce their energy footprint.

1. **Optimized Resource Usage**:

- Serverless encourages the efficient use of computing resources, only consuming resources when a function is triggered. This minimizes wasted energy and server overprovisioning.

Summary

Serverless architecture offers compelling benefits that make it an attractive choice for modern application development. Its cost-efficiency, automatic scalability, and flexibility give developers the freedom to focus on building features without worrying about infrastructure management. Moreover, the pay-per-use model ensures organizations can optimize both their budget and resource usage, scaling seamlessly to meet demand.

1.4 Popular Serverless Providers: AWS Lambda, Google Cloud Functions, and More

In the realm of serverless computing, several cloud providers have established themselves as leaders, each offering a unique set of services and capabilities to help developers build, deploy, and manage serverless applications. In this section, we will explore some of the most popular serverless platforms: **AWS Lambda, Google Cloud Functions, Microsoft Azure Functions**, and a few other notable providers. We will look at the key features of each platform, their integrations, and why they are widely adopted in modern application development.

1.4.1 AWS Lambda

AWS Lambda, introduced by Amazon Web Services (AWS) in 2014, is one of the pioneers of serverless computing. It allows developers to run code in response to various triggers or events without the need to provision or manage servers.

Key Features:

1. **Event-Driven Architecture**:

- AWS Lambda is designed to respond to events triggered by other AWS services, such as S3 (file uploads), DynamoDB (database changes), API Gateway (HTTP requests), and CloudWatch (monitoring). This makes it ideal for building event-driven applications and microservices.

1. **Language Support**:

- AWS Lambda supports several programming languages, including Node.js (JavaScript), Python, Java, Ruby, Go, and .NET (C#). This flexibility allows developers to choose the best language for their specific needs.

1. **Integrated with AWS Ecosystem**:

- One of the key advantages of AWS Lambda is its deep integration with the broader AWS ecosystem. Developers can seamlessly connect their Lambda functions to a wide range of services such as S3 (storage), DynamoDB (NoSQL database), SNS (messaging), SQS (queue), and more.

1. **Scalability**:

- AWS Lambda scales automatically based on the number of incoming requests. When traffic spikes, Lambda provisions more instances of your function to handle the load, making it ideal for highly variable workloads.

1. **Pricing Model**:

- AWS Lambda follows a pay-per-use model, where you are billed based on the number of requests and the duration (in milliseconds) of each function execution. This makes Lambda cost-effective for both small-scale applications and large-scale, high-traffic services.

Use Cases:

- **Web and API Backends**: Lambda can be used to build scalable API backends, especially when combined with AWS API Gateway.
- **Data Processing**: Lambda is great for processing data streams from services like Amazon Kinesis or S3, allowing you to build data pipelines without managing servers.
- **Real-Time File Processing**: Applications that process files uploaded to S3, such as image resizing, video transcoding, or metadata extraction, can be easily automated using Lambda.

1.4.2 Google Cloud Functions

Google Cloud Functions is Google's answer to AWS Lambda, offering a fully managed serverless environment where you can run your code in response to events originating from Google Cloud services and HTTP requests.

Key Features:

1. **Event-Driven and HTTP Triggers**:

- Google Cloud Functions can be triggered by various events from Google services like Google Cloud Storage (file uploads), Firestore (database changes), and Pub/Sub (message queues). You can also trigger functions via HTTP requests, making it easy to build webhooks and APIs.

1. **Language Support**:

- Cloud Functions supports Node.js (JavaScript), Python, Go, and Java, giving developers the flexibility to choose from some of the most popular programming languages for serverless applications.

1. **Tight Integration with Google Cloud Services**:

- Google Cloud Functions integrates natively with Google Cloud services such as Firestore (NoSQL database), BigQuery (data warehouse), and Cloud Pub/Sub (messaging). This makes it an excellent choice for developers already using the Google Cloud ecosystem.

1. **Global Scale and Regional Availability**:

- Like AWS Lambda, Cloud Functions scale automatically in response to incoming events, and Google ensures low-latency responses by deploying functions across multiple regions.

1. **Developer Tools and Monitoring**:

- Google provides powerful developer tools and monitoring options, such as Stackdriver, to help you debug, log, and monitor your Cloud Functions effectively.

Use Cases:

- **Building APIs**: Google Cloud Functions are ideal for quickly building scalable APIs that interact with services like Firestore or Google Cloud Storage.

- **IoT Applications**: With integration into Google Pub/Sub, Cloud Functions can be used to process data from IoT devices, enabling real-time data pipelines.
- **Machine Learning Pipelines**: Cloud Functions can trigger machine learning tasks such as image analysis or sentiment analysis in real time when new data is uploaded.

1.4.3 Microsoft Azure Functions

Azure Functions, part of Microsoft's cloud platform, provides serverless compute capabilities and is known for its powerful integrations within the Azure ecosystem. It shares many similarities with AWS Lambda and Google Cloud Functions but also offers a few unique features.

Key Features:

1. **Extensive Trigger Options**:

- Azure Functions supports a wide variety of trigger options, including HTTP requests, Azure Storage (blobs and queues), Event Hubs (real-time event streaming), and even third-party services via webhooks.

1. **Flexible Language Support**:

- Azure Functions support JavaScript (Node.js), Python, C#, Java, PowerShell, and TypeScript, making it one of the most flexible serverless platforms in terms of programming languages.

1. **Integration with Azure Services**:

- Azure Functions integrates with services like Azure Blob Storage, Cosmos DB (NoSQL), and Event Grid, making it well-suited for building event-driven applications in the Azure cloud.

1. **Durable Functions for Long-Running Workflows**:

- One standout feature of Azure Functions is *Durable Functions*, which allows you to build workflows that can run for extended periods of time. This is particularly useful for tasks like order processing, multi-step workflows, or stateful operations.

1. **Enterprise-Grade Security and Compliance**:

- Azure Functions benefits from Microsoft's focus on enterprise security and compliance, making it a good choice for organizations with strict regulatory requirements.

Use Cases:

- **Real-Time Data Processing**: Azure Functions can handle real-time data from IoT devices, processing streams from Event Hubs or Azure Blob Storage.
- **Serverless Microservices**: You can build serverless microservices architectures that scale automatically with Azure Functions and Azure API Management.
- **Enterprise Automation**: Azure Functions can be used to automate various enterprise tasks, such as data synchronization or automated backups.

1.4.4 Other Notable Providers

Beyond the major cloud players, there are several other platforms offering serverless computing solutions, each catering to different niches or providing unique capabilities.

1. **IBM Cloud Functions**:

- Based on Apache OpenWhisk, IBM Cloud Functions provides a robust serverless platform with support for multiple programming languages. It integrates well with IBM Watson for AI-driven serverless applications.

CHAPTER 1: UNDERSTANDING SERVERLESS ARCHITECTURE

1. **Netlify Functions**:

- For web developers, Netlify Functions provides a simple way to deploy serverless functions alongside static websites. It's particularly popular for Jamstack sites and integrates seamlessly with Git-based workflows.

1. **Vercel (formerly Zeit Now)**:

- Vercel provides serverless functions as part of its hosting platform, focused on performance and scalability for frontend developers. It's an excellent option for building full-stack React applications with serverless backends.

Conclusion:

Each serverless provider offers distinct features and capabilities, making it essential to choose the one that best fits your specific use case, development language, and cloud ecosystem preferences. AWS Lambda, Google Cloud Functions, and Azure Functions are the top choices for most developers due to their mature ecosystems, integrations, and scalability. However, niche platforms like Netlify or Vercel offer unique advantages for frontend-focused or static site deployments.

1.5 Common Use Cases for Serverless Architecture

Serverless architecture has emerged as a powerful solution for modern application development due to its flexibility, scalability, and cost-efficiency. Many businesses and developers have adopted serverless computing to simplify infrastructure management while focusing on writing code that delivers value. In this section, we'll explore some of the most common use cases where serverless architecture excels.

1.5.1 Web Applications and APIs

One of the most popular use cases for serverless architecture is building **web applications** and **APIs**. Serverless computing allows developers to build scalable backend services without worrying about provisioning and maintaining servers.

Key Benefits:

- **Automatic Scaling**: Serverless applications automatically scale based on demand, making it ideal for variable or unpredictable traffic patterns.
- **Event-Driven**: Serverless functions like AWS Lambda or Google Cloud Functions can be triggered by HTTP requests or events from other services, making them perfect for creating API endpoints.
- **Cost-Efficient**: Serverless functions are only charged for execution time, which makes them very cost-effective for applications with irregular or low traffic.

Use Case Examples:

- **RESTful APIs**: Building REST APIs using serverless functions allows for rapid deployment and seamless scaling.
- **Single Page Applications (SPAs)**: Serverless functions can handle backend logic for SPAs built with frameworks like React or Angular, interacting with databases and authentication services.

1.5.2 Data Processing and Transformation

Serverless architecture is particularly well-suited for **data processing tasks**, where functions are triggered in response to data events, such as the arrival of new files or changes in a database. This is especially useful for **real-time data processing** and **batch jobs**.

Key Benefits:

- **Event-Driven**: Serverless platforms support event-driven architectures, making it easy to trigger data processing functions whenever new data is available.
- **Concurrent Processing**: Functions can run concurrently, making serverless architecture ideal for handling high volumes of data.
- **Seamless Integration with Cloud Storage**: Serverless platforms integrate with cloud storage services (e.g., AWS S3, Google Cloud Storage)

to automate data processing workflows.

Use Case Examples:

- **ETL Pipelines**: Extracting, transforming, and loading (ETL) data in real-time or in batches can be automated using serverless functions that process data as it arrives in cloud storage.
- **File Processing**: Serverless functions can process files (e.g., images, videos, or documents) as soon as they are uploaded to a storage bucket. Common tasks include resizing images, transcoding videos, or extracting metadata.

1.5.3 IoT (Internet of Things) Applications

The **Internet of Things (IoT)** generates vast amounts of data that need to be processed and analyzed in real-time. Serverless architecture is a perfect fit for IoT applications, as it allows developers to quickly react to incoming data from connected devices.

Key Benefits:

- **Real-Time Data Processing**: Serverless functions can be triggered by data streams from IoT devices, enabling real-time processing of sensor data or device events.
- **Scaling for Large Device Networks**: Serverless functions can automatically scale to handle a large number of connected devices sending data simultaneously.
- **Low Latency**: The distributed nature of serverless functions ensures low-latency processing, crucial for real-time IoT applications.

Use Case Examples:

- **Smart Home Automation**: IoT devices in smart homes (e.g., thermostats, lights, cameras) can send data to serverless functions, which process the data and trigger automation rules (e.g., turning on lights when

motion is detected).
- **Predictive Maintenance**: Serverless architecture can monitor sensor data from industrial machines and trigger alerts or maintenance tasks when anomalies are detected.

1.5.4 Real-Time File and Media Processing

Serverless architecture is commonly used to automate tasks like image resizing, video transcoding, and document processing in response to new files being uploaded to cloud storage.

Key Benefits:

- **Instant Scalability**: Serverless functions can instantly scale to process large batches of files or media in parallel.
- **Cost Efficiency**: You only pay for the time your function is actively processing files, making it cost-effective for workloads that vary over time.
- **Event-Driven Processing**: File processing can be triggered automatically whenever new files are uploaded to storage buckets (e.g., AWS S3 or Google Cloud Storage).

Use Case Examples:

- **Image Processing**: A serverless function can automatically resize, compress, or watermark images as soon as they are uploaded to cloud storage.
- **Video Transcoding**: Serverless functions can transcode video files into different formats and resolutions for streaming on various devices.
- **Document Processing**: Serverless functions can extract text, metadata, or other structured information from uploaded documents (e.g., PDFs, Word documents) and store the results in a database.

1.5.5 Automation and Task Scheduling

Serverless architecture is a great choice for building **automation work-**

flows and **task schedulers**. These tasks may include sending emails, generating reports, or running scheduled jobs at specific intervals.

Key Benefits:

- **Scheduled Execution**: Most serverless platforms offer scheduling capabilities, allowing functions to run on a regular interval (e.g., cron jobs).
- **Easy Automation**: Serverless functions can automate repetitive tasks, such as triggering daily backups, sending out regular reports, or performing database maintenance.
- **Low Maintenance**: Since the cloud provider handles scaling, developers can focus on building the logic for their tasks without worrying about infrastructure.

Use Case Examples:

- **Cron Jobs**: Serverless functions can be scheduled to run at specific times (e.g., every hour, day, or week) to execute tasks like database cleanups or generating periodic reports.
- **Notifications and Alerts**: Automating notifications based on events, such as sending an email or SMS when a certain condition is met (e.g., low inventory in an e-commerce system).

1.5.6 Backend for Mobile and Web Applications

Many mobile and web applications rely on serverless functions for **backend logic**, such as handling user authentication, interacting with databases, or processing payment transactions.

Key Benefits:

- **Authentication and Authorization**: Serverless functions can integrate with authentication services (e.g., AWS Cognito, Firebase Authentication) to handle user login, registration, and authorization.
- **Database Interactions**: Serverless functions can interact with cloud-

based databases (e.g., AWS DynamoDB, Google Firestore) to read and write data for applications.
- **Payment Processing**: Serverless functions can handle payment transactions securely by integrating with payment gateways (e.g., Stripe, PayPal).

Use Case Examples:

- **User Authentication**: Serverless functions handle user login and registration workflows, interacting with a cloud-based authentication service.
- **E-Commerce Transactions**: A serverless function can process customer orders, interact with payment gateways, and update inventory in real time.

Summary

The flexibility and cost-efficiency of serverless architecture have enabled its widespread adoption across many industries and applications. From building web APIs to processing real-time data and automating tasks, serverless computing empowers developers to focus on coding while the cloud provider handles infrastructure management. These use cases represent just a glimpse of the potential of serverless computing, and as the ecosystem continues to evolve, more innovative applications will undoubtedly emerge.

1.6 The Role of JavaScript in Serverless Applications

JavaScript plays a significant role in the world of serverless architecture, particularly due to its versatility, popularity, and the increasing demand for event-driven, asynchronous systems. As one of the most widely used programming languages, JavaScript has become a dominant force in serverless development, both on the frontend and backend, thanks to frameworks like **Node.js**.

1.6.1 Why JavaScript?

JavaScript's ubiquity across both client-side and server-side development makes it a natural choice for serverless functions. With platforms like **AWS Lambda**, **Google Cloud Functions**, and **Azure Functions** supporting

Node.js, developers can write their serverless code in JavaScript or TypeScript, benefiting from the following advantages:

- **Single Language Across the Stack**: Using JavaScript means that developers can handle both frontend (browser-based) and backend logic with a unified language, streamlining the development process.
- **Large Ecosystem**: The JavaScript ecosystem is rich with open-source libraries and frameworks that can easily be integrated into serverless functions to extend functionality.
- **Event-Driven Nature**: Serverless functions are inherently event-driven, reacting to triggers such as HTTP requests, file uploads, or database changes. JavaScript, particularly with **Node.js**, excels in handling asynchronous events and I/O operations, making it ideal for serverless use cases.
- **Developer Familiarity**: JavaScript is already familiar to millions of developers worldwide, reducing the learning curve for those transitioning to serverless computing.

1.6.2 How JavaScript Powers Serverless Functions

JavaScript can be used to write serverless functions that handle everything from **HTTP requests** to **database queries** and **real-time processing**. Here are some key areas where JavaScript shines in serverless development:

- **APIs and Microservices**: JavaScript, using frameworks like **Express.js** on Node.js, can create microservices and API endpoints that are lightweight and scalable in a serverless environment. Functions can be designed to handle specific API routes, triggered by incoming HTTP requests.
- **Real-Time Data Processing**: JavaScript's non-blocking I/O and event-driven architecture make it perfect for building real-time applications, such as IoT data processing or live content updates.
- **Integration with Cloud Services**: Serverless functions written in JavaScript can interact seamlessly with other cloud services, such as

AWS S3, **DynamoDB**, and **Google Cloud Storage**, using SDKs provided by cloud vendors.
- **Automation and Task Scheduling**: JavaScript can be used to create automated workflows, such as triggering tasks on a schedule (e.g., cron jobs) or in response to specific events (e.g., new file uploads).

1.6.3 JavaScript and the Future of Serverless

As serverless architecture continues to evolve, JavaScript will remain central to this growth, especially with the rise of frameworks and platforms designed to make serverless development easier. With **Node.js**'s efficient runtime, the vast ecosystem of JavaScript libraries, and the increasing popularity of serverless computing, JavaScript developers will find themselves at the forefront of creating scalable, event-driven applications without needing to manage infrastructure.

Conclusion

In this chapter, we explored the fundamental concepts of serverless architecture and its key benefits, including cost efficiency, scalability, and flexibility. We also discussed the differences between serverless and traditional architectures, and examined the leading serverless platforms such as **AWS Lambda** and **Google Cloud Functions**. Additionally, we reviewed common use cases for serverless computing, demonstrating its wide range of applications from web APIs to IoT systems and real-time data processing.

Finally, we emphasized the critical role that JavaScript plays in the serverless ecosystem. As an accessible, event-driven language, JavaScript enables developers to build robust, scalable applications without the overhead of server management. Its strong integration with serverless platforms and cloud services ensures that JavaScript will continue to be a key driver of serverless innovation.

CHAPTER 2: SETTING UP YOUR SERVERLESS ENVIRONMENT

To build efficient serverless applications, it's crucial to have the right development environment. In this chapter, we will walk through setting up your local environment, configuring cloud provider tools, and ensuring you have the necessary software and dependencies installed. We'll cover everything from installing Node.js to setting up the development tools that will facilitate seamless serverless development.

2.1 Installing Node.js and JavaScript Development Tools

2.1.1 Why Node.js for Serverless Development?

Node.js is a JavaScript runtime built on **Chrome's V8 JavaScript engine**, designed for building scalable, event-driven applications. It's particularly well-suited for serverless computing because:

- **Asynchronous and Non-blocking I/O**: Node.js is optimized for handling multiple requests simultaneously, making it ideal for the event-driven nature of serverless applications.
- **Lightweight and Fast**: Node.js applications are lightweight, enabling fast cold starts when serverless functions are triggered.
- **JavaScript Ecosystem**: As a JavaScript runtime, Node.js leverages the vast ecosystem of JavaScript libraries, frameworks, and tools, making development more efficient.

2.1.2 Installing Node.js

1. **Download and Install**:

- Navigate to the official Node.js website.
- Download the **LTS (Long-Term Support)** version, which is more stable and reliable for production applications.
- Follow the installation instructions for your operating system (Windows, macOS, or Linux).

1. **Verify Installation**:

- Once installed, verify that Node.js and **npm** (Node Package Manager) are installed correctly by opening your terminal or command prompt and typing the following commands:

node -v

npm -v

These commands should return the versions of Node.js and npm, respectively.

2.1.3 Installing JavaScript Development Tools

While Node.js provides the core runtime, several development tools will help streamline your workflow:

1. **Text Editor/IDE**:

- Install a **text editor** or **Integrated Development Environment (IDE)** that supports JavaScript development. Popular options include:
- **Visual Studio Code (VS Code)**: A highly popular, free text editor with extensive JavaScript support and serverless plugins.
- **WebStorm**: A powerful IDE tailored for JavaScript development, with robust debugging and testing tools.
- Set up extensions for linting and formatting, such as **ESLint** and **Prettier**,

which ensure consistent and error-free code.

1. **Version Control (Git)**:

- Install **Git** for version control. It allows you to track changes in your codebase, collaborate with others, and deploy your projects seamlessly.
- On Windows, download Git from the official Git website, while macOS and Linux users can use their package manager.
- Verify your installation by typing the following in your terminal:

css

git —version

1. **Node Package Manager (npm) or Yarn**:

- **npm** comes bundled with Node.js and allows you to manage libraries and dependencies in your project.
- Alternatively, you can install **Yarn**, a fast, reliable, and secure package manager for JavaScript. Install Yarn by running:

npm install -g yarn

1. **Serverless Framework**:

- For managing your serverless projects efficiently, install the **Serverless Framework**, which provides a powerful CLI to deploy and manage serverless applications.
- Install the Serverless Framework using npm:

npm install -g serverless

- Verify the installation with:

css

serverless —version

2.1.4 Creating Your First Node.js Project

1. **Initialize a Node.js Project**:

- To start building a serverless application, navigate to your project folder and initialize it as a Node.js project using:

csharp

npm init

- Follow the prompts to set up your project, which creates a package.json file. This file will store metadata about your project and manage its dependencies.

1. **Install Dependencies**:

- You can now install any JavaScript libraries or frameworks required for your serverless functions, such as **Express.js** (for HTTP requests) or **Axios** (for API calls). For example:

npm install express axios

By completing the above steps, you've successfully set up Node.js and the necessary development tools to build serverless applications. Next, we'll configure your cloud environment and set up CLI tools to start deploying your functions.

2.2 Setting Up AWS for Serverless Development

CHAPTER 2: SETTING UP YOUR SERVERLESS ENVIRONMENT

To effectively deploy and manage serverless applications, you need to set up and configure your AWS environment. **AWS Lambda** is one of the most popular serverless platforms, allowing you to run code without provisioning or managing servers. In this section, we'll guide you through setting up AWS for serverless development, from creating an AWS account to configuring the necessary credentials using the AWS CLI.

2.2.1 Creating an AWS Account

Before you can begin deploying serverless functions with **AWS Lambda**, you'll need an AWS account. If you don't have one yet, follow these steps:

1. **Sign Up for AWS**:

- Go to the AWS Signup Page and click on **Create an AWS Account**.
- Enter your email address, create a password, and provide your contact and payment information. AWS offers a **Free Tier** that allows you to experiment with serverless functions for free, but make sure to monitor usage to avoid unexpected charges.

1. **Sign in to the AWS Management Console**:

- After creating your account, you can access the **AWS Management Console**. The console allows you to interact with AWS services such as Lambda, S3, DynamoDB, and more.

2.2.2 Setting Up AWS Identity and Access Management (IAM)

To securely interact with AWS services, it's important to configure your **IAM (Identity and Access Management)** settings. IAM allows you to create users, assign permissions, and manage access to AWS resources.

1. **Create a New IAM User**:

- In the AWS Management Console, search for **IAM** in the search bar, then click on **Users** and select **Add User**.

- Create a new user for your serverless projects, giving it a meaningful name (e.g., serverless-developer).
- For **Access Type**, choose **Programmatic access**. This generates an access key ID and a secret access key, which you'll use later to configure the AWS CLI.

1. **Assign Permissions**:

- Attach an existing policy directly to the user by selecting **Attach policies directly**.
- Search for and select the following policies to grant the appropriate permissions for serverless development:
- **AWSLambdaFullAccess**
- **AmazonS3FullAccess** (for using S3 with Lambda)
- **CloudWatchFullAccess** (for logging)
- Review and create the user.

1. **Download Access Credentials**:

- Once the user is created, download the **Access Key ID** and **Secret Access Key**. These keys will be used to configure your AWS CLI in the next step.

2.2.3 Installing and Configuring the AWS CLI

The **AWS Command Line Interface (CLI)** is a powerful tool that allows you to interact with AWS services directly from your terminal or command prompt. With the CLI, you can deploy Lambda functions, manage AWS resources, and much more.

1. **Install AWS CLI**:

- Download and install the AWS CLI from the AWS CLI installation page. Follow the installation instructions for your operating system (Windows, macOS, or Linux).

CHAPTER 2: SETTING UP YOUR SERVERLESS ENVIRONMENT

1. **Verify Installation**:

- To ensure the AWS CLI was installed correctly, run the following command in your terminal:

css

aws —version

- This command should return the installed AWS CLI version.

1. **Configure AWS CLI**:

- Now, configure your AWS CLI with the IAM credentials you generated earlier. Run:

aws configure

- You will be prompted to enter:
- **AWS Access Key ID**: Enter the access key ID you created.
- **AWS Secret Access Key**: Enter the secret access key.
- **Default region name**: Set the region where you want to deploy your Lambda functions (e.g., us-east-1 or eu-west-1).
- **Default output format**: Set this to json.

1. **Test Configuration**:

- To confirm that your AWS CLI is configured correctly, you can list the available Lambda functions (which should return nothing if none exist yet) using:

python

aws lambda list-functions

2.2.4 Setting Up AWS Lambda for Your First Function

Once your AWS CLI is configured, you're ready to deploy your first serverless function using **AWS Lambda**. Here's a quick overview of how to set up a simple Lambda function:

1. **Create a Basic Node.js Function**:

- Start by writing a basic Lambda function in Node.js that can be triggered by an event, such as an HTTP request or an S3 upload.

1. **Deploy the Function with AWS CLI**:

- Using the CLI, you can deploy your function to AWS Lambda, along with specifying the appropriate triggers and permissions.

1. **Test Your Lambda Function**:

- After deployment, use the AWS Management Console or the CLI to test your function by manually triggering it or invoking it via an API Gateway.

We'll cover these deployment steps in detail in later chapters, where you'll learn how to integrate Lambda with other AWS services and monitor your function's performance using **CloudWatch**.

By setting up AWS and configuring the necessary tools, you've laid the foundation for building and deploying serverless applications. With your IAM user configured and AWS CLI installed, you're now prepared to start working with AWS Lambda and other serverless services.

Next, we'll move on to setting up **Google Cloud Functions** and comparing the differences in workflow.

2.3 Getting Started with Google Cloud for Serverless

In addition to AWS, **Google Cloud** provides a robust platform for building serverless applications through its **Google Cloud Functions**. Google Cloud's serverless environment allows you to build scalable applications with ease, without worrying about managing infrastructure.

2.3.1 Creating a Google Cloud Account

To begin working with Google Cloud Functions, you'll need a Google Cloud account.

1. **Sign Up for Google Cloud**:

- Go to the Google Cloud Platform and click on **Get Started for Free**. If you don't already have an account, you can sign up for a free trial with $300 in credits to explore Google Cloud services.
- Follow the prompts to enter your details, including billing information. Google Cloud provides a **Free Tier** with access to Cloud Functions and other services.

1. **Access the Google Cloud Console**:

- Once you've created your account, log in to the **Google Cloud Console**. This web-based interface lets you manage your serverless projects and other Google Cloud resources.

2.3.2 Setting Up Google Cloud SDK

The **Google Cloud SDK** is a command-line tool that allows you to interact with Google Cloud services, including Cloud Functions, Compute Engine, and more. It's essential for deploying and managing your serverless applications.

1. **Install Google Cloud SDK**:

- To install the SDK, go to the Google Cloud SDK documentation and follow the installation instructions for your operating system (Windows, macOS, or Linux).
- After installing the SDK, you'll have access to the gcloud command-line

tool, which is used to manage Google Cloud resources.

1. **Initialize the SDK:**

- After installation, open your terminal and run the following command to initialize the SDK:

csharp

gcloud init

- This will guide you through selecting a Google Cloud project, setting up authentication, and configuring default settings like your preferred region.

1. **Authenticate with Google Cloud:**

- During the initialization process, you'll be prompted to authenticate your account. You can do this by following the provided link, signing in with your Google credentials, and copying the authentication token back into the terminal.

2.3.3 Setting Up Google Cloud Functions

Once the SDK is installed and initialized, you can start deploying serverless functions with **Google Cloud Functions**.

1. **Enable Cloud Functions API:**

- In the Google Cloud Console, you'll need to enable the **Cloud Functions API**. Go to the **API & Services** section, search for **Cloud Functions**, and click **Enable**.

1. **Creating a Google Cloud Project:**

CHAPTER 2: SETTING UP YOUR SERVERLESS ENVIRONMENT

- In Google Cloud, each serverless application or set of resources is organized under a **project**.
- To create a project, use the following command:

css

gcloud projects create [PROJECT_ID]

- Replace [PROJECT_ID] with a unique identifier for your project.
- You can set the project as your default with:

arduino

gcloud config set project [PROJECT_ID]

1. **Deploying a Cloud Function**:

- Let's create a simple Cloud Function using Node.js. First, create a JavaScript file (e.g., index.js) with the following code:

js

```
exports.helloWorld = (req, res) => {
  res.send('Hello, World!');
};
```

- This basic function will respond to HTTP requests with "Hello, World!".

1. **Deploying the Function Using gcloud**:

- In your terminal, navigate to the folder containing your index.js file and deploy the function with:

css

gcloud functions deploy helloWorld —runtime nodejs16 —trigger-http —allow-unauthenticated

- The —trigger-http flag specifies that the function will be triggered by HTTP requests. The —allow-unauthenticated flag allows anyone to invoke the function without authentication.

1. **Testing the Function**:

- After deployment, you'll receive a URL for your function. You can test it by visiting the URL in your browser or using a tool like curl to send an HTTP request:

css

curl [YOUR_FUNCTION_URL]

2.3.4 Setting Up IAM Roles in Google Cloud

To manage access and permissions for your serverless applications, you'll need to configure **IAM (Identity and Access Management)** in Google Cloud. IAM allows you to control who can deploy functions, access resources, and more.

1. **Create an IAM User**:

- In the **IAM & Admin** section of the Google Cloud Console, create a new user and assign them the necessary permissions to manage Cloud Functions.
- Common roles include **Cloud Functions Admin** and **Viewer**.

1. **Assigning Permissions**:

- You can assign roles to specific users or service accounts, allowing them to deploy, invoke, or manage your serverless applications.

2.3.5 Monitoring and Logging with Google Cloud

Google Cloud provides integrated monitoring and logging tools to track the performance of your serverless functions.

1. **Cloud Logging**:

- **Cloud Logging** automatically captures logs generated by your functions. You can view logs in the **Google Cloud Console** by going to **Logging** under **Operations**.
- Use the following command to view logs for a specific function:

bash

gcloud functions logs read helloWorld

1. **Cloud Monitoring**:

- **Cloud Monitoring** offers real-time insights into the performance and health of your serverless functions. You can track metrics like execution time, errors, and more.

By setting up Google Cloud for serverless development, you're now ready to deploy, monitor, and scale serverless functions with Google Cloud Functions. In the next section, we'll explore how to configure and manage serverless environments with **Microsoft Azure**.

2.4 Exploring Other Cloud Platforms (Azure, IBM, etc.)

While AWS and Google Cloud are two of the most popular platforms for serverless development, there are several other cloud providers that offer robust serverless solutions. Each of these platforms has unique features, pricing models, and integrations that can suit different business needs or technical requirements. In this section, we will briefly explore **Microsoft Azure, IBM Cloud**, and other alternatives for serverless architecture.

2.4.1 Microsoft Azure for Serverless Development

Microsoft Azure offers a suite of serverless computing options under the **Azure Functions** framework. Azure Functions allows you to run event-driven code without having to manage servers. It supports multiple programming languages, including JavaScript, C#, Python, and Java.

1. **Getting Started with Azure Functions**:

- Like AWS and Google Cloud, Azure requires an account. You can sign up at the Azure portal and access a **Free Tier** to explore its serverless capabilities.
- After signing up, go to the **Azure Functions** section to start creating serverless applications.

1. **Azure CLI and SDK**:

- Install the **Azure CLI** for command-line management of Azure resources. You can download it from the Azure documentation.
- Once installed, log in to Azure using:

az login

- You can now create and manage Azure Functions using the command-line interface.

1. **Deploying a Serverless Function on Azure**:

- A simple JavaScript function can be deployed in Azure Functions using the Azure CLI:

CHAPTER 2: SETTING UP YOUR SERVERLESS ENVIRONMENT

bash

az functionapp create —resource-group [ResourceGroup] —name [Function-AppName] —storage-account [StorageAccountName] —consumption-plan-location [Location] —runtime node

- This command sets up an Azure Function App for Node.js runtime.
- Azure provides built-in monitoring tools to track performance, including **Application Insights**.

1. **Azure Logic Apps for Workflow Automation**:

- Azure Logic Apps is a powerful tool for automating workflows and integrating applications with serverless architecture. It allows you to design workflows using a visual interface, integrating various services like Azure Functions, APIs, and databases.

2.4.2 IBM Cloud Functions

IBM Cloud Functions is built on the open-source **Apache OpenWhisk** project and provides a fully managed platform for running serverless functions.

1. **Getting Started with IBM Cloud Functions**:

- You can sign up for an IBM Cloud account at IBM Cloud and start using IBM Cloud Functions for free.
- IBM Cloud provides a comprehensive CLI for managing serverless functions. Install the CLI from the IBM Cloud documentation and log in with:

ibmcloud login

1. **Deploying a Cloud Function**:

- IBM Cloud Functions support multiple runtimes, including Node.js, Python, and Java.
- A simple Node.js function can be deployed using:

bash

ibmcloud fn action create helloWorld hello.js —kind nodejs:14

- The —kind flag specifies the runtime, and you can invoke the function using:

bash

ibmcloud fn action invoke helloWorld —result

1. **Integrating with IBM Services**:

- IBM Cloud offers deep integration with AI and machine learning services, such as **Watson**. You can trigger Cloud Functions based on events from services like **IBM Cloudant** (NoSQL database) and **IBM Watson** (for AI services like language processing and image recognition).

2.4.3 Other Serverless Platforms

Beyond the major cloud providers, there are several other serverless platforms worth considering for specialized use cases or multi-cloud strategies.

1. **Oracle Cloud Functions**:

- **Oracle Cloud** offers **Oracle Functions**, which is also built on **Apache OpenWhisk** and allows for serverless deployments on Oracle's cloud infrastructure.

- Oracle Cloud Functions is tightly integrated with Oracle's suite of enterprise applications and services, such as Oracle Autonomous Database, making it a great choice for businesses using Oracle software.

1. **Alibaba Cloud Function Compute**:

- **Alibaba Cloud** is one of the leading cloud providers in Asia and offers **Function Compute** as part of its serverless offerings.
- It supports a variety of languages, including JavaScript, and integrates seamlessly with other Alibaba Cloud services, making it a strong choice for organizations with a presence in the Chinese market.

1. **DigitalOcean Functions**:

- **DigitalOcean** is popular for its simplicity and low-cost hosting options. **DigitalOcean Functions** offers serverless capabilities with a developer-friendly interface, supporting Node.js and Python.

1. **Vercel and Netlify**:

- **Vercel** and **Netlify** are popular for static site hosting and offer **serverless functions** as part of their toolset. These platforms are highly optimized for front-end developers who want to integrate serverless functionality into their web applications.

2.4.4 Key Considerations for Choosing a Serverless Provider

When selecting a cloud platform for your serverless architecture, it's important to consider the following:

1. **Language Support**:

- Ensure the provider supports the programming language you plan to use, especially JavaScript/Node.js.

1. **Integrations and Ecosystem**:

- Different providers have varying levels of integration with other services. If you are already using services from a particular provider, such as **AWS S3** or **Google Cloud BigQuery**, it might make sense to choose that provider for serverless functions to simplify integration.

1. **Pricing Models**:

- Each platform has its pricing structure. Some offer more generous free tiers, while others provide competitive pricing for large-scale applications. Consider both short-term and long-term costs.

1. **Global Reach and Latency**:

- If your application has users in different regions, consider the provider's global reach and ability to deploy serverless functions across multiple regions.

1. **Tooling and Developer Experience**:

- Some platforms offer more advanced development tools and monitoring services, which can improve your productivity and ability to manage serverless applications effectively.

Summary

In this section, we explored the setup process for several major serverless platforms, including **AWS**, **Google Cloud**, **Microsoft Azure**, and others. By understanding how to configure these environments and leverage the tools provided by each cloud platform, you are now equipped to build and deploy serverless applications using a variety of cloud providers.

This section has provided a foundational understanding of how to set up Node.js and your development tools, deploy functions to various cloud platforms, and manage dependencies and integrations.

2.5 Configuring Local Development Environments for Serverless Applications

Developing serverless applications typically involves setting up a local environment where you can write, test, and debug your code before deploying it to the cloud. Although serverless functions are designed to run in cloud environments, having a well-configured local environment can speed up development by allowing you to simulate serverless execution without repeatedly deploying code.

In this section, we will walk through how to configure a local development environment for serverless applications, covering the tools and practices you need for AWS Lambda, Google Cloud Functions, Azure Functions, and other platforms.

2.5.1 Why Use a Local Development Environment?

Before diving into setup, let's highlight the benefits of using a local development environment for serverless applications:

1. **Speed**: Deploying to the cloud every time you make a small change can be time-consuming. Running functions locally allows for faster iterations.
2. **Cost Savings**: Frequent deployments can incur cloud usage costs. A local environment eliminates this concern during development.
3. **Debugging**: Cloud environments often have limited debugging capabilities. Local environments allow you to use standard debugging tools like breakpoints and logs.
4. **Version Control**: You can manage changes more effectively with version control systems (e.g., Git) when working in a local environment.

2.5.2 Key Tools for Local Development

To create an efficient local development environment for serverless applications, you will need a combination of development tools, cloud emulators, and function frameworks. Below are some of the most important tools:

1. **Node.js and NPM**:

- Since JavaScript and Node.js are central to serverless development, ensure that you have **Node.js** installed. Most serverless platforms use Node.js as a runtime environment.
- You can install it by downloading from Node.js or using a package manager like **Homebrew** on macOS or **nvm** (Node Version Manager) for managing multiple Node.js versions.

1. **Serverless Framework**:

- The **Serverless Framework** is a popular open-source tool for developing serverless applications. It provides a consistent interface for deploying functions across multiple cloud providers, including AWS, Google Cloud, and Azure.
- Install the Serverless Framework globally:

bash

npm install -g serverless

- After installation, you can scaffold a new project for AWS Lambda using:

bash

serverless create —template aws-nodejs —path my-service

- The framework allows you to run functions locally:

bash

serverless invoke local —function myFunction

CHAPTER 2: SETTING UP YOUR SERVERLESS ENVIRONMENT

1. **AWS SAM (Serverless Application Model)**:

- The **AWS SAM CLI** allows you to simulate AWS Lambda functions locally, making it easier to test functions before deploying them.
- Install AWS SAM by following the [SAM CLI installation guide](#).
- Once installed, you can run the function locally with:

bash

sam local invoke

- This allows you to emulate AWS Lambda events (such as API Gateway requests or DynamoDB triggers) on your local machine.

1. **Google Cloud Functions Emulator**:

- **Google Cloud Functions** can be tested locally using the **Functions Framework**.
- Install it via npm:

bash

npm install @google-cloud/functions-framework

- You can then run the framework locally with:

bash

functions-framework —target=myFunction

1. **Azure Functions Core Tools**:

- **Azure Functions Core Tools** allow you to develop and test Azure

Functions locally.
- You can install it from Azure Functions Documentation.
- Once installed, you can create a new function app and run it locally:

bash

func init MyFunctionApp —worker-runtime node
func start

1. **Docker**:

- Some serverless platforms, like AWS Lambda, allow functions to be packaged and deployed as Docker containers. Docker also enables you to simulate serverless environments on your machine.
- If your application requires a custom runtime or specific dependencies, Docker can be used to develop locally and test in a consistent containerized environment.

2.5.3 Setting Up Emulators for Cloud Services

In many serverless applications, functions interact with various cloud services, such as databases, message queues, and storage. Setting up emulators for these services locally can give you a complete development environment. Here are a few emulators for popular services:

1. **DynamoDB Local (AWS)**:

- AWS offers a local version of **DynamoDB** that can be used for testing database interactions.
- Download and run it locally:

bash

docker run -p 8000:8000 amazon/dynamodb-local

CHAPTER 2: SETTING UP YOUR SERVERLESS ENVIRONMENT

- You can connect your AWS Lambda functions to this local instance of DynamoDB instead of the cloud-based version.

1. **Google Cloud Datastore Emulator**:

- **Google Cloud Datastore** provides a local emulator for testing database interactions.
- You can start the emulator using:

bash

gcloud beta emulators datastore start

1. **Azure Storage Emulator**:

- **Azure Storage Emulator** is useful when building applications that use **Blob, Queue**, or **Table storage**.
- Install the emulator via Azure Storage Documentation.

2.5.4 Best Practices for Local Development

1. **Environment Variables**:

- Serverless applications often rely on environment variables for configuring services like databases, authentication, and third-party APIs.
- Use a .env file to store environment variables locally, and use packages like dotenv to load them in your application:

bash

npm install dotenv

- Example .env file:

makefile

DB_HOST=localhost
  DB_USER=root
  DB_PASSWORD=password

- Load them in your application:

javascript

require('dotenv').config();

1. **Unit Testing**:

- While local emulators are great for integration testing, unit tests are essential for testing individual functions and logic.
- Frameworks like **Jest** or **Mocha** can be used to create comprehensive test suites for your functions. Here's an example with Jest:

bash

npm install jest
  Add a test script in package.json:
  json

"scripts": {
  "test": "jest"
  }

1. **Continuous Integration**:

- Set up continuous integration (CI) pipelines with tools like **GitHub Actions** or **CircleCI** to run tests, linting, and automated deployment to

serverless platforms.
- CI pipelines help ensure that your serverless functions are always ready for production deployment.

Summary

This summary provided a comprehensive guide to setting up your serverless environment across various cloud platforms, including **AWS**, **Google Cloud**, **Microsoft Azure**, and others. We walked through the installation of tools and emulators for local development, enabling you to build and test serverless applications efficiently without needing to constantly deploy to the cloud.

By now, you should have a functional development environment that supports both local testing and cloud deployment. You've also gained insights into best practices for configuring your environment, using emulators for cloud services, and applying testing strategies for serverless development.

2.6 Creating Your First AWS Lambda and Google Cloud Function

In this section, we will guide you through the steps of creating your very first **AWS Lambda** and **Google Cloud Function**. Both platforms offer easy ways to set up serverless functions that can scale automatically based on demand. By the end of this section, you will have successfully created and deployed a basic function on both platforms.

2.6.1 Creating an AWS Lambda Function

To create your first AWS Lambda function, follow these steps:

1. **Log in to the AWS Management Console**:

- Navigate to the **AWS Lambda** service by searching for "Lambda" in the console search bar.

1. **Create a New Function**:

- Click "**Create function**".
- Choose the option "**Author from scratch**".
- Provide a **function name** (e.g., MyFirstLambda).

- Set the **runtime** to **Node.js** (e.g., Node.js 14.x).
- Set an **execution role**. You can use an existing role or create a new one with basic Lambda permissions.

1. **Write Your Lambda Function**:

- AWS will present a code editor where you can write your first Lambda function.
- Use the following simple **Hello World** example:

javascript

```
exports.handler = async (event) => {
  const response = {
  statusCode: 200,
  body: JSON.stringify('Hello from Lambda!'),
  };
  return response;
};
```

1. **Test Your Lambda Function**:

- AWS Lambda allows you to test your function directly from the console.
- Click the **Test** button and provide an event (leave it as default for now).
- You should see the response:

json

```
{
  "statusCode": 200,
  "body": "\"Hello from Lambda!\""
}
```

1. **Deploy Your Lambda Function**:

- Once you're satisfied with the function, deploy it by clicking **"Deploy"**.

1. **Invoke the Lambda Function**:

- You can invoke the function using the **Lambda Console**, or if you've set it up to be triggered by an event (e.g., API Gateway, S3, DynamoDB), it will run in response to that event.

2.6.2 Creating a Google Cloud Function
Creating a Google Cloud Function is quite similar. Follow these steps:

1. **Log in to the Google Cloud Console**:

- Navigate to **Cloud Functions** by searching for it in the Google Cloud Console.

1. **Create a New Cloud Function**:

- Click **"Create Function"**.
- Choose a **function name** (e.g., MyFirstCloudFunction).
- Set the **region** and **runtime** to **Node.js** (e.g., Node.js 14).

1. **Write Your Cloud Function**:

- Google Cloud will provide a code editor similar to AWS Lambda.
- Write the following simple function:

javascript

```
exports.helloWorld = (req, res) => {
  res.status(200).send('Hello from Google Cloud Function!');
```

};

1. **Trigger and Deploy Your Function**:

- Set the trigger to **HTTP** (default for simple functions).
- Click **"Deploy"** to deploy the function to Google Cloud.

1. **Invoke the Google Cloud Function**:

- Once the function is deployed, Google will provide you with an HTTP URL to trigger the function.
- Open the URL in a browser or use a tool like **cURL** or **Postman** to invoke it.
- You should see the response:

javascript

Hello from Google Cloud Function!

2.6.3 Testing and Debugging

Both AWS Lambda and Google Cloud Functions provide mechanisms to test your functions:

- **AWS Lambda** has a test feature built into the AWS Console where you can pass mock events and see the output.
- **Google Cloud Functions** provide an **HTTP endpoint** (for HTTP-triggered functions) to test with real or simulated requests.

In addition to the native tools, you can test functions locally using the **Serverless Framework, AWS SAM CLI,** or **Google Cloud Functions Framework** as discussed in the previous section.

Summary

In this section, you have successfully set up your environment for serverless development and created your first **AWS Lambda** and **Google Cloud**

Function. By installing the required tools, configuring local development environments, and deploying basic functions, you now have a solid foundation for building more complex serverless applications.

Throughout this section, we covered:

- Installing and configuring **Node.js** and various JavaScript development tools.
- Setting up environments for **AWS Lambda**, **Google Cloud**, and other platforms like **Azure**.
- Using cloud emulators and local development tools to simulate serverless environments.
- Finally, deploying your first simple serverless functions on both AWS and Google Cloud.

With this foundational knowledge, you're ready to dive deeper into serverless architecture. In the next chapter, we'll explore how to build and deploy more sophisticated serverless applications, including event-driven architectures, integrating with third-party services, and optimizing performance.

CHAPTER 3: AWS LAMBDA FUNDAMENTALS

3.1 What is AWS Lambda?

AWS Lambda is Amazon Web Services' serverless compute service that lets you run code without provisioning or managing servers. The idea behind Lambda is simple: you write and upload your function (code), set the event triggers, and AWS handles the scaling, infrastructure, and management automatically.

Lambda is event-driven, meaning it executes your code in response to specific events. These events could come from various AWS services, such as **S3** (when a file is uploaded), **DynamoDB** (when data changes), or **API Gateway** (when an API request is made). You only pay for the execution time of your code, making Lambda a cost-efficient solution for running backend services, automation tasks, or microservices.

Key features of AWS Lambda include:

- **Serverless**: No need to worry about underlying infrastructure.
- **Scalable**: AWS Lambda scales automatically, handling thousands of requests per second.
- **Pay-as-you-go**: You're only billed for the compute time used by your function.
- **Event-driven**: It responds to events from other AWS services or external HTTP requests.

In the following sections, we will explore how AWS Lambda operates, what makes it unique, and its key role in the modern serverless landscape.

How AWS Lambda Works

When an event occurs, such as an HTTP request or an S3 upload, AWS Lambda responds by:

1. **Triggering the function**: Based on predefined rules or event listeners, AWS Lambda initiates your function.
2. **Executing the function**: Your JavaScript code runs within the Lambda execution environment. AWS manages the computing resources necessary for this execution.
3. **Returning the output**: After processing the event, Lambda either returns the output to the invoking service or triggers another event in your architecture (e.g., sending a message to SNS or updating a DynamoDB table).

Lambda abstracts the underlying infrastructure, allowing you to focus on writing code rather than maintaining or scaling servers.

Use Cases for AWS Lambda

AWS Lambda is commonly used in a variety of real-world scenarios:

- **File processing**: Automatically process uploaded files in S3 (e.g., resizing images, transcribing audio).
- **Data pipelines**: Respond to events in a data stream (e.g., real-time analytics on incoming data in Kinesis).
- **API backends**: Handle API requests via API Gateway (e.g., implementing RESTful APIs).
- **Automation**: Create scheduled tasks with **Amazon CloudWatch** to perform routine maintenance, clean-up, or backups.
- **Chatbots and voice assistants**: Power intelligent responses through AWS Lambda for services like **Alexa**.

Now that we have an overview of what AWS Lambda is, let's dive deeper into how it contrasts with other architectures and why it's a vital component of the serverless paradigm.

3.2 Creating and Deploying Lambda Functions with JavaScript

AWS Lambda supports multiple programming languages, but using **JavaScript** with **Node.js** is one of the most popular approaches due to JavaScript's versatility in both frontend and backend development. In this section, we will walk through the steps required to create, deploy, and invoke an AWS Lambda function using JavaScript.

3.2.1 Step-by-Step Guide to Creating Your First Lambda Function with JavaScript

Step 1: Access the AWS Lambda Console

To get started, log in to the **AWS Management Console** and navigate to the **Lambda** service. You can find Lambda by searching for it in the AWS search bar.

Step 2: Create a New Lambda Function

Once in the Lambda dashboard:

1. Click on the **"Create function"** button.
2. Select **"Author from scratch"** as the option.
3. Set a **Function name** (e.g., MyFirstLambdaFunction).
4. Choose **Node.js** as the **runtime** (e.g., **Node.js 18.x**).
5. Set the **Execution role**: You can either choose an existing role or create a new one with basic Lambda permissions (e.g., AWSLambdaBasicExecutionRole).
6. Click **Create function**.

Step 3: Write the Lambda Function in JavaScript

Once the function is created, you will be presented with a code editor in the AWS Console. Here's a simple example of a **Hello World** Lambda function in JavaScript:

javascript

exports.handler = async (event) => {

```
const response = {
statusCode: 200,
body: JSON.stringify('Hello from AWS Lambda!'),
};
return response;
};
```
This function:

- Returns a statusCode of 200, indicating success.
- Returns a JSON string in the body saying, "Hello from AWS Lambda!"

Step 4: Configure Triggers (Optional)

You can set up triggers for your Lambda function. For example, you could have the function trigger every time an object is uploaded to an S3 bucket or when an API call is made via API Gateway. For now, we'll leave this as-is and manually invoke the function later.

Step 5: Deploy the Function

Once you've written your code, click **Deploy** to save the function and push the changes to AWS Lambda.

3.2.2 Testing Your Lambda Function

After deploying your function, it's time to test it.

Step 1: Set Up a Test Event

1. In the **AWS Lambda Console**, navigate to the **Test** tab.
2. Click **"Configure test event"**.
3. Choose the **Event template**. You can leave the default test event as-is or create a custom one.
4. Click **Save**.

Step 2: Invoke the Function

Once your test event is configured:

- Click **Test** to invoke the Lambda function using the test event.

- You should see a successful response in the **Execution results** pane, showing:

json

```
{
  "statusCode": 200,
  "body": "\"Hello from AWS Lambda!\""
}
```

3.2.3 Deploying Lambda Functions via the AWS CLI

While the AWS Management Console is user-friendly, deploying Lambda functions through the **AWS Command Line Interface (CLI)** offers more flexibility, especially for automating deployments in development pipelines.

Step 1: Install the AWS CLI

Before you begin, ensure that you have the AWS CLI installed and configured:

- Install the AWS CLI by following instructions from the AWS CLI installation guide.
- Configure the CLI with your AWS credentials:

bash

```
aws configure
```

Step 2: Create a Lambda Function Package

To deploy a function via the CLI, you'll need to package it into a **.zip** file:

1. Create a directory for your Lambda function:

bash

```
mkdir my-lambda-function
cd my-lambda-function
```

1. Create a index.js file with the following code:

javascript

```javascript
exports.handler = async (event) => {
  const response = {
  statusCode: 200,
  body: JSON.stringify('Hello from AWS Lambda!'),
  };
  return response;
};
```

1. Zip the contents of the directory:

bash

```bash
zip -r function.zip .
```

Step 3: Deploy the Function Using AWS CLI

Use the AWS CLI to create a new Lambda function:

bash

```bash
aws lambda create-function \
  —function-name MyFirstLambdaFunctionCLI \
  —runtime nodejs18.x \
  —role arn:aws:iam::123456789012:role/execution_role \
  —handler index.handler \
  —zip-file fileb://function.zip
```

- Replace MyFirstLambdaFunctionCLI with the name of your function.
- Ensure that execution_role is replaced with the correct **IAM role ARN** for Lambda execution.

3.2.4 Invoking the Lambda Function via AWS CLI

To invoke your Lambda function using the AWS CLI:
bash

aws lambda invoke \
 —function-name MyFirstLambdaFunctionCLI \
 output.txt

- This command will execute the Lambda function and store the response in the output.txt file.

You should see the output Hello from AWS Lambda! inside the output.txt file.

Summary

In this section, we covered how to create, deploy, and test AWS Lambda functions written in JavaScript. You can create and deploy Lambda functions through both the AWS Management Console and the AWS CLI, providing flexibility depending on your use case. As you begin deploying more complex applications, automating these deployments with CLI commands or scripts can greatly improve productivity.

3.3 Understanding Event-Driven Architecture in AWS Lambda

AWS Lambda is a core component of **event-driven architectures**, where services or applications respond to events in near real-time. In a traditional architecture, you may have to manage and scale servers or processes that continuously listen for incoming requests. However, in an event-driven model, actions (or **events**) trigger functions, allowing you to build more efficient, decoupled, and scalable systems.

In this section, we will delve deeper into how AWS Lambda leverages event-driven design principles and integrates with various AWS services to execute code in response to events.

3.3.1 What is Event-Driven Architecture?

Event-driven architecture (EDA) is a software design paradigm in which the flow of the program is determined by events. These events can be anything from an HTTP request, a file upload, a database update, or a message in a queue. EDA allows applications to react to changes or actions and is widely used in **asynchronous systems** where responses to events are processed separately.

The core components of event-driven architecture include:

- **Event Producers**: Systems or services that generate events. This could be an S3 bucket, API Gateway, or user interaction in a frontend.
- **Event Consumers**: These are systems or services that respond to or process the events. AWS Lambda functions typically serve as event consumers, executing code when the event occurs.
- **Event Channels**: The medium through which the event data is passed between producers and consumers. In AWS, these channels could be services like **SNS (Simple Notification Service)**, **SQS (Simple Queue Service)**, or **EventBridge**.

3.3.2 AWS Lambda's Role in Event-Driven Architectures

AWS Lambda plays the role of the event consumer in an event-driven system. It listens for events from AWS services or external sources, executes the corresponding function, and then terminates when the task is complete.

Key characteristics that make AWS Lambda ideal for event-driven architectures:

- **Automatic execution**: Lambda automatically invokes your function when an event is detected, without requiring manual intervention.
- **Scalability**: Lambda can scale automatically to handle high volumes of events. If multiple events occur simultaneously, Lambda will scale horizontally to ensure that all events are processed.
- **Asynchronous execution**: Lambda can be invoked asynchronously, meaning you don't need to wait for the function to complete before continuing with other tasks.
- **Event sources**: Lambda integrates seamlessly with many AWS services, acting as the backend for processing events from S3, DynamoDB, Kinesis, and many more.

3.3.3 Common Event Sources in AWS Lambda

AWS Lambda can be triggered by a variety of **event sources**, which include both AWS services and custom events from external systems. Let's explore some of the most common event sources for Lambda functions:

1. S3 (Simple Storage Service)

When an object is created, deleted, or modified in an S3 bucket, it can trigger a Lambda function. Common use cases include:

- Automatically resizing images upon upload.
- Running virus scans on files uploaded to a bucket.
- Processing log files or data after they are stored.

2. API Gateway

You can use AWS **API Gateway** to create RESTful or HTTP-based APIs that invoke Lambda functions. This is often used to build **serverless APIs** where Lambda functions handle backend processing.

- Use case: When a client sends an HTTP request to the API, the Gateway forwards the request to Lambda, which processes it and returns a response.

3. DynamoDB

Changes in a **DynamoDB table** (such as adding or modifying items) can trigger Lambda functions. This is particularly useful for real-time data processing or analytics.

- Use case: When a new item is added to a table, Lambda can process the data and push it to other services, such as Elasticsearch for indexing.

4. SQS (Simple Queue Service)

SQS is a message queuing service that allows asynchronous communication between distributed systems. Lambda functions can process messages from an SQS queue, enabling scalable, decoupled services.

- Use case: A Lambda function processes messages from a queue to complete tasks, such as order fulfillment in an e-commerce system.

5. SNS (Simple Notification Service)

Lambda can subscribe to **SNS topics**, which are used for messaging and notifications. When a message is published to the topic, Lambda functions can be triggered to process or relay that message.

- Use case: Sending notifications based on specific events or alerts.

6. Kinesis

Amazon Kinesis allows real-time processing of streaming data. Lambda can consume data from a Kinesis stream and perform analytics or transformations in real-time.

- Use case: Processing log data from multiple sources or monitoring data streams for real-time insights.

7. CloudWatch Events and CloudWatch Logs

Lambda can respond to scheduled events or alarms using **CloudWatch Events**. For example, a Lambda function could be triggered to perform system maintenance or send alerts based on predefined thresholds.

- Use case: Running daily reports, performing backups, or automatically scaling infrastructure in response to CloudWatch metrics.

3.3.4 How to Configure Event Sources for Lambda

There are two primary ways to set up event sources for Lambda functions:

1. Configuring Event Sources in the AWS Console

1. Navigate to your Lambda function in the **AWS Management Console**.
2. Scroll down to the **Triggers** section and click **"Add trigger"**.
3. Choose an event source (e.g., **S3, API Gateway, DynamoDB**).

4. Set up the specific event configuration (e.g., for S3, specify the bucket and event type).
5. Click **Add** to finalize the trigger configuration.

2. Configuring Event Sources with AWS CLI

You can also use the **AWS CLI** to add event sources programmatically. For example, to set up a trigger for an S3 event, you can use the following command:

bash

aws lambda create-event-source-mapping \
 —function-name MyLambdaFunction \
 —event-source arn:aws:s3:::my-bucket \
 —starting-position LATEST

This flexibility allows for more dynamic and automated deployments, especially in larger systems.

3.3.5 Benefits of Event-Driven Architecture with AWS Lambda

1. **Scalability**: Lambda automatically scales in response to the volume of events, handling multiple invocations simultaneously without manual intervention.
2. **Cost Efficiency**: With Lambda's pay-per-use pricing model, you only incur charges when your function is triggered, making it highly cost-effective.
3. **Reduced Infrastructure Management**: Since Lambda is fully managed, you don't need to worry about managing or scaling servers. AWS handles the infrastructure, allowing you to focus on your application's functionality.
4. **Real-Time Processing**: Event-driven architectures are ideal for real-time data processing. Lambda functions can be triggered by events the moment they occur, ensuring timely processing of data or requests.

Summary

Understanding how AWS Lambda integrates into event-driven architectures is essential for creating responsive, scalable, and cost-efficient applications. By leveraging various AWS services as event sources, you can build powerful serverless applications that respond to events in real-time without manual scaling or server management.

3.4 Triggering AWS Lambda with API Gateway

Amazon API Gateway is a fully managed service that enables developers to create and publish RESTful and HTTP-based APIs that act as a "front door" for applications. One of the most powerful use cases for API Gateway is integrating it with AWS Lambda, where API requests trigger Lambda functions to handle the backend logic. This combination allows you to build fully serverless web applications and microservices with no infrastructure to manage.

In this section, we'll dive into how you can use API Gateway to trigger AWS Lambda functions, explore common use cases, and set up a simple example to connect the two services.

3.4.1 What is API Gateway?

API Gateway acts as a bridge between clients (such as browsers, mobile apps, or other services) and AWS Lambda functions. It allows you to expose a public API that clients can use to send HTTP or HTTPS requests, which are then routed to Lambda for processing.

Key features of API Gateway include:

- **Request Routing**: Routes HTTP requests to appropriate backend services (such as Lambda).
- **Throttling and Rate Limiting**: Protects your API from excessive usage or abuse by limiting the number of requests allowed per second.
- **Authorization**: Supports various forms of authentication and authorization, including AWS IAM, Cognito, and OAuth 2.0.
- **Caching**: Reduces latency by caching responses to repeat requests.
- **Logging and Monitoring**: Provides built-in CloudWatch monitoring to track API usage and performance.

3.4.2 Setting Up API Gateway to Trigger Lambda Functions

Let's go through the process of connecting API Gateway to Lambda in a few steps:

Step 1: Creating a Lambda Function

First, you'll need a Lambda function that will be triggered by the API. If you already have one, you can skip this step.

Here's an example of a simple Lambda function that returns a JSON response when triggered:

javascript

```
exports.handler = async (event) => {
  const response = {
  statusCode: 200,
  body: JSON.stringify({ message: "Hello, world!" }),
  };
  return response;
};
```

You can create this function in the AWS Management Console:

1. Go to **AWS Lambda** in the console.
2. Click on **Create Function**.
3. Name your function (e.g., HelloWorldFunction) and choose **Node.js** as the runtime.
4. In the function editor, replace the default code with the example code above.
5. Click **Deploy** to save your function.

Step 2: Creating an API Gateway

Now that we have a Lambda function, the next step is to create an API Gateway to trigger it.

1. In the **API Gateway** console, click **Create API**.
2. Choose **HTTP API** or **REST API** depending on your needs. For this

example, we'll use **HTTP API** for simplicity.
3. Click **Build**.
4. In the **Configure routes** section, click **Add integration** and select **Lambda**.
5. Select your Lambda function (HelloWorldFunction) and click **Add**.
6. Configure the route for your API:

- **Method**: GET
- **Resource path**: /hello

1. Review and click **Create**.

Step 3: Testing the API Gateway

Now that the API is set up to trigger your Lambda function, you can test it.

1. In the **API Gateway** console, navigate to your newly created API and find the **Invoke URL**.
2. Copy the **Invoke URL** and append /hello to it (e.g., https://abc123.execute-api.us-east-1.amazonaws.com/hello).
3. Open your browser or use a tool like **Postman** or **cURL** to send a GET request to this URL.

If everything is set up correctly, the Lambda function will be triggered, and you should receive the following JSON response:

json

```
{
  "message": "Hello, world!"
}
```

3.4.3 Common Use Cases for API Gateway and Lambda Integration

The integration of API Gateway and Lambda unlocks a wide range of use cases for building serverless APIs, microservices, and backend logic. Some of the most common use cases include:

1. **Serverless Web Applications**: Use API Gateway to handle HTTP requests from frontend clients (e.g., Single Page Applications) and invoke Lambda functions for backend processing.

   - **Example**: A weather app that queries weather data via API Gateway and retrieves weather information through a Lambda function.

1. **Microservices Architecture**: API Gateway acts as the entry point for different microservices, with each service mapped to a corresponding Lambda function.

   - **Example**: An e-commerce system where separate Lambda functions handle product searches, user authentication, and payment processing.

1. **Webhook Receivers**: API Gateway can be used to receive and process webhooks from third-party services, triggering Lambda functions to process or store the data.

   - **Example**: Integrating with a payment gateway to process transactions via webhooks and trigger Lambda functions for order fulfillment.

1. **Mobile and IoT Applications**: API Gateway can be used as the backend for mobile and IoT applications, forwarding requests from these devices to Lambda for processing.

   - **Example**: A mobile app that sends user location data to an API, where Lambda functions process and store it in a database.

3.4.4 Securing Your API Gateway with Lambda Integration

One of the critical aspects of building APIs is ensuring proper security measures. With API Gateway, you can apply various security mechanisms to protect your Lambda functions and ensure only authorized clients can access them.

1. **AWS IAM Authorization**: You can use **IAM roles** and policies to restrict access to your API. Only users or services with the appropriate IAM permissions can invoke your Lambda functions.
2. **AWS Cognito Authentication**: For user-based authentication, **Amazon Cognito** can be integrated with API Gateway to manage user sign-up, sign-in, and access controls.
3. **API Keys and Throttling**: You can create **API keys** for clients that need to access your API and set up **usage plans** that limit the number of requests to prevent abuse.
4. **OAuth 2.0 and Custom Authorizers**: If you want to implement a custom authentication mechanism, you can create **Lambda Authorizers** (formerly known as custom authorizers) that check tokens, verify user credentials, or perform any other necessary logic before allowing access.

3.4.5 Benefits of Using API Gateway with AWS Lambda

1. **Simplified Backend Development**: With API Gateway, you can avoid the complexities of managing servers and focus solely on writing the logic in your Lambda functions.
2. **Scalability**: API Gateway can automatically scale to handle thousands or even millions of requests, and Lambda will scale accordingly to process each event.
3. **Cost Efficiency**: Since you're only billed for the API requests made and the Lambda executions, you can drastically reduce infrastructure costs, especially for applications with intermittent usage.
4. **Security and Monitoring**: API Gateway integrates seamlessly with AWS security services like IAM, CloudWatch, and WAF, providing comprehensive monitoring and security controls.

Summary

By integrating AWS Lambda with API Gateway, you can build highly scalable, secure, and cost-efficient APIs without the overhead of managing servers. API Gateway serves as the bridge between clients and Lambda functions, providing robust features such as request routing, throttling, and security controls.

3.5 Managing Permissions with IAM for AWS Lambda

In any serverless application, security is paramount, and managing permissions effectively ensures that your AWS Lambda functions operate securely and as intended. AWS Identity and Access Management (IAM) is a key service that allows you to control access to AWS services and resources, including Lambda functions.

In this section, we'll explore how to manage permissions for AWS Lambda using IAM, understand the various roles and policies involved, and look at best practices for securing your Lambda functions.

3.5.1 Introduction to IAM

AWS Identity and Access Management (IAM) is a service that enables you to manage access to AWS resources securely. Using IAM, you can:

- Control who can access specific AWS resources (such as Lambda functions, S3 buckets, or DynamoDB tables).
- Define what actions users or services can perform on those resources.
- Securely delegate access to external users and applications.

For AWS Lambda, IAM plays a crucial role in both:

- **Assigning permissions** to your Lambda functions to allow them to access other AWS services.
- **Controlling access** to who can invoke and manage your Lambda functions.

3.5.2 Key IAM Concepts for AWS Lambda

Before we dive into setting up permissions, it's important to understand the key IAM components relevant to Lambda.

- **IAM Users**: These are individual users (such as developers) who may need access to manage Lambda functions or other AWS resources.
- **IAM Roles**: These are sets of permissions that are assigned to AWS

resources. Lambda functions use IAM roles to access other AWS services (e.g., S3, DynamoDB). You can also assign IAM roles to users or services.
- **IAM Policies**: These are JSON documents that define permissions for an IAM role or user. Policies specify what actions are allowed (or denied) and on which resources. For Lambda, you'll create policies that grant specific access to services like S3, API Gateway, and others.
- **Resource-Based Policies**: These are policies that are directly attached to resources, such as Lambda functions. They specify who can invoke the function or access its resources.

3.5.3 Setting Up an IAM Role for AWS Lambda

Every Lambda function requires an **execution role** that grants it permission to access AWS resources like S3, DynamoDB, or SNS. Let's walk through the process of creating a role for a Lambda function.

Step 1: Creating an IAM Role for Lambda

1. In the **IAM Console**, navigate to **Roles** and click **Create Role**.
2. Under **Trusted Entity Type**, select **AWS Service**, and then choose **Lambda** from the list of services.
3. Click **Next** to add permissions.

Step 2: Adding Permissions to the Role

Next, you'll need to assign permissions to the role, determining what AWS services the Lambda function can access. For instance, if your Lambda function needs to read from an S3 bucket, you'll grant it s3:ListBucket and s3:GetObject permissions.

1. Click **Attach Policies** and search for the relevant service (e.g., **AmazonS3FullAccess**).
2. Add the required policies (you can also create custom policies if needed).
3. Click **Next** and give your role a meaningful name (e.g., LambdaS3AccessRole).

Step 3: Assigning the Role to a Lambda Function

Once the role is created, you can assign it to your Lambda function:

1. Navigate to your **Lambda function** in the AWS Console.
2. Under the **Configuration** tab, go to **Permissions** and click on **Execution Role**.
3. Select **Use an Existing Role** and choose the role you just created (LambdaS3AccessRole).
4. Save the changes.

Now your Lambda function has permission to interact with the specified AWS resources (in this case, S3).

3.5.4 Granting Permissions to Invoke Lambda Functions

IAM policies can also control who is allowed to invoke your Lambda functions. For example, you may want to grant permission for an API Gateway, S3 events, or specific IAM users to trigger your Lambda function.

Example 1: Granting API Gateway Permission to Invoke a Lambda Function

To allow API Gateway to invoke a Lambda function, you need to add an **AWS Lambda Resource Policy**. Here's an example policy that grants API Gateway permission:

json

```
{
  "Version": "2012-10-17",
  "Statement": [
    {
      "Effect": "Allow",
      "Principal": {
        "Service": "apigateway.amazonaws.com"
      },
      "Action": "lambda:InvokeFunction",
      "Resource": "arn:aws:lambda:us-east-1:123456789012:function:MyFuncti
```

on"
   }
  ]
}

1. In the AWS Lambda Console, go to your **Lambda function**.
2. Under the **Configuration** tab, select **Permissions** and then click on **Resource-based policies**.
3. Add the above policy, replacing the **ARN** of your Lambda function.

Example 2: Granting S3 Permission to Invoke a Lambda Function

If you're using S3 to trigger Lambda functions (e.g., in response to file uploads), you'll need to add permissions for S3 to invoke the Lambda function. The process is similar to API Gateway, but the **Principal** changes to s3.amazonaws.com.

json

{
"Version": "2012-10-17",
"Statement": [
{
"Effect": "Allow",
"Principal": {
"Service": "s3.amazonaws.com"
},
"Action": "lambda:InvokeFunction",
"Resource": "arn:aws:lambda:us-east-1:123456789012:function:MyS3Triggered Function"
  }
 ]
}

3.5.5 Best Practices for Managing IAM Permissions for Lambda

1. **Principle of Least Privilege**: Always assign the minimum permissions necessary for your Lambda function to operate. This reduces the attack surface and minimizes the risk of security vulnerabilities.
2. **Use Managed Policies**: AWS provides pre-built **managed policies** that contain commonly used permissions for Lambda. These can simplify permission management but ensure that you review the policies to confirm they meet your security requirements.
3. **Monitor and Audit IAM Roles**: Regularly audit the roles assigned to your Lambda functions and monitor their use with AWS CloudTrail. This helps detect any unauthorized or unusual access patterns.
4. **Avoid Hardcoding Credentials**: Never hardcode AWS credentials (e.g., access keys) into your Lambda code. Instead, use IAM roles and policies to manage permissions securely.
5. **Use Resource-Based Policies Where Appropriate**: For finer-grained control, use **resource-based policies** on your Lambda functions. This is particularly useful when external services or cross-account access is needed.

Summary

Managing permissions with IAM is crucial for ensuring that your Lambda functions are both secure and functional. By understanding how to assign roles, manage policies, and enforce the principle of least privilege, you can protect your serverless applications from potential security threats while ensuring they have the necessary access to AWS services.

3.6 Logging and Monitoring Lambda Functions with CloudWatch

Monitoring the performance and behavior of your AWS Lambda functions is essential for identifying issues, optimizing performance, and maintaining the overall health of your serverless applications. Amazon CloudWatch, a powerful monitoring service, is a key tool in your AWS toolkit for logging, tracking metrics, and setting up alarms to monitor Lambda functions in real-time.

In this section, we will cover the basics of logging and monitoring AWS Lambda functions using CloudWatch, explore how to set up log groups and metrics, and discuss best practices for monitoring Lambda performance and error handling.

3.6.1 Introduction to Amazon CloudWatch

Amazon CloudWatch is a monitoring and observability service that provides real-time data and actionable insights into AWS resources, applications, and services. For AWS Lambda, CloudWatch can:

- **Log function invocations**, errors, and output.
- **Track performance metrics** like invocation duration, error rates, and throttling.
- **Set alarms** to alert you when certain thresholds are exceeded (e.g., high error rates or excessive execution time).
- **Create dashboards** to visualize Lambda performance and other AWS resources in one place.

3.6.2 CloudWatch Logs for AWS Lambda

Whenever a Lambda function is invoked, AWS automatically creates **log streams** for that function in CloudWatch. These log streams capture everything from the function's execution start and end times to any output, errors, or custom log messages generated by the function.

How to Enable Logging for Lambda Functions

By default, Lambda is integrated with CloudWatch Logs. When a Lambda function runs, log entries are automatically generated and stored in **log groups**.

1. **Log Group Creation**: Each Lambda function has an associated log group, typically named /aws/lambda/<function-name>. A new log stream is created for each new invocation.
2. **Viewing Logs**: To view logs, go to the **CloudWatch Console**, select **Logs** from the navigation pane, and find the log group for your Lambda function. Each log group contains individual log streams for each function invocation.

Custom Logging Using console.log()

In addition to system logs, you can add custom log entries within your Lambda functions using JavaScript's console.log() or console.error() functions. This is especially useful for debugging or tracking specific events during function execution.

Example of logging custom messages:
javascript

```javascript
exports.handler = async (event) => {
  console.log('Lambda function started');
  try {
    // Function logic here
    console.log('Processing event:', JSON.stringify(event));

    // Simulate function processing
    let result = processEvent(event);

    console.log('Processing complete:', result);
    return result;
  } catch (error) {
    console.error('Error occurred:', error);
    throw error;
  }
};
```

Handling Errors in Logs

Whenever an unhandled error occurs in your Lambda function, CloudWatch Logs will capture the error message and stack trace. It's a good practice to monitor these error logs regularly and use them to troubleshoot issues.

3.6.3 CloudWatch Metrics for AWS Lambda

In addition to logs, AWS Lambda automatically generates **metrics** that help track the performance of your function over time. These metrics can be viewed and analyzed in the CloudWatch Metrics Console.

Common Lambda metrics include:

- **Invocations**: The number of times your function is invoked.
- **Duration**: The time your function takes to execute (measured in milliseconds).
- **Errors**: The number of invocations that resulted in an error.
- **Throttles**: The number of requests that were throttled due to hitting concurrency limits.
- **Iterator Age**: For stream-based invocations (e.g., from Kinesis or DynamoDB), this metric tracks the time between when an event was added to the stream and when the function processes it.

Viewing Lambda Metrics in CloudWatch

1. Open the **CloudWatch Console** and click on **Metrics** in the navigation pane.
2. Under **Browse**, select **Lambda** to see all metrics associated with your Lambda functions.
3. You can filter by specific function names, regions, and timeframes to track key performance indicators.

Setting Alarms on Metrics

You can set up **CloudWatch Alarms** to receive notifications when certain thresholds are breached, such as high error rates or increased function duration.

To create an alarm:

1. In the CloudWatch Console, go to **Alarms** and click **Create Alarm**.
2. Select a metric (e.g., **Errors** or **Duration**) and set the threshold.
3. Configure notifications to trigger an email or SNS alert when the alarm state is triggered.

This proactive monitoring can help you quickly address performance issues before they affect your users.

3.6.4 Best Practices for Logging and Monitoring AWS Lambda

To ensure optimal performance and reliability, consider these best practices when using CloudWatch for logging and monitoring:

1. **Log Only Necessary Data**: While logging is essential for debugging and monitoring, excessive logging can increase costs and clutter your logs. Use logging strategically to capture important events and errors, but avoid logging every detail unless necessary.
2. **Monitor Critical Metrics**: Pay close attention to critical Lambda metrics like **Error Rate**, **Duration**, **Throttling**, and **Memory Usage**. These metrics provide insights into performance bottlenecks, resource constraints, and potential issues with your function.
3. **Use Filters for Error Detection**: CloudWatch Logs Insights allows you to create queries and filters to search through log data quickly. You can use filters to detect patterns such as failed invocations or specific error types, enabling faster troubleshooting.
4. **Enable Enhanced Monitoring**: For more granular insights, consider enabling enhanced monitoring for Lambda. This provides additional metrics, such as memory usage, execution breakdowns, and network activity.
5. **Set Up Alarms and Alerts**: Don't rely solely on manual monitoring. Use CloudWatch Alarms to notify your team when critical thresholds are exceeded, ensuring you can address issues in real-time.

Summary

Effective logging and monitoring are vital to maintaining the health and performance of AWS Lambda functions. By leveraging Amazon CloudWatch, you can gain real-time visibility into your functions' behavior, track performance over time, and receive alerts when something goes wrong.

3.7 Lambda Performance Optimization Techniques

Optimizing the performance of AWS Lambda functions is crucial for ensuring that your serverless applications run efficiently and cost-effectively. There are several strategies and best practices you can implement to improve the performance of your Lambda functions. In this section, we will explore key techniques for optimizing execution time, resource utilization, and overall efficiency.

3.7.1 Optimize Function Code

The way you write and structure your code can significantly impact the performance of your Lambda functions. Here are some coding best practices to consider:

1. **Minimize Package Size**: Large deployment packages can increase cold start times. Use tools like Webpack or Rollup to bundle your code and dependencies, and only include what's necessary for your function.
2. **Reduce Cold Starts**: Cold starts occur when AWS Lambda must initialize a new execution environment for a function, which can introduce latency. To minimize cold starts:

- Use lighter runtimes if applicable (e.g., Node.js over heavier languages).
- Keep your function's dependencies minimal.
- Use **Provisioned Concurrency**, which keeps a specified number of Lambda instances warm and ready to respond.

1. **Use Asynchronous Code**: Take advantage of JavaScript's asynchronous capabilities (such as Promises and async/await) to prevent blocking execution. Non-blocking code can improve response times and handle more requests simultaneously.
2. **Avoid Heavy Computations**: Offload heavy computations to other services (e.g., AWS Batch or EC2). This keeps your Lambda function lightweight and responsive.

3.7.2 Efficiently Manage Memory and Timeout Settings

AWS Lambda allows you to configure the memory allocation and execution timeout for each function. Here's how to optimize these settings:

1. **Choose Appropriate Memory Size**: Increasing the memory size not only allows your function to process more data but also provides

additional CPU power. AWS allocates CPU power proportionally to the amount of memory assigned. If your function is CPU-intensive, allocating more memory can significantly reduce execution time.
2. **Set Reasonable Timeout Values**: Configure your function's timeout settings to the minimum necessary duration. This ensures that any stuck or inefficient code doesn't run indefinitely, incurring unnecessary costs.
3. **Test and Monitor Performance**: Use CloudWatch metrics to monitor the function's performance. Adjust memory and timeout settings based on the observed performance and resource usage patterns.

3.7.3 Utilize Caching and Database Connections

Managing connections to databases or other external services efficiently can significantly enhance performance:

1. **Connection Pooling**: For database connections, establish connections outside the main handler code. This allows your function to reuse existing connections, reducing the time needed to establish a new connection for each invocation.
2. **Caching Data**: Use caching solutions like Amazon ElastiCache or AWS Lambda's built-in caching features (via the API Gateway) to store frequently accessed data. Caching can greatly reduce the number of calls to backend services, speeding up response times.

3.7.4 Optimize API Gateway Integration

If your Lambda function is invoked via API Gateway, optimizing this integration can also enhance performance:

1. **Enable Caching in API Gateway**: API Gateway allows you to enable caching for your endpoints, which can reduce the number of requests made to your Lambda function for frequently requested data.
2. **Use HTTP APIs for Low Latency**: If your application allows, use HTTP APIs instead of REST APIs in API Gateway. HTTP APIs have lower latency and cost compared to REST APIs.

3.7.5 Monitor and Iterate

Performance optimization is an ongoing process. Regularly monitor your Lambda functions using CloudWatch metrics and logs to identify bottlenecks or areas for improvement. Set performance goals and iterate on your optimizations based on real-world usage data.

1. **Conduct Load Testing**: Use load testing tools to simulate different levels of traffic and evaluate how your Lambda functions perform under stress. This helps identify performance limitations before they impact users.
2. **Gather User Feedback**: Collect feedback from users regarding application responsiveness and performance. This insight can guide further optimizations.

Conclusion

In this chapter, we explored the fundamentals of AWS Lambda, focusing on its unique architecture, event-driven capabilities, and the essential role of IAM for managing permissions. We also delved into logging and monitoring with Amazon CloudWatch, emphasizing the importance of visibility into function performance and error handling. Finally, we covered various techniques for optimizing Lambda performance, including code optimization, efficient resource management, and leveraging caching.

By implementing these best practices, you can enhance the efficiency, scalability, and reliability of your serverless applications, ultimately providing a better experience for your users. As we move forward, the next chapter will introduce **Google Cloud Functions** and explore how to build serverless applications in the Google Cloud ecosystem.

4.1 Introduction to Google Cloud Functions

Google Cloud Functions is a serverless compute service that enables you to run event-driven applications without the need to manage the underlying infrastructure. By using Google Cloud Functions, developers can focus on writing code and deploying their functions while Google Cloud automatically handles the scaling, load balancing, and fault tolerance.

In this section, we will provide an overview of Google Cloud Functions, explore its core features, and discuss its integration within the Google Cloud ecosystem.

4.1.1 What Are Google Cloud Functions?

Google Cloud Functions allows you to execute JavaScript (Node.js), Python, Go, and Java code in response to events from various Google Cloud services and third-party sources. With Cloud Functions, you can quickly build and deploy microservices that automatically scale based on demand.

Key characteristics of Google Cloud Functions include:

- **Event-Driven**: Functions can be triggered by a variety of events, such as HTTP requests, Cloud Pub/Sub messages, changes in Cloud Storage, or other Google Cloud services.
- **Fully Managed**: There's no need to provision or manage servers, allowing you to focus on writing code. Google Cloud takes care of server management, scaling, and load balancing.
- **Scalable**: Google Cloud Functions can automatically scale up to handle increased load and scale down when not in use, ensuring cost efficiency.

4.1.2 Core Features of Google Cloud Functions

Google Cloud Functions comes with several features designed to simplify the development and deployment of serverless applications:

1. **Support for Multiple Languages**: Developers can choose from various supported runtimes, including Node.js, Python, Go, and Java, allowing them to use their preferred programming language.
2. **Integrated with Google Cloud Services**: Functions can easily integrate with other Google Cloud services, such as Firestore, Pub/Sub, BigQuery, and more. This seamless integration allows you to build robust applications that leverage the power of Google Cloud.
3. **Triggers and Event Sources**: Cloud Functions can be triggered by various events, such as:

- **HTTP triggers**: Invoke functions through HTTP requests.
- **Cloud Pub/Sub triggers**: Respond to messages published to Cloud Pub/Sub topics.
- **Cloud Storage triggers**: Execute functions in response to file changes (e.g., uploads, deletions) in Cloud Storage buckets.
- **Firebase triggers**: Automatically run functions in response to Firebase events, such as database changes or user authentication.

4.1.2 CORE FEATURES OF GOOGLE CLOUD FUNCTIONS

1. **Automatic Scaling**: Cloud Functions scales automatically based on incoming traffic, ensuring your application can handle sudden spikes in requests without manual intervention.
2. **Monitoring and Logging**: Integration with Google Cloud's operations suite (formerly Stackdriver) provides comprehensive logging and monitoring capabilities, making it easy to track function performance and troubleshoot issues.

4.1.3 Use Cases for Google Cloud Functions

Google Cloud Functions is suitable for a wide range of applications, including but not limited to:

- **Webhooks**: Handle webhook events from third-party services, such as payment processing or messaging platforms.
- **Data Processing**: Process and transform data in real time as it is ingested from various sources, such as Cloud Pub/Sub or Cloud Storage.
- **API Development**: Build serverless APIs that can be triggered by HTTP requests, allowing you to create scalable microservices.
- **Automation**: Automate tasks such as image processing, sending notifications, or performing scheduled tasks using Cloud Scheduler.

Summary

In this section, we introduced Google Cloud Functions as a powerful serverless compute platform that allows developers to build and deploy applications in response to various events. With its fully managed infrastructure, automatic scaling, and seamless integration with other Google Cloud services, Cloud Functions provides an efficient way to develop event-driven applications.

4.2 Creating and Deploying Google Cloud Functions with JavaScript

In this section, we will explore the process of creating and deploying Google Cloud Functions using JavaScript. We will cover the steps required to set up your development environment, write your first function, and deploy it to Google Cloud.

4.2.1 Setting Up Your Environment

Before creating a Google Cloud Function, ensure you have the following prerequisites:

1. **Google Cloud Account**: If you don't have one, sign up for a free account on Google Cloud.
2. **Google Cloud SDK**: Install the Google Cloud SDK, which includes the command-line tools required to interact with Google Cloud services. You can download it from Google Cloud SDK.
3. **Node.js**: Ensure that Node.js is installed on your machine. You can download it from Node.js.
4. **Enable Google Cloud Functions API**: In the Google Cloud Console, enable the Cloud Functions API for your project. You can do this by navigating to the **APIs & Services** section and selecting **Library**. Search for "Cloud Functions API" and click **Enable**.

4.2.2 Creating Your First Google Cloud Function

Now, let's create a simple HTTP-triggered Cloud Function in JavaScript.

1. **Create a New Directory**:

bash

```
mkdir my-cloud-function
  cd my-cloud-function
```

1. **Initialize a Node.js Project**:

bash

```
npm init -y
```

1. **Create a JavaScript File**: Create a new file named index.js:

javascript

```
exports.helloWorld = (req, res) => {
  res.send('Hello, World!');
```

4.2.2 CREATING YOUR FIRST GOOGLE CLOUD FUNCTION

};

In this simple function, we are exporting a function named helloWorld, which sends a "Hello, World!" response when triggered.

1. **Create a package.json File**: You may not need any additional dependencies for this simple function, but it's good practice to create a package.json file to define your function's metadata.

If needed, add dependencies in your package.json file, for example, express if you want to use a framework for building HTTP functions.

4.2.3 Deploying Your Google Cloud Function

With your function written, it's time to deploy it to Google Cloud.

1. **Authenticate with Google Cloud**: If you haven't already authenticated, run:

bash

gcloud auth login

1. **Set Your Project**: Set the project where you want to deploy your function:

bash

gcloud config set project YOUR_PROJECT_ID

1. **Deploy the Function**: Use the following command to deploy your function:

bash

gcloud functions deploy helloWorld —runtime nodejs14 —trigger-http

4.2.3 DEPLOYING YOUR GOOGLE CLOUD FUNCTION

—allow-unauthenticated
In this command:

- helloWorld is the name of your function.
- —runtime nodejs14 specifies the Node.js version you are using (check the latest version available).
- —trigger-http indicates that this function will be triggered via HTTP requests.
- —allow-unauthenticated allows public access to the function (you can omit this for restricted access).

1. **Get the Function URL**: Once the deployment is complete, you will see a URL where your function is hosted. You can test your function by sending a request to that URL.

4.2.4 Testing Your Cloud Function

To test your deployed function, open a web browser or use a tool like curl or Postman to send an HTTP GET request to the function's URL:

```bash
curl https://REGION-PROJECT_ID.cloudfunctions.net/helloWorld
```

You should receive a response that says "Hello, World!"

4.2.5 Updating and Managing Your Function

If you need to update your function:

1. Make changes to the index.js file.
2. Deploy again using the same gcloud functions deploy command. Google Cloud will automatically update your existing function with the new code.

To delete a function, use:
  bash

gcloud functions delete helloWorld

Summary

In this section, we walked through the process of creating and deploying your first Google Cloud Function using JavaScript. We covered the prerequisites, setup, and deployment steps, demonstrating how simple it is to build and run serverless applications on Google Cloud.

4.3 Integrating Google Cloud Functions with Other Google Cloud Services

Google Cloud Functions can be seamlessly integrated with a variety of Google Cloud services, allowing you to build robust, event-driven applications. This integration enables your functions to respond to events from different sources, process data, and interact with various services efficiently. In this section, we will explore how to integrate Google Cloud Functions with several key Google Cloud services, including Cloud Pub/Sub, Cloud Storage, Firestore, and others.

4.3.1 Integrating with Cloud Pub/Sub

Cloud Pub/Sub is a messaging service that allows you to send and receive messages between independent applications. You can use Cloud Functions to process messages published to a Pub/Sub topic.

Steps to Create a Pub/Sub Triggered Function:

1. **Create a Pub/Sub Topic**:

bash

```
gcloud pubsub topics create my-topic
```

1. **Write Your Function**: In your index.js file, add a new function to process messages from the Pub/Sub topic:

javascript

```
exports.processMessage = (message, context) => {
  const data = Buffer.from(message.data, 'base64').toString();
  console.log(`Message ID: ${context.eventId}`);
  console.log(`Message Data: ${data}`);
};
```

1. **Deploy the Function with Pub/Sub Trigger**: Deploy the function using the Pub/Sub topic as a trigger:

4.3.1 INTEGRATING WITH CLOUD PUB/SUB

bash

gcloud functions deploy processMessage —runtime nodejs14 —trigger-topic my-topic

1. **Publish Messages to the Topic**: You can publish messages to the topic using the following command:

bash

gcloud pubsub topics publish my-topic —message "Hello, Pub/Sub!"

When a message is published to the topic, your Cloud Function will automatically trigger and process the message.

4.3.2 Integrating with Cloud Storage

Google Cloud Storage is used for storing and retrieving large amounts of data, such as images, videos, and backups. You can set up Cloud Functions to respond to events in Cloud Storage, such as file uploads or deletions.

Steps to Create a Cloud Storage Triggered Function:

1. **Create a Cloud Storage Bucket**:

bash

```
gsutil mb gs://my-bucket
```

1. **Write Your Function**: In your index.js file, add a function to respond to file uploads:

javascript

```
exports.processFileUpload = (file, context) => {
  const fileName = file.name;
  console.log('File uploaded: ${fileName}');
};
```

1. **Deploy the Function with Storage Trigger**: Deploy the function with a trigger for the bucket:

4.3.2 INTEGRATING WITH CLOUD STORAGE

bash

gcloud functions deploy processFileUpload —runtime nodejs14 —trigger-resource my-bucket —trigger-event google.storage.object.finalize

1. **Upload a File**: Upload a file to the bucket using:

bash

gsutil cp localfile.txt gs://my-bucket

Your Cloud Function will trigger upon the file upload, allowing you to process the file accordingly.

4.3.3 Integrating with Firestore

Cloud Firestore is a NoSQL database that allows you to store and sync data for client- and server-side development. You can use Cloud Functions to react to changes in Firestore documents.

Steps to Create a Firestore Triggered Function:

1. **Write Your Function**: In your index.js, add a function to respond to document changes:

javascript

```
const admin = require('firebase-admin');
admin.initializeApp();

exports.onDocumentCreate = (snap, context) => {
  const newValue = snap.data();
  console.log('New document created: ${JSON.stringify(newValue)}');
};
```

1. **Deploy the Function with Firestore Trigger**: Deploy the function to listen for document creation in a Firestore collection:

bash

gcloud functions deploy onDocumentCreate —runtime nodejs14 —trigger-

4.3.3 INTEGRATING WITH FIRESTORE

resource YOUR_FIRESTORE_COLLECTION —trigger-event google.firestore.document.create

1. **Add a Document to Firestore**: Use the Firestore console or Firebase SDK to add a document to the specified collection. The function will trigger and log the newly created document.

4.3.4 Additional Integrations

Beyond the services mentioned, Google Cloud Functions can integrate with various other Google Cloud services, such as:

- **Cloud SQL**: Access and manipulate data in Cloud SQL databases.
- **Firebase Authentication**: Handle authentication events and manage user accounts.
- **Google Analytics**: Process and analyze analytics data in real time.

Summary

In this section, we explored how to integrate Google Cloud Functions with other key Google Cloud services, such as Cloud Pub/Sub, Cloud Storage, and Firestore. These integrations enable developers to build powerful, event-driven applications that leverage the capabilities of the Google Cloud ecosystem.

By harnessing the capabilities of Google Cloud Functions and its integrations, you can create efficient, scalable applications that respond to real-time events and manage data effectively. In the next section, we will discuss error handling, monitoring, and best practices for managing Google Cloud Functions effectively.

4.4 Securing Google Cloud Functions with IAM Roles

Security is a critical aspect of developing serverless applications, especially when your functions interact with sensitive data or are exposed to the internet. Google Cloud offers Identity and Access Management (IAM) roles to help you manage access control for Google Cloud Functions effectively. In this section, we will explore how to secure your Google Cloud Functions using IAM roles, allowing you to specify who can invoke your functions and what resources they can access.

4.4.1 Understanding IAM Roles and Permissions

IAM allows you to grant specific permissions to users, groups, or service accounts. Each permission defines an action that can be performed on a resource. For Google Cloud Functions, IAM roles can be broadly categorized into three types:

1. **Basic Roles**: These are the broadest roles, including Owner, Editor, and Viewer.
2. **Predefined Roles**: These roles are created by Google and include specific permissions for certain services. For example, the Cloud Functions Invoker role allows users to invoke a Cloud Function.
3. **Custom Roles**: You can create your own roles with a specific set of permissions tailored to your needs.

When deploying a Cloud Function, it is essential to assign the appropriate IAM role to limit access to authorized users only.

4.4.2 Securing HTTP Triggered Functions

For HTTP-triggered functions, you can control access using IAM roles. By default, functions are publicly accessible, but you can restrict access to only authenticated users or specific IAM roles.

Steps to Secure an HTTP Triggered Function:

1. **Deploy the Function with IAM Restrictions**: When deploying your function, avoid using the —allow-unauthenticated flag. This will ensure that only users with the appropriate IAM roles can access the function.

bash

gcloud functions deploy helloWorld —runtime nodejs14 —trigger-http

1. **Assign the Invoker Role**: To grant access to a user or service account, assign the Cloud Functions Invoker role. For example, to allow a specific user to invoke your function:

bash

gcloud functions add-iam-policy-binding helloWorld \
    —member='user:example@example.com' \
    —role='roles/cloudfunctions.invoker'

1. **Invoke the Function**: When invoking the function, ensure the request

4.4.2 SECURING HTTP TRIGGERED FUNCTIONS

includes an authentication token. You can obtain this token using the gcloud command:

bash

gcloud auth print-access-token
 Use this token in your request headers to authenticate:
 bash

curl -H "Authorization: Bearer ACCESS_TOKEN" https://REGION-PROJECT_ID.cloudfunctions.net/helloWorld

4.4.3 Securing Functions Triggered by Cloud Events

For functions triggered by Cloud Pub/Sub or Cloud Storage, you can control access at the resource level.

1. **Grant IAM Permissions**: When a function is triggered by Cloud Pub/Sub, ensure that the Pub/Sub topic or subscription has the appropriate IAM roles assigned. For example:

bash

```
gcloud pubsub topics add-iam-policy-binding my-topic \
  —member='serviceAccount:YOUR_SERVICE_ACCOUNT_EMAIL' \
  —role='roles/pubsub.publisher'
```

1. **Cloud Storage Integration**: For functions triggered by Cloud Storage, you should also set IAM permissions on the bucket. Grant the necessary roles to the service account that your function runs under:

bash

```
gsutil iam ch serviceAccount:YOUR_SERVICE_ACCOUNT_EMAIL:object Viewer gs://my-bucket
```

4.4.4 Best Practices for Securing Google Cloud Functions

- **Principle of Least Privilege**: Always grant the minimum permissions necessary for a user or service account to perform their tasks. Avoid using overly permissive roles.
- **Monitor IAM Permissions**: Regularly review IAM permissions assigned to ensure they align with current security policies and practices.
- **Enable Audit Logging**: Google Cloud provides audit logging features that allow you to track access to your functions. Enable audit logging for better security and compliance monitoring.
- **Use Service Accounts**: When functions need to access other Google Cloud resources, use service accounts with the necessary roles instead of user accounts. This approach enhances security and simplifies permission management.

Summary

In this section, we discussed the importance of securing Google Cloud Functions using IAM roles. By understanding IAM roles and permissions, you can effectively manage access to your functions, ensuring that only authorized users or service accounts can invoke them.

Implementing security best practices not only protects your functions and data but also helps you comply with organizational security policies. As you build more complex serverless applications, maintaining security will be crucial to ensuring reliability and trust in your services.

4.5 Monitoring and Debugging Google Cloud Functions

Monitoring and debugging are essential components of maintaining the performance and reliability of serverless applications. Google Cloud Functions provides various tools and services to help you monitor your functions, troubleshoot issues, and ensure they are operating correctly. In this section, we will explore the monitoring and debugging capabilities of Google Cloud Functions and how to utilize them effectively.

4.5.1 Monitoring with Google Cloud Monitoring

Google Cloud Monitoring (formerly known as Stackdriver) is a powerful tool that allows you to monitor the performance of your Cloud Functions and receive alerts based on predefined conditions. With Cloud Monitoring, you can track metrics such as invocation counts, error rates, and execution times.

Steps to Set Up Monitoring:

1. **Access Google Cloud Monitoring**: Navigate to the Google Cloud Console and select the Monitoring service from the left-hand menu.
2. **Create Dashboards**: You can create custom dashboards to visualize key metrics for your Cloud Functions. For example, you might track:

- Invocation count
- Error count
- Execution duration
- Memory usage

1. **Set Up Alerts**: To proactively manage your functions, set up alerting policies based on specific thresholds. For instance, you can create an alert to notify you when the error rate exceeds a certain percentage:

- Go to the Alerting section in the Monitoring dashboard.

4.5.1 MONITORING WITH GOOGLE CLOUD MONITORING

- Click on "Create Policy."
- Define the conditions for your alert (e.g., error rate > 5% for 5 minutes).
- Specify notification channels (e.g., email, SMS) to receive alerts.

4.5.2 Logging with Google Cloud Logging

Google Cloud Logging allows you to view and analyze logs generated by your Cloud Functions. Logging is critical for debugging and understanding how your functions behave in production.

Steps to Enable and Access Logging:

1. **Write Logs in Your Function**: Use the built-in logging functionality in your function. For example, in Node.js:

javascript

```javascript
const { Logging } = require('@google-cloud/logging');
const logging = new Logging();

exports.myFunction = (req, res) => {
  console.log('Function invoked!');
  // Additional processing...
  res.send('Hello, World!');
};
```

1. **View Logs in the Cloud Console**: Navigate to the Logging section in the Google Cloud Console:

- Click on "Logs Explorer."
- Select your Cloud Function from the resource type drop-down.

4.5.2 LOGGING WITH GOOGLE CLOUD LOGGING

- You can filter logs by severity level (INFO, ERROR, etc.) to find specific entries.

1. **Log-Based Metrics**: Create log-based metrics to track specific events or errors within your logs. This can help you monitor unusual behavior or issues in your functions:

- In the Logging dashboard, select "Log-based metrics."
- Click on "Create Metric" and define the conditions based on log entries.

4.5.3 Debugging Google Cloud Functions

Debugging serverless functions can be challenging due to their ephemeral nature. However, Google Cloud offers tools to assist with debugging:

1. **Error Reporting**: Google Cloud Error Reporting automatically aggregates and displays the errors that occur in your functions. You can view the error details, including stack traces, to help identify the root cause.

- Navigate to the Error Reporting section in the Google Cloud Console.
- Review the errors and click on an individual error to see more details.

1. **Using Stackdriver Debugger**: Google Cloud Debugger lets you inspect the state of your application at any point without stopping it. This is particularly useful for investigating issues that occur in production:

- Enable Stackdriver Debugger for your project.
- Set breakpoints in your code to pause execution and inspect variables.

1. **Unit Testing and Local Development**: To avoid issues in production, consider implementing unit tests for your functions. Use frameworks like Mocha or Jest to test your code locally before deploying it to the cloud.

Summary

In this section, we explored the monitoring and debugging capabilities of Google Cloud Functions. Utilizing Google Cloud Monitoring and Logging enables you to keep track of your functions' performance and identify issues quickly. By implementing proactive monitoring, logging best practices, and debugging tools, you can ensure the reliability and robustness of your serverless applications.

As your serverless architecture grows, maintaining visibility into function performance and behavior becomes increasingly crucial. In the next section, we will discuss **4.6 Best Practices for Google Cloud Functions** to help you optimize and enhance your serverless applications.

4.6 Google Cloud Functions vs. AWS Lambda: Key Differences

As serverless architecture continues to gain traction, developers often find themselves choosing between Google Cloud Functions and AWS Lambda as their preferred serverless computing solution. Both platforms offer powerful features and capabilities for building and deploying serverless applications. However, they also have key differences that may influence your decision based on your project requirements and existing infrastructure. In this section, we will compare Google Cloud Functions and AWS Lambda across several dimensions.

4.6.1 Language Support

Google Cloud Functions:

- Supports multiple languages, including Node.js, Python, Go, and Java.
- Allows you to deploy functions written in any language that can run on a supported runtime (e.g., custom runtimes via Docker).

AWS Lambda:

- Supports a wide range of programming languages, including Node.js, Python, Java, C#, Go, Ruby, and PowerShell.
- Offers custom runtimes, enabling you to run applications written in other languages by packaging your code in a compatible format.

Conclusion: Both platforms offer strong language support, but AWS Lambda provides a broader range of languages natively supported.

4.6.2 Triggering Mechanisms

Google Cloud Functions:

- Can be triggered by HTTP requests, Cloud Pub/Sub events, Cloud Storage changes, and other Google Cloud services.
- Supports background events from Google Cloud services, making it easy to integrate with other parts of the Google Cloud ecosystem.

AWS Lambda:

- Offers a wide variety of triggers, including Amazon API Gateway, AWS S3, DynamoDB Streams, Kinesis Streams, and more.
- Has extensive support for event-driven architecture, allowing seamless integration with other AWS services.

AWS Lambda provides more flexibility in triggering mechanisms, especially for integrations with various AWS services.

4.6.3 Deployment and Management Tools

Google Cloud Functions:

- Deployment can be performed via the Google Cloud Console, gcloud command-line tool, or through CI/CD pipelines.
- Integrated with Google Cloud Console for monitoring, logging, and debugging.

AWS Lambda:

- Offers deployment through the AWS Management Console, AWS CLI, AWS SDKs, or AWS CloudFormation for infrastructure as code.
- Integrates with AWS CloudWatch for monitoring and logging, along with AWS X-Ray for debugging and tracing.

Both platforms provide robust deployment options, but AWS Lambda has a more extensive ecosystem for infrastructure management and deployment.

4.6.4 Pricing Models

Google Cloud Functions:

- Charged based on the number of invocations, compute time (CPU and memory used), and network egress.
- Offers a free tier that includes a certain number of invocations and GB-seconds of compute time.

AWS Lambda:

- Pricing is based on the number of requests, duration of execution (GB-seconds), and data transfer.
- Also provides a free tier with a specific number of requests and compute time.

Both services use a pay-as-you-go pricing model, but it's essential to evaluate the specifics based on your usage patterns, as the costs can vary significantly depending on the workload.

4.6.5 Cold Start Performance

Google Cloud Functions:

- Generally exhibits faster cold start times compared to AWS Lambda, especially for smaller functions.
- However, cold starts can still be noticeable, particularly for larger functions or those with a more extensive initialization process.

AWS Lambda:

- Cold starts can be longer, especially for functions using languages like Java or C# due to the larger runtime environment.
- AWS has introduced provisioned concurrency, which allows you to keep a certain number of instances warm to minimize cold starts.

Google Cloud Functions may have an edge in cold start performance, but AWS Lambda's provisioned concurrency feature offers a solution for minimizing cold starts.

4.6.6 Ecosystem and Integration

Google Cloud Functions:

- Seamlessly integrates with other Google Cloud services, such as Firestore, Firebase, and BigQuery.
- Strongly supports data processing and analytics tasks, leveraging the capabilities of Google Cloud's data services.

AWS Lambda:

- Integrates well with a vast range of AWS services, making it suitable for building complex applications using multiple services.
- Has a more extensive ecosystem with numerous third-party tools and frameworks that enhance the serverless experience.

AWS Lambda benefits from a broader ecosystem and better integration capabilities across a wide array of services, making it ideal for more complex applications.

Summary

In this section, we compared Google Cloud Functions and AWS Lambda, examining their differences in language support, triggering mechanisms, deployment tools, pricing models, cold start performance, and integration capabilities.

Choosing between the two platforms will largely depend on your specific use case, familiarity with the ecosystem, and the services you plan to utilize. Both Google Cloud Functions and AWS Lambda offer robust serverless solutions, so consider your project requirements and existing infrastructure when making a decision.

4.7 Best Practices for Google Cloud Functions

To ensure that your serverless applications using Google Cloud Functions run efficiently and effectively, following best practices is essential. This section outlines key strategies to optimize performance, maintainability, and cost-effectiveness for your functions.

4.7.1 Keep Functions Small and Focused

Design your functions to perform a single, specific task. This practice promotes reusability and simplifies debugging and maintenance. A smaller function is easier to understand and can be invoked independently, enhancing scalability.

Example: Instead of creating a monolithic function that handles user authentication, database operations, and notifications, break it down into smaller functions—one for authentication, one for database operations, and another for sending notifications.

4.7.2 Optimize Function Performance

1. **Use the Right Memory and Timeout Settings**: Allocate sufficient memory and adjust timeout settings based on the function's requirements. More memory can lead to faster execution times, as it provides more CPU power.
2. **Reduce Cold Start Times**: Minimize cold start times by keeping your functions lightweight and using smaller libraries. Consider using Google Cloud's "always on" feature for frequently accessed functions.
3. **Efficient Code Practices**: Write efficient and clean code. Avoid unnecessary computations, and optimize your code paths for performance.

4.7.3 Leverage Environment Variables

Use environment variables to manage configuration settings, such as API keys and database connection strings, instead of hardcoding them in your functions. This practice enhances security and simplifies changes to configuration settings without redeploying your functions.

Example: Store API keys in environment variables and access them in your code like this:

javascript

```
const apiKey = process.env.API_KEY;
```

4.7.4 Implement Proper Error Handling

Robust error handling is crucial in serverless applications. Use try-catch blocks to handle exceptions gracefully, and return meaningful error messages to the caller. Consider implementing retries for transient errors to enhance resilience.

Example:
javascript

```
exports.myFunction = async (req, res) => {
  try {
    // Perform actions
  } catch (error) {
    console.error('Error occurred:', error);
    res.status(500).send('Internal Server Error');
  }
};
```

4.7.5 Monitor and Log Effectively

Utilize Google Cloud Logging and Monitoring to track your function's performance and troubleshoot issues. Implement structured logging to make it easier to search and analyze logs.

- Create log entries for important events, errors, and performance metrics.
- Set up alerts based on thresholds for error rates or execution times to proactively manage your functions.

4.7.6 Secure Your Functions

1. **Use IAM Roles and Policies**: Assign the least privilege principle when granting permissions to your functions. Use IAM roles to control access to resources.
2. **Validate Inputs**: Always validate and sanitize inputs to prevent security vulnerabilities such as injection attacks.
3. **Secure Communication**: Use HTTPS for all communications with your functions to protect data in transit.

Conclusion

In this chapter, we explored the fundamentals of Google Cloud Functions, covering their creation, deployment, integration with other services, security measures, and monitoring capabilities. We also compared Google Cloud Functions with AWS Lambda, highlighting key differences in language support, triggering mechanisms, pricing, and integration capabilities.

Finally, we discussed best practices to ensure your Google Cloud Functions are optimized for performance, security, and maintainability. By following these guidelines, you can build scalable, efficient, and reliable serverless applications on Google Cloud.

CHAPTER 5: SERVERLESS STORAGE SOLUTIONS

In serverless architectures, efficiently managing data storage is crucial. This chapter will explore various storage solutions that work seamlessly with serverless applications, focusing on popular options like AWS S3 and Google Cloud Storage. We'll also discuss best practices for data management in a serverless environment.

5.1 Storing Data with AWS S3 in Serverless Applications

AWS S3 (Simple Storage Service) is an object storage service that provides highly scalable, durable, and secure storage for a variety of data types. It is widely used in serverless applications for storing files, images, backups, and data for analytics.

5.1.1 Key Features of AWS S3

- **Scalability**: S3 can handle virtually unlimited amounts of data and can scale automatically as your application grows.
- **Durability**: With an average annual durability of 99.999999999% (11 nines), S3 is designed to ensure that your data is safe and available.
- **Security**: Provides multiple layers of security, including bucket policies, IAM policies, and server-side encryption options.
- **Data Management**: Offers features like versioning, lifecycle policies, and event notifications for better data management.

5.1.2 Using AWS S3 with Serverless Applications

1. **Setting Up an S3 Bucket**:

- Log in to the AWS Management Console and navigate to S3.
- Click on "Create Bucket," choose a unique name, and select your region.
- Configure options such as versioning, logging, and encryption based on your needs.

1. **Interacting with S3 in Lambda Functions**: To interact with S3 from AWS Lambda, use the AWS SDK for JavaScript. Here's how to upload a file to S3 from a Lambda function:

- javascript

```
const AWS = require('aws-sdk');
const s3 = new AWS.S3();

exports.handler = async (event) => {
  const bucketName = 'your-bucket-name';
  const fileName = 'example.txt';
  const fileContent = 'Hello, this is a test file!';
```

```javascript
const params = {
  Bucket: bucketName,
  Key: fileName,
  Body: fileContent,
};

try {
  await s3.putObject(params).promise();
  console.log('File uploaded successfully to ${bucketName}/${fileName}');
} catch (error) {
  console.error('Error uploading file:', error);
}
};
```

1. **Retrieving Data from S3**: You can also retrieve objects stored in S3. Here's an example of how to read a file:

javascript

```javascript
const params = {
  Bucket: bucketName,
  Key: fileName,
};

try {
  const data = await s3.getObject(params).promise();
  const fileContent = data.Body.toString('utf-8');
  console.log('File content:', fileContent);
} catch (error) {
  console.error('Error retrieving file:', error);
}
```

5.1.3 Best Practices for Using AWS S3

- **Use Versioning**: Enable versioning on your S3 buckets to keep track of changes to objects and protect against accidental deletions.
- **Implement Lifecycle Policies**: Use lifecycle policies to automatically transition objects to lower-cost storage classes or delete them after a specific period.
- **Optimize for Performance**: Consider using S3 Transfer Acceleration for faster uploads, especially for large files or data coming from remote locations.
- **Monitor and Audit**: Utilize AWS CloudTrail and S3 logging to monitor access and modifications to your data for security and compliance purposes.

Summary

AWS S3 is a powerful and versatile storage solution for serverless applications, offering scalability, durability, and security. By understanding how to interact with S3 using AWS Lambda and following best practices for data management, you can ensure your serverless applications are efficient and reliable.

5.2 Using Google Cloud Storage with Serverless Architecture

Google Cloud Storage (GCS) is a scalable and secure object storage service designed for storing and accessing data in the cloud. It is a critical component of serverless architectures, allowing applications to manage and store unstructured data, including files, images, and backups.

5.2.1 Key Features of Google Cloud Storage

- **Scalability**: GCS can scale to handle petabytes of data with no limits on the number of objects.
- **Durability**: Offers a 99.999999999% (11 nines) durability across multiple locations, ensuring data is reliably stored.
- **Security**: Provides robust security features, including IAM roles, bucket policies, and data encryption at rest and in transit.
- **Integrated Services**: Seamlessly integrates with other Google Cloud services, such as BigQuery and Cloud Functions.

5.2.2 Setting Up Google Cloud Storage

1. **Creating a Cloud Storage Bucket**:

- Log in to the Google Cloud Console.
- Navigate to "Cloud Storage" and click on "Create Bucket."
- Choose a globally unique name, select a location, and configure storage class and access control settings.

1. **Interacting with Google Cloud Storage from Cloud Functions**: You can use the Google Cloud Client Library for JavaScript to interact with Cloud Storage from your Cloud Functions. Here's an example of how to upload a file:

```javascript
const { Storage } = require('@google-cloud/storage');
const storage = new Storage();

exports.uploadFile = async (req, res) => {
  const bucketName = 'your-bucket-name';
  const fileName = 'example.txt';
  const fileContent = 'Hello, this is a test file!';

  try {
```

```
await storage.bucket(bucketName).file(fileName).save(fileContent);
console.log('File ${fileName} uploaded to ${bucketName}.');
res.status(200).send('File uploaded successfully: ${fileName}');
} catch (error) {
console.error('Error uploading file:', error);
res.status(500).send('Error uploading file');
}
};
```

1. **Retrieving Data from Google Cloud Storage**: Here's how to read a file stored in GCS:

javascript

```
exports.readFile = async (req, res) => {
  const bucketName = 'your-bucket-name';
  const fileName = 'example.txt';

try {
  const file = storage.bucket(bucketName).file(fileName);
  const data = await file.download();
  const fileContent = data[0].toString('utf-8');
  console.log('File content:', fileContent);
  res.status(200).send('File content: ${fileContent}');
} catch (error) {
  console.error('Error retrieving file:', error);
  res.status(500).send('Error retrieving file');
  }
};
```

5.2.3 Best Practices for Using Google Cloud Storage

- **Use Object Lifecycle Management**: Implement lifecycle management rules to automatically transition objects to lower-cost storage classes or delete them after a specified time.
- **Leverage Regional Buckets for Latency**: Choose the right location for your buckets based on your application's access patterns to minimize latency.
- **Optimize for Cost**: Select the appropriate storage class (e.g., Standard, Nearline, Coldline) based on your data access frequency to optimize costs.
- **Implement Strong Security Measures**: Use IAM roles to enforce the principle of least privilege, ensuring that users and services only have access to the necessary resources.

Summary

Google Cloud Storage is an essential tool for managing data in serverless architectures, offering flexibility, scalability, and strong security features. By effectively using GCS in conjunction with Cloud Functions, developers can create robust serverless applications that handle various data types efficiently.

5.3 Integrating AWS DynamoDB with Lambda Functions

AWS DynamoDB is a fully managed NoSQL database service that provides fast and predictable performance with seamless scalability. It is commonly used in serverless applications to store and retrieve data due to its low latency and high availability.

5.3.1 Key Features of DynamoDB

- **Managed Service**: AWS takes care of operational tasks such as hardware provisioning, setup, configuration, and backups.
- **Scalability**: DynamoDB can automatically scale up and down to adjust for capacity and maintain performance.
- **Integrated Security**: Provides encryption at rest and in transit, along with fine-grained access control using IAM.
- **Global Tables**: Supports multi-region, fully replicated tables for low-latency access to data.

5.3.2 Setting Up DynamoDB

1. **Creating a DynamoDB Table**:

- Log in to the AWS Management Console and navigate to DynamoDB.
- Click on "Create Table" and define the table name and primary key attributes.
- Configure settings such as read/write capacity and enable auto-scaling if needed.

1. **Integrating DynamoDB with AWS Lambda**: To interact with DynamoDB from a Lambda function, you can use the AWS SDK for JavaScript. Here's how to put an item into a DynamoDB table:

```javascript
const AWS = require('aws-sdk');
const dynamoDB = new AWS.DynamoDB.DocumentClient();

exports.handler = async (event) => {
  const params = {
    TableName: 'your-table-name',
    Item: {
      id: '1', // Primary key
      name: 'John Doe',
```

```
    age: 30,
  },
};

try {
  await dynamoDB.put(params).promise();
  console.log('Item added to DynamoDB:', params.Item);
  return {
  statusCode: 200,
  body: JSON.stringify('Item added successfully!'),
  };
} catch (error) {
  console.error('Error adding item:', error);
  return {
  statusCode: 500,
  body: JSON.stringify('Error adding item'),
  };
  }
};
```

1. **Retrieving Data from DynamoDB**: Here's how to read an item from the DynamoDB table:

javascript

```
exports.handler = async (event) => {
  const params = {
  TableName: 'your-table-name',
  Key: {
  id: '1', // Primary key
  },
  };
```

5.3.2 SETTING UP DYNAMODB

```
try {
    const data = await dynamoDB.get(params).promise();
    console.log('Item retrieved from DynamoDB:', data.Item);
    return {
    statusCode: 200,
    body: JSON.stringify(data.Item),
    };
    } catch (error) {
    console.error('Error retrieving item:', error);
    return {
    statusCode: 500,
    body: JSON.stringify('Error retrieving item'),
    };
    }
};
```

5.3.3 Best Practices for Using DynamoDB with Lambda

- **Use Batch Operations**: When dealing with multiple items, utilize batch operations (e.g., BatchWriteItem, BatchGetItem) to reduce the number of calls to DynamoDB.
- **Design Efficient Table Structures**: Plan your table schema and access patterns upfront to minimize the need for complex queries. Use composite primary keys and secondary indexes as needed.
- **Leverage DynamoDB Streams**: Enable DynamoDB Streams to capture item-level changes in your tables. This allows you to trigger Lambda functions in response to changes, enabling real-time data processing.
- **Monitor and Optimize**: Use Amazon CloudWatch to monitor DynamoDB performance metrics and adjust read/write capacity accordingly. Optimize your queries to ensure they are efficient and cost-effective.

Summary

Integrating AWS DynamoDB with Lambda functions allows developers to build scalable and high-performance serverless applications. By leveraging DynamoDB's key features and adhering to best practices, you can efficiently manage and retrieve data in a serverless environment.

5.4 Google Cloud Firestore and Serverless Integration

Google Cloud Firestore is a flexible, scalable NoSQL database designed for mobile, web, and server development. It is part of the Firebase platform and offers seamless integration with other Google Cloud services. Firestore is a popular choice for serverless applications due to its real-time capabilities and easy scaling.

5.4.1 Key Features of Google Cloud Firestore

- **Real-Time Synchronization**: Firestore allows data to be synchronized in real time across clients, making it suitable for applications that require instant updates.
- **Flexible Data Model**: Supports hierarchical data structures, allowing developers to store data in documents and collections.
- **Offline Support**: Clients can access data even when offline, with Firestore automatically syncing changes once connectivity is restored.
- **Integrated Security**: Offers robust security features through Firebase Authentication and Firestore Security Rules.

5.4.2 Setting Up Google Cloud Firestore

1. **Creating a Firestore Database**:

- Log in to the Google Cloud Console and navigate to "Firestore."
- Click on "Create Database" and choose between "Native mode" or "Datastore mode."
- Configure security rules and set up the database location.

1. **Integrating Firestore with Cloud Functions**: Use the Firebase Admin SDK to interact with Firestore from Cloud Functions. Here's how to add a document to a Firestore collection:

- javascript

```javascript
const admin = require('firebase-admin');
admin.initializeApp();

exports.addDocument = async (req, res) => {
  const db = admin.firestore();
  const docRef = db.collection('users').doc('user_1');

const userData = {
  name: 'Jane Doe',
  age: 28,
```

5.4.2 SETTING UP GOOGLE CLOUD FIRESTORE

```
};

try {
  await docRef.set(userData);
  console.log('Document added to Firestore:', userData);
  res.status(200).send('Document added successfully!');
} catch (error) {
  console.error('Error adding document:', error);
  res.status(500).send('Error adding document');
}
};
```

1. **Retrieving Data from Firestore**: To read a document from Firestore, use the following code:

javascript

```
exports.getDocument = async (req, res) => {
  const db = admin.firestore();
  const docRef = db.collection('users').doc('user_1');

try {
  const doc = await docRef.get();
  if (!doc.exists) {
  console.log('No such document!');
  return res.status(404).send('Document not found');
  } else {
  console.log('Document data:', doc.data());
  res.status(200).send(doc.data());
  }
} catch (error) {
  console.error('Error retrieving document:', error);
  res.status(500).send('Error retrieving document');
```

```
}
};
```

5.4.3 Best Practices for Using Firestore with Serverless Applications

- **Optimize Data Structure**: Plan your data model to take advantage of Firestore's capabilities, using collections and documents efficiently to minimize read and write operations.
- **Use Firestore Security Rules**: Implement fine-grained security rules to control access to your data based on user authentication and roles.
- **Leverage Batch Operations**: Use batch writes and transactions for atomic operations to ensure data consistency and integrity.
- **Monitor Usage**: Utilize Google Cloud Monitoring and Firestore usage metrics to keep track of your application's performance and optimize costs.

Summary

Integrating Google Cloud Firestore with serverless architectures provides a powerful solution for managing data in real-time applications. By leveraging Firestore's unique features and following best practices, developers can build responsive, scalable, and secure serverless applications.

5.5 Choosing Between SQL and NoSQL in Serverless Applications

When building serverless applications, one of the critical architectural decisions is selecting the right database type. The choice between SQL (relational) and NoSQL (non-relational) databases can significantly impact the application's performance, scalability, and data management capabilities. This section explores the strengths and weaknesses of each database type to help you make an informed decision.

5.5.1 Understanding SQL Databases

SQL databases, such as MySQL, PostgreSQL, and Microsoft SQL Server, store data in structured formats using tables with predefined schemas. They enforce ACID (Atomicity, Consistency, Isolation, Durability) properties, which ensure reliable transactions.

Advantages of SQL Databases:

- **Structured Data**: Ideal for applications requiring complex queries and structured data.
- **Relationships**: Strong support for relationships between tables via foreign keys and JOIN operations.
- **Data Integrity**: Ensures data integrity through constraints and validation rules.
- **Mature Ecosystem**: A vast array of tools and libraries available for management, querying, and reporting.

Disadvantages of SQL Databases:

- **Scalability Limitations**: Horizontal scaling can be challenging, leading to potential performance bottlenecks as the application grows.
- **Schema Rigidity**: Changes to the database schema can be complex and may require significant downtime.

5.5.2 Understanding NoSQL Databases

NoSQL databases, such as MongoDB, DynamoDB, and Google Firestore, offer a flexible schema design and can store various data formats, including key-value pairs, documents, and wide-column stores. They are designed for horizontal scaling and high availability.

Advantages of NoSQL Databases:

- **Scalability**: Easily scales horizontally to handle large amounts of data and high traffic loads.
- **Flexibility**: Supports dynamic schemas, allowing developers to modify the data structure without downtime.
- **Performance**: Optimized for fast read and write operations, especially for unstructured data and real-time applications.

Disadvantages of NoSQL Databases:

- **Data Consistency**: Most NoSQL databases sacrifice some ACID properties in favor of availability and partition tolerance (CAP theorem), which can lead to eventual consistency issues.
- **Complex Querying**: Limited support for complex queries and transactions compared to SQL databases.

5.5.3 Factors to Consider When Choosing

1. **Data Structure**:

- If your data is highly structured and requires complex relationships, SQL may be the better choice.
- For unstructured or semi-structured data with flexible schemas, NoSQL offers more agility.

1. **Scalability Needs**:

- If you anticipate rapid growth and need to scale out, NoSQL databases are generally more adept at handling large volumes of data.
- SQL databases can also scale but may require more planning and configuration.

1. **Use Case**:

- For applications like financial systems requiring strict data integrity, SQL is preferable.
- For applications with real-time analytics, user-generated content, or IoT data, NoSQL may be more suitable.

1. **Team Expertise**:

5.5.3 FACTORS TO CONSIDER WHEN CHOOSING

- Consider your team's familiarity with SQL or NoSQL technologies. Leveraging existing knowledge can reduce the learning curve and accelerate development.

1. **Cost Considerations**:

- Evaluate the pricing models of different database services on cloud platforms, as costs can vary significantly between SQL and NoSQL options.

Summary

Choosing between SQL and NoSQL databases in serverless applications involves weighing the advantages and disadvantages of each type against the specific needs of your application. By understanding the data structure, scalability requirements, use cases, and your team's expertise, you can make a more informed decision that aligns with your project goals.

5.6 Handling Large Datasets and File Uploads in Serverless Applications

In serverless architectures, managing large datasets and handling file uploads can pose unique challenges. However, by leveraging cloud services and best practices, developers can efficiently process, store, and serve large volumes of data without compromising performance.

5.6.1 Strategies for Handling Large Datasets

1. **Data Partitioning**:

- Break down large datasets into smaller, more manageable chunks. This can improve performance by allowing parallel processing and reducing latency during data retrieval.
- Use techniques such as sharding or creating multiple tables/collections based on data characteristics (e.g., date ranges, user IDs).

1. **Batch Processing**:

- Implement batch processing to handle large volumes of data at once. This approach can minimize the number of individual requests made to your database or storage system, leading to more efficient processing.
- Tools like AWS Batch or Google Cloud Dataflow can be used to orchestrate batch jobs in serverless environments.

1. **Data Streaming**:

- For real-time processing, consider using streaming data services such as AWS Kinesis or Google Cloud Pub/Sub. These services allow you to process data as it arrives, making it suitable for applications that require

5.6.1 STRATEGIES FOR HANDLING LARGE DATASETS

immediate insights.

1. **Using Data Lakes**:

- Store large datasets in data lakes (e.g., AWS S3 or Google Cloud Storage) and query them using serverless data processing frameworks like AWS Athena or Google BigQuery. This allows you to work with large volumes of data without the need for a traditional database.

5.6.2 Handling File Uploads

1. **Direct Uploads to Cloud Storage**:

- Instead of routing file uploads through your serverless functions, allow clients to upload files directly to cloud storage (e.g., AWS S3 or Google Cloud Storage). This can significantly reduce latency and offload processing from your functions.
- Generate pre-signed URLs to enable secure, temporary access for clients to upload files directly.

javascript

```
const AWS = require('aws-sdk');
const s3 = new AWS.S3();

exports.generatePresignedUrl = async (req, res) => {
  const params = {
  Bucket: 'your-bucket-name',
  Key: 'uploads/file.txt',
  Expires: 60, // URL expires in 60 seconds
  ContentType: 'text/plain',
  };

  try {
```

5.6.2 HANDLING FILE UPLOADS

```
const url = await s3.getSignedUrlPromise('putObject', params);
res.status(200).send({ url });
} catch (error) {
console.error('Error generating pre-signed URL:', error);
res.status(500).send('Error generating URL');
}
};
```

1. **Processing Uploaded Files**:

- After files are uploaded, use serverless functions to trigger processing workflows. For example, you can use S3 event notifications to invoke a Lambda function that processes the uploaded file.

javascript

```
exports.processUploadedFile = async (event) => {
  const bucket = event.Records[0].s3.bucket.name;
  const key = event.Records[0].s3.object.key;

// Implement your file processing logic here
  console.log('Processing file from bucket: ${bucket}, key: ${key}');
};
```

1. **Managing Large File Transfers**:

- For applications that require the transfer of large files, consider using multipart uploads or resumable uploads to ensure reliability and efficiency. Both AWS S3 and Google Cloud Storage support multipart upload functionality.

Conclusion

Chapter 5 explored various strategies for managing large datasets and handling file uploads in serverless applications. By leveraging cloud storage solutions, data partitioning, batch processing, and streaming technologies, developers can effectively work with large volumes of data while ensuring optimal performance and scalability. Additionally, implementing direct file uploads to cloud storage can streamline the upload process, allowing for more efficient resource utilization in serverless environments.

CHAPTER 6: API DEVELOPMENT IN A SERVERLESS ENVIRONMENT

Building APIs is a fundamental aspect of modern application development, and serverless architectures provide a flexible and scalable approach to creating RESTful APIs. This chapter will explore how to build RESTful APIs using AWS Lambda and API Gateway, focusing on best practices, integration, and real-world examples.

6.1.1 Overview of RESTful APIs

REST (Representational State Transfer) is an architectural style for designing networked applications. RESTful APIs adhere to a set of principles that allow for scalable and stateless communication between clients and servers. They use standard HTTP methods (GET, POST, PUT, DELETE) to perform CRUD (Create, Read, Update, Delete) operations on resources.

6.1.2 Setting Up AWS Lambda for API Development

1. **Creating a Lambda Function**:

- Go to the AWS Lambda console and click "Create function."
- Choose "Author from scratch," provide a name, select the runtime (Node.js), and set up execution permissions with an appropriate IAM role.

Example of a simple Lambda function to handle a GET request:
javascript

```
exports.handler = async (event) => {
const response = {
statusCode: 200,
body: JSON.stringify({ message: 'Hello, World!' }),
};
return response;
};
```

1. **Configuring API Gateway**:

- Navigate to the Amazon API Gateway console and click "Create API."

- Choose "HTTP API" for a simpler setup or "REST API" for more advanced features.
- Define your API endpoints and link them to the Lambda function created earlier.

6.1.3 Creating API Endpoints

1. **Defining Resources and Methods**:

- For a RESTful API, define resources (e.g., /users, /products) and specify the HTTP methods to be used (GET, POST, etc.).
- For example, to create a /users resource with a GET method:

```javascript
const express = require('express');
const app = express();

app.get('/users', async (req, res) => {
  // Fetch users from a database or service
  res.json([{ id: 1, name: 'Jane Doe' }]);
});

exports.handler = serverless(app);
```

1. **Deploying the API**:

- Once your API is configured, deploy it by clicking on the "Deploy" button in the API Gateway console. This process creates a public URL for your API, which can be used to send requests.

6.1.4 Testing the API

- Use tools like Postman or cURL to send requests to your API endpoints. Verify that the responses are as expected, and troubleshoot any issues that arise.

Example of using cURL to test the GET endpoint:
bash

```
curl -X GET https://your-api-id.execute-api.region.amazonaws.com/users
```

6.1.5 Integrating with Other AWS Services

- Enhance your API by integrating it with other AWS services:
- **DynamoDB**: Use AWS Lambda to interact with DynamoDB for data persistence.
- **S3**: Store files and media uploads directly to S3, triggered by API calls.
- **SNS**: Send notifications or messages via AWS Simple Notification Service (SNS) based on API events.

Example of fetching data from DynamoDB within a Lambda function:
javascript

```javascript
const AWS = require('aws-sdk');
const dynamoDB = new AWS.DynamoDB.DocumentClient();

exports.handler = async (event) => {
  const params = {
    TableName: 'Users',
  };
  const data = await dynamoDB.scan(params).promise();

  return {
    statusCode: 200,
    body: JSON.stringify(data.Items),
  };
```

};

6.1.6 Security Best Practices for APIs

- **Authentication**: Implement API authentication using AWS Cognito or API keys to secure access to your endpoints.
- **Authorization**: Define user roles and permissions to control access to specific resources.
- **Input Validation**: Always validate and sanitize input to prevent injection attacks and ensure data integrity.
- **Rate Limiting**: Configure usage plans in API Gateway to limit the number of requests per user to prevent abuse.

Summary

Building RESTful APIs with AWS Lambda and API Gateway provides a powerful approach to developing serverless applications. By leveraging AWS services, developers can create scalable and efficient APIs that integrate seamlessly with various data sources and enhance application functionality. Understanding the principles of REST, setting up Lambda functions, and implementing security best practices are essential for successful API development in a serverless environment.

Next, we will move to **6.2 Building GraphQL APIs with AWS AppSync**, where we will explore the capabilities of GraphQL and how to implement it in a serverless architecture.

6.2 Creating Serverless APIs with Google Cloud Functions and Google API Gateway

Google Cloud provides powerful tools for building serverless APIs, including **Google Cloud Functions** and **Google API Gateway**. This section will guide you through the process of creating, deploying, and managing APIs using these services, focusing on leveraging JavaScript for the development of Google Cloud Functions.

6.2.1 Overview of Google Cloud Functions

Google Cloud Functions is a lightweight, event-driven serverless compute service that enables you to run JavaScript code in response to events, such as HTTP requests or triggers from other Google Cloud services.

Key features of Google Cloud Functions:

- Event-driven architecture
- Fully managed infrastructure
- Native integration with Google Cloud services like Cloud Storage, Firestore, Pub/Sub, etc.
- Pay-per-use pricing

6.2.2 Setting Up Google API Gateway for Cloud Functions

Google API Gateway allows you to expose Google Cloud Functions as RESTful APIs, enabling you to manage traffic, enforce security, and monitor API performance.

Steps to set up Google API Gateway:

1. **Create a Google Cloud Project**: Start by creating a new project in the Google Cloud Console. This project will house your functions and APIs.
2. **Enable Google API Gateway**: Go to the **API Gateway** section and enable it for your project.
3. **Create an API**: Define your API configuration in a YAML file, specifying the API's routes, methods, and integrations with your Cloud Functions.
4. **Deploy the API**: Once the configuration is ready, deploy the API and integrate it with your Cloud Functions.

6.2.3 Creating a Simple Google Cloud Function

Start by creating a basic function that responds to HTTP requests. Here's an example using Node.js:

javascript

```
/**
 * Responds to any HTTP request.
 * @param {Object} req Cloud Function request context.
 * @param {Object} res Cloud Function response context.
 */
exports.helloWorld = (req, res) => {
  res.status(200).send('Hello from Google Cloud Functions!');
};
```

To deploy this function, run the following command in your terminal:

bash

```
gcloud functions deploy helloWorld —runtime nodejs14 —trigger-http —allow-unauthenticated
```

This command deploys the function and exposes it via an HTTP trigger.

6.2.4 Integrating Google API Gateway with Cloud Functions

Once your Cloud Function is ready, you can expose it via Google API Gateway for better management and security.

1. **Create a New API Configuration**: Create a YAML file to define your API. Here's an example for a simple GET endpoint:

yaml

```
swagger: '2.0'
  info:
  title: My API
  description: API for managing Google Cloud Functions
  version: 1.0.0
  paths:
  /hello:
  get:
  summary: Responds with a greeting
  operationId: helloWorld
  x-google-backend:
  address: https://REGION-PROJECT_ID.cloudfunctions.net/helloWorld
```

1. **Deploy the API**: Use the following command to deploy the API:

bash

gcloud api-gateway apis create my-api —api-config=my-api-config.yaml —project=PROJECT_ID

1. **Test Your API**: Once deployed, Google API Gateway will provide a public URL for your API. Use this URL to test your function with tools like Postman or cURL:

bash

curl -X GET https://API_GATEWAY_URL/hello

This should trigger the helloWorld function and return the response "Hello from Google Cloud Functions!"

6.2.5 Managing Authentication and Permissions

Google API Gateway allows you to secure your API using authentication mechanisms like **OAuth2**, **API Keys**, and **IAM Roles**.

1. **Securing with API Keys**:

- Create an API key in the Google Cloud Console under the API Gateway section.
- Configure your API to require the key for authentication by updating your API configuration YAML.

1. **IAM Roles for Fine-Grained Control**: You can assign specific IAM roles to control who can invoke your Google Cloud Functions. This is particularly useful when integrating your API with other Google Cloud services or when managing access within your organization.

6.2.6 Monitoring and Logging Google Cloud Functions

Monitoring and debugging are critical to maintaining serverless APIs. Google Cloud offers several tools to help:

1. **Cloud Logging**: View detailed logs for every Cloud Function invocation. Logs include the function's execution time, errors, and status codes.

- To view logs for your function, use the Cloud Console or the gcloud CLI:

bash

gcloud functions logs read helloWorld

1. **Cloud Monitoring**: Set up performance metrics, such as function latency, memory usage, and execution frequency. This helps you understand the health of your API and optimize its performance.

6.2.7 Handling Errors and Retries in Cloud Functions

Error handling in Google Cloud Functions can be managed using custom error responses. For example, if your function fails due to an invalid input, you can return a 400 status code:

javascript

```
exports.helloWorld = (req, res) => {
  if (!req.query.name) {
  res.status(400).send('Name is required!');
  } else {
  res.status(200).send('Hello, ${req.query.name}!');
  }
};
```

You can also configure retry policies for failed invocations, especially if your function is triggered by asynchronous events such as Pub/Sub messages or Cloud Storage uploads.

Summary

Creating serverless APIs with Google Cloud Functions and Google API Gateway offers a powerful way to build scalable and secure applications. By leveraging Google Cloud's ecosystem, you can easily integrate serverless APIs with other services, secure your endpoints, and monitor their performance. Mastering the setup and deployment of these APIs ensures efficient development in a serverless environment.

6.3 Securing APIs with OAuth and JWT in Serverless Applications

As serverless applications become more complex and handle sensitive data, securing APIs is a critical task. Two common methods for securing APIs in a serverless environment are **OAuth 2.0** and **JSON Web Tokens (JWT)**. Both approaches enable robust authentication and authorization mechanisms that protect your serverless applications from unauthorized access.

In this section, we will explore how OAuth and JWT work, and how to implement them in APIs using **AWS Lambda** and **Google Cloud Functions**.

6.3.1 Overview of OAuth 2.0 for Serverless Applications

OAuth 2.0 is an industry-standard protocol for authorization, allowing users to grant third-party applications access to their resources without sharing credentials. In a serverless context, OAuth 2.0 is often used to secure APIs and provide access control for different levels of users.

Key components of OAuth 2.0:

- **Authorization Server**: Handles the generation of tokens after verifying user credentials (e.g., Google, AWS Cognito).
- **Client Application**: Your serverless application that requests access to resources.
- **Resource Owner**: The user granting access to their data.
- **Access Token**: A token provided by the authorization server, granting access to the protected resource.

OAuth Flow for Serverless APIs:

1. **User Authentication**: The user logs in using an identity provider like Google, Facebook, or AWS Cognito.
2. **Token Generation**: Once authenticated, the OAuth server generates an access token and returns it to the client.
3. **API Request**: The client includes the access token in each API request as an authentication header.
4. **Resource Access**: The API server verifies the token and grants access to the resource if valid.

6.3.2 Implementing OAuth 2.0 in AWS Lambda

To implement OAuth 2.0 for an AWS Lambda-based API, you can use **AWS Cognito** as the identity provider. Follow these steps:

1. **Create a User Pool in AWS Cognito**:

- Go to the AWS Cognito Console and create a user pool.
- Define user attributes (e.g., email, username) and configure user sign-up/sign-in settings.

1. **Configure an OAuth 2.0 App Client**:

- Create an app client in Cognito that supports OAuth 2.0 flows such as Authorization Code or Implicit Flow.
- You can also configure allowed callback URLs and scopes.

1. **Secure Lambda APIs with OAuth**:

- In **API Gateway**, add an authorizer that verifies OAuth 2.0 access tokens.
- In the Lambda function, retrieve the access token from the request header and validate it using AWS SDK:

javascript

6.3.2 IMPLEMENTING OAUTH 2.0 IN AWS LAMBDA

```javascript
const AWS = require('aws-sdk');
const cognitoIdentityServiceProvider = new AWS.CognitoIdentityServiceProvider();

exports.handler = async (event) => {
  const token = event.headers.Authorization;

  try {
    // Verify the token with Cognito
    const params = {
      AccessToken: token
    };
    const result = await cognitoIdentityServiceProvider.getUser(params).promise();
    return {
      statusCode: 200,
      body: JSON.stringify({ message: 'Access granted', user: result })
    };
  } catch (err) {
    return {
      statusCode: 401,
      body: JSON.stringify({ message: 'Unauthorized' })
    };
  }
};
```

6.3.3 Implementing OAuth 2.0 in Google Cloud Functions

In Google Cloud Functions, OAuth 2.0 can be implemented by leveraging **Google Identity Platform** or external providers like GitHub or Facebook.

Steps for implementing OAuth in Google Cloud Functions:

1. **Set up OAuth 2.0 in Google Cloud Console**:

- Enable the **Identity and Access Management (IAM)** API in your Google Cloud project.
- Create OAuth credentials and configure authorized redirect URIs for your app.

1. **Authenticate Users and Verify Tokens**:

- After user login, the client app will receive an access token.
- Use the token in Google Cloud Functions to authorize access:

javascript

```
const {OAuth2Client} = require('google-auth-library');
  const client = new OAuth2Client(CLIENT_ID);
```

6.3.3 IMPLEMENTING OAUTH 2.0 IN GOOGLE CLOUD FUNCTIONS

```
exports.verifyToken = async (req, res) => {
  const token = req.headers.authorization.split(' ')[1];

try {
  const ticket = await client.verifyIdToken({
  idToken: token,
  audience: CLIENT_ID
  });
  const payload = ticket.getPayload();
  res.status(200).send('Hello, ${payload.name}');
  } catch (error) {
  res.status(401).send('Unauthorized');
  }
  };
```

6.3.4 Introduction to JSON Web Tokens (JWT)

JSON Web Tokens (JWT) is another widely-used standard for securely transmitting information between parties. JWTs are compact, URL-safe tokens that can be used for authentication and data exchange. A typical JWT contains three parts:

- **Header**: Specifies the type of token and the hashing algorithm.
- **Payload**: Contains claims (user data) encoded in base64.
- **Signature**: A cryptographic signature that verifies the token's authenticity.

6.3.5 Securing Serverless APIs with JWT

JWTs are often used for securing serverless APIs because they allow stateless authentication. Unlike OAuth, which typically involves third-party authorization servers, JWTs can be generated and verified by the API server itself, making it suitable for microservices and event-driven architectures.

Steps for JWT Authentication:

1. **Generating a JWT**:

- On user login, the server generates a JWT with user information and signs it with a secret key or private key.

javascript

```
const jwt = require('jsonwebtoken');
const token = jwt.sign({ userId: 123 }, 'secret-key', { expiresIn: '1h' });
```

1. **Securing API Endpoints**:

- The client includes the JWT in the HTTP Authorization header for each request:

bash

```
GET /api/resource HTTP/1.1
Authorization: Bearer your.jwt.token.here
```

1. **Verifying JWT in AWS Lambda**:

- Use the jsonwebtoken package to verify the JWT in AWS Lambda:

STEPS FOR JWT AUTHENTICATION:

javascript

```
const jwt = require('jsonwebtoken');

exports.handler = async (event) => {
  const token = event.headers.Authorization.split(' ')[1];

try {
  const decoded = jwt.verify(token, 'secret-key');
  return {
  statusCode: 200,
  body: JSON.stringify({ message: 'Access granted', user: decoded })
  };
} catch (err) {
  return {
  statusCode: 401,
  body: JSON.stringify({ message: 'Unauthorized' })
  };
  }
};
```

1. **Verifying JWT in Google Cloud Functions**:

   - Google Cloud Functions can also validate JWTs using similar logic:

javascript

```
const jwt = require('jsonwebtoken');

exports.verifyToken = async (req, res) => {
  const token = req.headers.authorization.split(' ')[1];

try {
```

```
const decoded = jwt.verify(token, 'secret-key');
res.status(200).send('Hello, ${decoded.userId}');
} catch (error) {
res.status(401).send('Unauthorized');
}
};
```

6.3.6 Securing API Endpoints with Role-Based Access Control (RBAC)

Role-based access control (RBAC) allows fine-grained access control by associating permissions with user roles.

1. **Defining Roles and Permissions**:

- Define user roles (e.g., Admin, User, Guest) and assign specific actions to each role.

1. **Integrating RBAC with JWT**:

- Include user roles in the JWT payload when generating tokens:

javascript

const token = jwt.sign({ userId: 123, role: 'Admin' }, 'secret-key', { expiresIn: '1h' });

- In the API, check the user's role before granting access:

javascript

if (decoded.role === 'Admin') {

// Grant access to admin resources
}

Summary

By implementing OAuth 2.0 and JWT for securing serverless APIs, you can ensure that your applications are well-protected against unauthorized access. OAuth is ideal for scenarios where third-party authentication is required, while JWT offers a stateless, scalable solution for internal authentication in serverless environments.

Both methods offer flexibility and can be integrated with **AWS Lambda** and **Google Cloud Functions**, making them powerful tools for securing modern serverless applications.

6.4 Rate Limiting and Throttling in Serverless APIs

As serverless architectures gain popularity, ensuring the stability and performance of APIs becomes increasingly important. One effective strategy for managing traffic and preventing abuse is **rate limiting and throttling**. This section will explore what these concepts mean, their significance in serverless environments, and how to implement them in both AWS Lambda and Google Cloud Functions.

6.4.1 Understanding Rate Limiting and Throttling

- **Rate Limiting**: This technique restricts the number of requests a user or application can make to an API over a specified time period. For example, you might limit a user to 100 requests per hour. When the user exceeds this limit, further requests are rejected, typically returning a 429 Too Many Requests HTTP status code.
- **Throttling**: Throttling is a broader concept that limits the number of requests at any given time, rather than over a specific period. This approach helps smooth traffic spikes by queuing excess requests or delaying them, allowing the server to handle traffic more effectively.

Both techniques aim to protect your serverless applications from excessive load, improve overall performance, and ensure fair usage among all clients.

6.4.2 Importance of Rate Limiting and Throttling in Serverless Environments

Serverless architectures, such as AWS Lambda and Google Cloud Functions, inherently scale to meet demand. However, they can still be vulnerable to:

- **Denial-of-Service (DoS) Attacks**: Malicious actors may attempt to overwhelm your API with a flood of requests, causing downtime.
- **Cost Management**: Excessive API calls can lead to unexpectedly high costs due to pay-per-use billing models in serverless environments.
- **Fairness**: Rate limiting ensures that all users receive equitable access to resources without being affected by others' high usage.

Implementing rate limiting and throttling is essential for maintaining the integrity, reliability, and cost-effectiveness of your serverless applications.

6.4.3 Implementing Rate Limiting in AWS Lambda

To implement rate limiting in AWS Lambda, you can utilize **API Gateway**'s built-in throttling features. Here's how to set it up:

1. **Create or Update API Gateway**:

- Navigate to the AWS API Gateway Console and select your API or create a new one.
- Under **Usage Plans**, create a new usage plan that specifies the throttle limits, such as requests per second (RPS) or requests per minute (RPM).

1. **Associate API Stages with the Usage Plan**:

- Attach the usage plan to specific API stages (e.g., development, production) and specify usage limits for each stage.

1. **Integrate with AWS Lambda**:

- When requests exceed the defined rate limit, API Gateway returns a 429 Too Many Requests response without invoking the Lambda function.

1. **Monitoring and Adjustments**:

- Monitor usage patterns using AWS CloudWatch to analyze traffic and adjust the rate limits as necessary.

Example:

In the AWS API Gateway, you can set a usage plan with a burst limit of 200 RPS and a steady state of 100 RPS. This way, your API can handle sudden spikes while ensuring overall stability.

6.4.4 Implementing Throttling in Google Cloud Functions

Google Cloud Functions can also utilize rate limiting and throttling mechanisms, primarily through the **Google Cloud API** and additional tools such as **Cloud Endpoints** or **API Gateway**. Here's how to implement throttling:

1. **Set Up Google Cloud API Gateway**:

- Create an API Gateway in the Google Cloud Console and connect it to your Cloud Function.
- Define the endpoint for your API and configure throttling limits in the API Gateway settings.

1. **Use Quotas and Limits**:

- Set quotas on your Cloud Functions to define the maximum number of requests per minute, hour, or day for individual users or applications.

1. **Implementing Custom Logic**:

- If you need more granular control over throttling, you can implement custom logic within your Cloud Function to monitor and manage the rate of incoming requests.

6.4.4 IMPLEMENTING THROTTLING IN GOOGLE CLOUD FUNCTIONS

javascript

```
const rateLimit = require('express-rate-limit');
const express = require('express');
const app = express();

// Set rate limit to 100 requests per hour
const limiter = rateLimit({
windowMs: 60 * 60 * 1000, // 1 hour
max: 100, // Limit each IP to 100 requests per windowMs
message: 'Too many requests from this IP, please try again later.'
});

app.use(limiter);

app.get('/api/resource', (req, res) => {
res.send('Resource accessed successfully.');
});

exports.handler = app;
```

6.4.5 Best Practices for Implementing Rate Limiting and Throttling

1. **Define Clear Limits**: Establish reasonable limits based on the expected usage patterns of your application. Consider both individual and overall API usage.
2. **Communicate Limits**: Inform users of any rate limits in your API documentation. Provide guidance on what to expect when limits are exceeded.
3. **Implement Exponential Backoff**: When returning a 429 Too Many Requests response, suggest users retry after a certain period using an exponential backoff strategy.
4. **Monitor Traffic**: Use monitoring tools like AWS CloudWatch or Google Cloud Monitoring to analyze API usage trends, adjust rate limits accordingly, and identify potential abuse.
5. **Graceful Error Handling**: Ensure that your API gracefully handles rate limit errors and provides meaningful messages to users.

Summary

Implementing rate limiting and throttling in serverless APIs is crucial for maintaining application performance and security. By leveraging the built-in features of AWS API Gateway and Google Cloud API Gateway, you can effectively manage traffic, prevent abuse, and ensure a seamless experience for all users.

6.5 Handling CORS Issues in Serverless APIs

Cross-Origin Resource Sharing (CORS) is a security feature implemented by web browsers that restricts web pages from making requests to a different domain than the one that served the web page. When developing serverless APIs, especially when they are consumed by web applications hosted on different domains, it's essential to properly configure CORS to avoid issues and ensure a smooth user experience. In this section, we will explore what CORS is, how it works, and how to manage CORS issues in both AWS Lambda and Google Cloud Functions.

6.5.1 Understanding CORS

- **What is CORS?**: CORS is a protocol that allows web applications to request resources from a different domain. It is primarily implemented to protect users from malicious websites attempting to access sensitive data from another origin.
- **Same-Origin Policy**: This policy restricts web pages from making requests to a domain different from the one that served the original web page. CORS provides a way to relax this restriction securely.
- **CORS Headers**: When a browser makes a cross-origin request, it sends an OPTIONS request first (preflight request) to determine whether the actual request is safe to send. The server must respond with specific CORS headers, such as:
- Access-Control-Allow-Origin: Specifies which origins are permitted to access the resource.
- Access-Control-Allow-Methods: Lists the HTTP methods (GET, POST, etc.) allowed when accessing the resource.
- Access-Control-Allow-Headers: Lists the headers that can be used in the actual request.

6.5.2 Importance of CORS in Serverless APIs

Handling CORS correctly is crucial for several reasons:

1. **Security**: Proper CORS configuration helps prevent unauthorized access to your API and protects user data.
2. **User Experience**: A well-configured API enhances the user experience by ensuring that requests succeed without unexpected errors.
3. **Interoperability**: Many modern web applications interact with multiple APIs across different domains. CORS enables this interaction while maintaining security.

6.5.3 Implementing CORS in AWS Lambda

To manage CORS issues in AWS Lambda when using API Gateway, follow these steps:

1. **Enable CORS in API Gateway**:

- In the AWS Management Console, navigate to API Gateway and select the API you are working with.
- Choose the resource (endpoint) for which you want to enable CORS.
- Click on the **Actions** dropdown and select **Enable CORS**.
- Configure the allowed origins, methods, and headers according to your application's requirements.

1. **Add CORS Headers in Lambda Response**:

- When returning a response from your Lambda function, include CORS headers in the response. Here's an example of how to do this:

javascript

```
exports.handler = async (event) => {
  const response = {
    statusCode: 200,
```

```
headers: {
"Access-Control-Allow-Origin": "*", // Allow all origins (adjust for production)
"Access-Control-Allow-Methods": "GET, POST, OPTIONS", // Allowed methods
"Access-Control-Allow-Headers": "Content-Type" // Allowed headers
},
body: JSON.stringify({ message: "Hello from Lambda!" }),
};
return response;
};
```

1. **Handle Preflight Requests**:

- Ensure that your Lambda function can respond to preflight OPTIONS requests. You can either set up a separate Lambda function for this purpose or handle it within your existing function.

6.5.4 Implementing CORS in Google Cloud Functions

For Google Cloud Functions, managing CORS is straightforward. Here's how to handle CORS issues:

1. **Set CORS Headers in Your Function**:

- Similar to AWS, you need to include the CORS headers in the response of your Cloud Function. Here's an example:

javascript

exports.myFunction = (req, res) => {
  // Set CORS headers
  res.set('Access-Control-Allow-Origin', '*'); // Allow all origins (adjust for production)
  res.set('Access-Control-Allow-Methods', 'GET, POST, OPTIONS'); // Allowed methods
  res.set('Access-Control-Allow-Headers', 'Content-Type'); // Allowed headers

// Handle preflight requests
  if (req.method === 'OPTIONS') {
  return res.status(204).send('');

}

// Your function logic
res.status(200).send({ message: 'Hello from Google Cloud Functions!' });
};

1. **Using Cloud Endpoints**:

- If you are using Cloud Endpoints, you can configure CORS in your OpenAPI specification. This allows you to define allowed origins, methods, and headers directly in the API definition.

6.5.5 Best Practices for CORS Configuration

1. **Limit Allowed Origins**: Instead of using a wildcard (*), specify the exact domains that should have access to your API to enhance security.
2. **Test CORS Behavior**: Use tools like Postman or browser developer tools to test the CORS behavior of your API and ensure it is functioning as expected.
3. **Handle OPTIONS Requests**: Make sure your server responds to preflight OPTIONS requests appropriately to avoid issues with certain HTTP methods.
4. **Monitor CORS Errors**: Keep an eye on CORS-related errors in your application logs to quickly identify and resolve any misconfigurations.
5. **Documentation**: Clearly document your CORS policies in your API documentation to inform users about which origins are allowed.

Summary

Effectively handling CORS issues in serverless APIs is vital for security and user experience. By properly configuring CORS in AWS Lambda and Google Cloud Functions, you can ensure that your API can be accessed securely and seamlessly from different domains.

6.6 Building GraphQL APIs in a Serverless Environment

GraphQL is a powerful query language for APIs that enables clients to request exactly the data they need. Unlike REST, where multiple endpoints are often required to fetch related resources, GraphQL allows clients to retrieve complex data structures in a single request. In this section, we will explore how to build GraphQL APIs in a serverless environment using AWS Lambda and Google Cloud Functions.

6.6.1 Understanding GraphQL Basics

- **What is GraphQL?**: Developed by Facebook in 2012, GraphQL provides a more efficient and flexible alternative to REST APIs. Clients can specify their data requirements in a single query, and the server responds with precisely the requested data.
- **Key Concepts**:
- **Schemas**: GraphQL APIs are defined by schemas that describe types and relationships.
- **Queries and Mutations**: Queries fetch data, while mutations modify data.
- **Resolvers**: Functions that resolve a specific field on a type in the schema, fetching the data as requested by the client.

6.6.2 Setting Up a GraphQL API with AWS Lambda

To create a GraphQL API on AWS Lambda, you can use libraries such as Apollo Server or Express-GraphQL. Here's how to set it up:

1. **Create Your Lambda Function**:

- Use the AWS Management Console or CLI to create a new Lambda function. Choose Node.js as the runtime.

1. **Install Dependencies**:

- Use npm to install Apollo Server and GraphQL:

bash

npm install apollo-server-lambda graphql

1. **Define Your Schema and Resolvers**:

- Create a GraphQL schema and define resolvers to handle queries and mutations.

javascript

```
const { ApolloServer, gql } = require('apollo-server-lambda');

const typeDefs = gql`
  type Query {
    hello: String
  }
`;

const resolvers = {
  Query: {
    hello: () => 'Hello, World!',
  },
};

const server = new ApolloServer({ typeDefs, resolvers });

exports.handler = server.createHandler();
```

1. **Deploy Your Function**:

- Deploy your function using the AWS CLI or via the AWS Management Console.

1. **Create API Gateway**:

- Set up an API Gateway to trigger your Lambda function and configure CORS as described in the previous section.

6.6.3 Building a GraphQL API with Google Cloud Functions

Similar to AWS, Google Cloud Functions can also host a GraphQL API. The setup is quite straightforward:

1. **Create Your Cloud Function**:

- Go to the Google Cloud Console and create a new Cloud Function. Select Node.js as the runtime.

1. **Install Dependencies**:

- Use npm to install Apollo Server and GraphQL:

bash

npm install apollo-server-cloud-functions graphql

1. **Define Your Schema and Resolvers**:

- Create your GraphQL schema and resolvers similarly to how it was done for AWS.

javascript

```javascript
const { ApolloServer, gql } = require('apollo-server-cloud-functions');

const typeDefs = gql`
  type Query {
    hello: String
  }
`;

const resolvers = {
  Query: {
    hello: () => 'Hello, Google Cloud!',
  },
};

const server = new ApolloServer({ typeDefs, resolvers });

exports.graphql = server.createHandler();
```

1. **Deploy Your Function**:

- Deploy your function using the Google Cloud Console or via the gcloud command-line tool.

1. **API Gateway Integration**:

- If needed, set up an API Gateway or Cloud Endpoints to manage routing and CORS.

6.6.4 Benefits of Using GraphQL in Serverless Architecture

1. **Reduced Overhead**: Clients can specify precisely what data they need, reducing the amount of data transferred over the network.
2. **Single Endpoint**: Unlike REST, where multiple endpoints are needed, GraphQL typically exposes a single endpoint, simplifying the API structure.
3. **Versioning**: With GraphQL, clients can request new data without requiring versioning, as they control the fields they query.
4. **Flexibility**: GraphQL's dynamic querying capabilities allow developers to evolve their APIs more easily.

Conclusion

In this chapter, we explored the fundamentals of API development in a serverless environment, focusing on both RESTful and GraphQL APIs. We covered key concepts such as securing APIs, handling CORS issues, and optimizing performance with rate limiting and error handling. We also discussed the benefits of leveraging GraphQL in serverless applications, highlighting its flexibility and efficiency.

As serverless architectures continue to gain traction, understanding how to build robust APIs will be essential for developers. With the knowledge gained in this chapter, you're now equipped to design and implement scalable and secure APIs in both AWS and Google Cloud environments.

7.1 Connecting AWS Lambda to AWS RDS and Aurora

In serverless applications, data management is critical, and AWS provides powerful relational database services like Amazon RDS (Relational Database Service) and Amazon Aurora, a MySQL- and PostgreSQL-compatible database. This section will explore how to connect AWS Lambda functions to these services, enabling seamless data operations.

7.1.1 Overview of Amazon RDS and Aurora

- **Amazon RDS**: A managed relational database service that supports various database engines, including MySQL, PostgreSQL, Oracle, and SQL Server. It automates tasks like backups, patching, and scaling.
- **Amazon Aurora**: A MySQL- and PostgreSQL-compatible database that offers enhanced performance, scalability, and durability. Aurora is designed for high availability and is fully managed by AWS.

7.1.2 Setting Up Amazon RDS or Aurora

1. **Create an RDS or Aurora Instance**:

- Navigate to the AWS Management Console.
- Choose RDS from the Services menu and click on "Create database."
- Select the desired database engine (e.g., MySQL or PostgreSQL).
- Configure the instance settings, including instance size, storage, and database name.
- Choose the VPC (Virtual Private Cloud) settings, ensuring that it allows connections from your Lambda function.

1. **Configure Security Groups**:

- Ensure that the security group associated with your RDS or Aurora instance allows inbound traffic from the Lambda function's security group or VPC.

1. **Set Up Database Credentials**:

- Create a master username and password for the database. Keep these credentials secure, as they will be required to connect from Lambda.

7.1.3 Connecting Lambda Functions to RDS/Aurora

To connect your AWS Lambda function to RDS or Aurora, you'll need to use a suitable database driver. Below is an example using Node.js and the MySQL driver.

1. **Install the MySQL Driver**:

- Add the mysql or mysql2 package to your Lambda function:

bash

npm install mysql2

1. **Create a Lambda Function**:

- In your Lambda function code, require the MySQL driver and establish a connection to the RDS/Aurora instance.

javascript

const mysql = require('mysql2');

const connection = mysql.createConnection({

7.1.3 CONNECTING LAMBDA FUNCTIONS TO RDS/AURORA

```
  host: 'your-db-instance-endpoint',
  user: 'your-username',
  password: 'your-password',
  database: 'your-database-name',
});

exports.handler = async (event) => {
  return new Promise((resolve, reject) => {
  connection.query('SELECT * FROM your_table', (error, results) => {
  if (error) {
  reject(error);
  } else {
  resolve(results);
  }
  });
  });
};
```

1. **Deploy the Lambda Function**:

- Deploy your Lambda function, ensuring it has the necessary permissions to access the RDS/Aurora instance.

1. **Test the Connection**:

- Trigger the Lambda function to verify that it can successfully connect to the database and return the expected results.

7.2 Using Amazon DynamoDB with AWS Lambda

In addition to relational databases, AWS Lambda works seamlessly with DynamoDB, a fully managed NoSQL database service. In this section, we will cover how to use DynamoDB with AWS Lambda for high-performance data operations.

7.2.1 Overview of Amazon DynamoDB

- **DynamoDB**: A NoSQL database service that provides fast and predictable performance with seamless scalability. It is designed for applications that require low-latency data access at any scale.

7.2.2 Setting Up DynamoDB

1. **Create a DynamoDB Table**:

- Go to the DynamoDB section in the AWS Management Console.
- Click on "Create table."
- Define the table name and primary key (partition key and optional sort key).

1. **Configure Throughput and Autoscaling**:

- Set the read and write capacity units for your table. Consider enabling autoscaling for dynamic workloads.

7.2.3 Connecting Lambda Functions to DynamoDB

1. **Install the AWS SDK**:

- The AWS SDK for JavaScript is available by default in AWS Lambda, but ensure your function can access DynamoDB.

1. **Create a Lambda Function**:

- Use the following code to connect to DynamoDB and perform CRUD operations.

```javascript
const AWS = require('aws-sdk');
const dynamoDB = new AWS.DynamoDB.DocumentClient();

exports.handler = async (event) => {
  const params = {
    TableName: 'your-table-name',
    Key: {
      'your-primary-key': event.key,
    },
```

};

try {
    const data = await dynamoDB.get(params).promise();
    return data.Item;
} catch (error) {
    throw new Error(`Unable to get item: ${error.message}`);
}
};

1. **Deploy the Lambda Function**:

- Deploy your Lambda function and ensure it has permissions to access the DynamoDB table.

1. **Test the Function**:

- Trigger the Lambda function and verify that it retrieves the expected data from DynamoDB.

7.3 Integrating Google Cloud Functions with Cloud SQL

Google Cloud Functions can also connect to Cloud SQL, a fully managed database service that supports MySQL, PostgreSQL, and SQL Server.

7.3.1 Overview of Cloud SQL

- **Cloud SQL**: A managed database service that allows you to run SQL databases in the cloud with high availability, automated backups, and seamless scaling.

7.3.2 Setting Up Cloud SQL

1. **Create a Cloud SQL Instance**:

- Navigate to the Google Cloud Console and create a new Cloud SQL instance.
- Choose your desired database engine and configure the instance settings.

1. **Configure Access Control**:

- Set up user accounts and passwords, and allow Cloud Functions to connect by configuring the appropriate network settings.

7.3.3 Connecting Cloud Functions to Cloud SQL

1. **Use the Cloud SQL Node.js Driver:**

- Install the appropriate database driver for your database engine.

```bash
npm install mysql2
```

1. **Create a Cloud Function:**

- Use the following code to connect to Cloud SQL and perform data operations.

```javascript
const mysql = require('mysql2');

const connection = mysql.createConnection({
  host: '/cloudsql/your-connection-name',
  user: 'your-username',
  password: 'your-password',
```

7.3.3 CONNECTING CLOUD FUNCTIONS TO CLOUD SQL

```
  database: 'your-database-name',
});

exports.handler = (req, res) => {
  connection.query('SELECT * FROM your_table', (error, results) => {
  if (error) {
  res.status(500).send(error.message);
  } else {
  res.status(200).send(results);
  }
});
};
```

1. **Deploy the Cloud Function**:

- Deploy your Cloud Function and ensure it has access to the Cloud SQL instance.

7.4 Best Practices for Database Management in Serverless Applications

1. **Connection Management**:

- Reuse database connections to minimize latency and optimize resource usage.
- For AWS, consider using a connection pool.

1. **Error Handling**:

- Implement robust error handling to manage database connection failures and query errors gracefully.

1. **Data Validation**:

- Always validate incoming data to protect against SQL injection and ensure data integrity.

1. **Scalability**:

- Choose the right database based on your application needs (SQL vs. NoSQL).
- Utilize autoscaling features provided by managed database services.

Summary

In this section, we explored how to manage databases in serverless applications using AWS and Google Cloud services. We covered connecting AWS Lambda to RDS and DynamoDB, as well as integrating Google Cloud Functions with Cloud SQL. The chapter highlighted best practices for connection management, error handling, and data validation, which are crucial for maintaining efficient and secure data operations in a serverless environment.

7.2 Google Cloud Functions with Cloud SQL and Cloud Firestore

Google Cloud Functions seamlessly integrates with both Cloud SQL and Cloud Firestore, allowing you to leverage the capabilities of these managed database services in your serverless applications. This section will cover how to connect Google Cloud Functions to these databases and perform data operations effectively.

7.2.1 Connecting Google Cloud Functions to Cloud SQL

Overview of Cloud SQL
Cloud SQL is a fully managed relational database service for MySQL, PostgreSQL, and SQL Server. It provides features such as automated backups, high availability, and scaling capabilities.

Setting Up Cloud SQL

1. **Create a Cloud SQL Instance**:

- In the Google Cloud Console, navigate to Cloud SQL and click on "Create instance."
- Choose the database engine (MySQL or PostgreSQL) and configure the instance settings, including region, database version, and instance ID.

1. **Configure Users and Access**:

- Create database users with strong passwords and assign them appropriate roles and permissions.
- Ensure that the Cloud Function can connect by allowing the required IP ranges or enabling the appropriate authentication methods.

Connecting Cloud Functions to Cloud SQL

1. **Use the Cloud SQL Node.js Driver**:

   - Install the required database driver for your chosen database engine, such as mysql2 for MySQL.

bash

npm install mysql2

1. **Create a Cloud Function**:

   - Write a Cloud Function that connects to Cloud SQL and performs database operations. Below is an example that retrieves data from a MySQL database.

javascript

```javascript
const mysql = require('mysql2/promise');

const connectionName = 'your-project-id:your-region:your-instance-id';
  const dbUser = 'your-db-user';
  const dbPassword = 'your-db-password';
  const dbName = 'your-database-name';

exports.handler = async (req, res) => {
  const connection = await mysql.createConnection({
  host: `/cloudsql/${connectionName}`,
  user: dbUser,
  password: dbPassword,
  database: dbName,
  });

const [rows] = await connection.execute('SELECT * FROM your_table');
```

7.2.1 CONNECTING GOOGLE CLOUD FUNCTIONS TO CLOUD SQL

res.status(200).send(rows);
await connection.end();
};

1. **Deploy the Cloud Function**:

- Use the Google Cloud Console or the gcloud command-line tool to deploy the Cloud Function, ensuring it has access to the Cloud SQL instance.

1. **Testing the Connection**:

- Trigger the Cloud Function via an HTTP request or other event sources to verify that it retrieves data as expected.

7.2.2 Using Cloud Firestore with Google Cloud Functions

Overview of Cloud Firestore

Cloud Firestore is a NoSQL document database that provides real-time synchronization and querying capabilities. It is ideal for applications that require a flexible, scalable database solution.

Setting Up Firestore

1. **Create a Firestore Database**:

- In the Google Cloud Console, navigate to Firestore and click "Create database."
- Choose between "Start in production mode" or "Start in test mode" based on your requirements.

1. **Set Up Security Rules**:

- Configure Firestore security rules to manage access to your database, ensuring that only authorized users can read or write data.

Connecting Cloud Functions to Cloud Firestore

1. **Install the Firebase Admin SDK**:

7.2.2 USING CLOUD FIRESTORE WITH GOOGLE CLOUD FUNCTIONS

- Add the Firebase Admin SDK to your project, which allows you to interact with Firestore.

bash

npm install firebase-admin

1. **Create a Cloud Function**:

- Write a Cloud Function that interacts with Firestore. Below is an example that retrieves documents from a Firestore collection.

javascript

```
const admin = require('firebase-admin');
  admin.initializeApp();

exports.handler = async (req, res) => {
  const db = admin.firestore();
  const snapshot = await db.collection('your_collection').get();
  const documents = [];

snapshot.forEach(doc => {
  documents.push({ id: doc.id, ...doc.data() });
  });

res.status(200).send(documents);
  };
```

1. **Deploy the Cloud Function**:

- Deploy your Cloud Function, ensuring it has permission to access Firestore. You may need to set up IAM roles for your function's service account.

1. **Testing Firestore Integration:**

- Trigger the Cloud Function to verify that it successfully retrieves data from Firestore.

7.2.3 Best Practices for Using Cloud SQL and Firestore in Google Cloud Functions

1. **Connection Management**:

- Use connection pooling where possible to manage database connections efficiently, reducing latency and resource consumption.

1. **Error Handling**:

- Implement comprehensive error handling to gracefully manage database connection failures and query errors.

1. **Data Validation**:

- Always validate incoming data to prevent issues such as SQL injection attacks and to ensure data integrity.

1. **Security**:

- Apply appropriate security measures, such as using environment variables for sensitive information (e.g., passwords) and configuring IAM roles correctly.

1. **Testing and Monitoring**:

- Continuously test and monitor your Cloud Functions to ensure they perform optimally and can handle expected loads.

Summary

In this section, we delved into the integration of Google Cloud Functions with Cloud SQL and Cloud Firestore, highlighting the processes for connecting to these databases and performing CRUD operations. We discussed best practices for managing database connections, handling errors, ensuring data security, and validating data.

7.3 Implementing Database Transactions in a Serverless Context

Database transactions are crucial in ensuring data integrity and consistency, particularly in applications that require multiple operations to be performed together as a single unit of work. In serverless architectures, managing transactions can be a bit different from traditional setups due to the stateless nature of serverless functions. This section discusses how to implement database transactions in both AWS Lambda and Google Cloud Functions.

7.3.1 Understanding Transactions

A transaction is a sequence of operations performed as a single logical unit of work. Transactions have four key properties, often referred to as ACID:

1. **Atomicity**: The entire transaction must be completed; if any part fails, the whole transaction fails.
2. **Consistency**: The database must remain in a consistent state before and after the transaction.
3. **Isolation**: Transactions should not interfere with each other; concurrent transactions must yield consistent results.
4. **Durability**: Once a transaction is committed, it remains so, even in the event of a failure.

7.3.2 Implementing Transactions in AWS Lambda with DynamoDB

AWS DynamoDB supports transactions through the TransactWriteItems and TransactGetItems operations. Here's how to implement a transaction in an AWS Lambda function:

1. **Setting Up DynamoDB**: Ensure you have a DynamoDB table ready for the operations you want to perform.
2. **Lambda Function Code**:

javascript

const AWS = require('aws-sdk');
  const dynamoDB = new AWS.DynamoDB.DocumentClient();

exports.handler = async (event) => {
  const params = {
  TransactItems: [
  {
  Put: {
  TableName: 'YourTable',
  Item: {
  id: '123',
  attribute1: 'value1',

7.3.2 IMPLEMENTING TRANSACTIONS IN AWS LAMBDA WITH DYNAMODB

```
        attribute2: 'value2',
      },
    },
  },
  {
    Update: {
      TableName: 'YourTable',
      Key: { id: '456' },
      UpdateExpression: 'set attribute1 = :val1',
      ExpressionAttributeValues: {
        ':val1': 'updatedValue',
      },
    },
  },
  ],
};

try {
  await dynamoDB.transactWrite(params).promise();
  return { statusCode: 200, body: 'Transaction Successful' };
} catch (error) {
  console.error('Transaction failed:', error);
  return { statusCode: 500, body: 'Transaction Failed' };
}
};
```

1. **Deploy and Test**: Deploy your function and invoke it to test the transaction. If any part of the transaction fails, the whole transaction is rolled back.

7.3.3 Implementing Transactions in Google Cloud Functions with Firestore

Firestore also supports atomic operations, but it does not support multi-document transactions in the same way that SQL databases do. Instead, you can use Firestore's batched writes and transactions for this purpose.

1. **Setting Up Firestore**: Ensure your Firestore database is set up with the required collections.
2. **Cloud Function Code**:

javascript

```
const admin = require('firebase-admin');
  admin.initializeApp();

exports.handler = async (req, res) => {
  const db = admin.firestore();
  const batch = db.batch();

const docRef1 = db.collection('YourCollection').doc('doc1');
  const docRef2 = db.collection('YourCollection').doc('doc2');

batch.set(docRef1, { attribute1: 'value1' });
```

7.3.3 IMPLEMENTING TRANSACTIONS IN GOOGLE CLOUD FUNCTIONS...

batch.update(docRef2, { attribute2: 'updatedValue' });

try {
  await batch.commit();
  res.status(200).send('Batch transaction successful');
  } catch (error) {
  console.error('Batch transaction failed:', error);
  res.status(500).send('Batch transaction failed');
  }
};

1. **Deploy and Test**: Deploy your Cloud Function and test the batch transaction. If any write operation fails, none of the operations in the batch will be applied.

7.3.4 Best Practices for Transactions in Serverless Applications

1. **Keep Transactions Short**: Minimize the number of operations in a transaction to reduce the chance of contention and improve performance.
2. **Use Appropriate Isolation Levels**: For SQL databases, select an isolation level that suits your application's needs, balancing performance and data integrity.
3. **Error Handling**: Implement robust error handling to manage transaction failures and retries gracefully.
4. **Monitoring**: Use monitoring tools to track transaction performance and diagnose issues, ensuring that your application remains reliable.
5. **Test Thoroughly**: Conduct thorough testing of transaction logic under various scenarios to ensure reliability and correctness.

Summary

In this section, we explored how to manage databases in serverless applications, focusing on integrating AWS Lambda with Cloud SQL and DynamoDB, as well as Google Cloud Functions with Firestore. We discussed implementing database transactions, ensuring data integrity and consistency, and highlighted best practices for effective transaction management.

7.4 Serverless Database Design Considerations

Designing databases for serverless applications involves unique considerations that differ from traditional architectures. In a serverless environment, the database must not only fulfill data storage and retrieval needs but also integrate seamlessly with the event-driven and stateless nature of serverless computing. This section discusses essential design considerations to keep in mind when building serverless databases.

7.4.1 Scalability

Serverless applications often experience unpredictable traffic patterns, making scalability a primary concern. When designing your database:

- **Choose a Scalable Database**: Opt for databases that automatically scale based on demand. For example, AWS DynamoDB and Google Cloud Firestore provide automatic scaling capabilities.
  - **Partitioning**: For SQL databases, consider partitioning data to distribute load effectively across multiple nodes, enhancing performance during high traffic.

7.4.2 Data Access Patterns

Understanding how your application accesses data is critical for optimal database design:

- **Read vs. Write Patterns**: Analyze whether your application will have more reads than writes (or vice versa) and design your database schema accordingly. For instance, you might optimize for read performance by denormalizing data when necessary.
  - **Data Modeling**: In NoSQL databases, adopt flexible schema designs that allow for easier modifications and accommodate varied data structures.

7.4.3 Latency and Performance

Latency can significantly affect user experience in serverless applications. To minimize latency:

- **Proximity to Services**: Choose a database that is located in the same region as your serverless functions to reduce network latency.
- **Use Caching**: Implement caching strategies using tools like Redis or DynamoDB Accelerator (DAX) to store frequently accessed data closer to your application logic.

7.4.4 Cost Management

While serverless architectures can be cost-effective, poor database design can lead to unexpected costs:

- **Understand Pricing Models**: Familiarize yourself with the pricing models of your chosen database. For instance, DynamoDB charges based on read/write capacity and storage, while Firestore charges based on document reads, writes, and deletes.
  - **Optimize Queries**: Ensure that your queries are efficient and that you are not reading more data than necessary. Use indexing and limit operations where appropriate to reduce costs.

7.4.5 Security and Access Control

Security is paramount in any application, especially when dealing with user data:

- **Fine-Grained Access Control**: Implement fine-grained access control using IAM roles in AWS or Firebase Authentication in Google Cloud to ensure that only authorized users and functions can access sensitive data.
  - **Data Encryption**: Utilize encryption for data at rest and in transit to protect user data from unauthorized access.

7.4.6 Backup and Recovery

Establishing a robust backup and recovery plan is crucial for data integrity:

- **Automated Backups**: Use built-in features for automated backups offered by cloud providers. For example, AWS RDS provides automated backups that can be configured easily.
- **Disaster Recovery Planning**: Design your database architecture with disaster recovery in mind, ensuring you have strategies for data restoration in case of failure.

Summary

In this section, we explored how to effectively manage databases in serverless applications, focusing on connecting AWS Lambda and Google Cloud Functions to various database services. We discussed implementing database transactions, best practices for transaction management, and essential design considerations for serverless databases.

Understanding these aspects will help ensure that your serverless applications are robust, scalable, and efficient.

7.5 Real-Time Data with Serverless Databases

In modern applications, real-time data processing and delivery are essential, especially for features like live updates, notifications, and interactive user experiences. Serverless databases can play a vital role in achieving real-time data capabilities, enabling developers to build responsive applications without the overhead of managing server infrastructure. This section explores how to implement real-time data solutions using serverless databases and technologies.

7.5.1 Understanding Real-Time Data Requirements

Before diving into implementation, it's important to define what real-time data means for your application:

- **Low Latency**: The data should be processed and delivered with minimal delay.
- **Event-Driven Architecture**: Changes in data should trigger events that notify clients or other services immediately.
- **Scalability**: The solution must handle fluctuations in user load without degradation in performance.

7.5.2 Utilizing WebSockets for Real-Time Communication

WebSockets provide a persistent connection between clients and servers, allowing for real-time bidirectional communication. While serverless architectures are inherently stateless, integrating WebSockets can enable real-time data delivery:

1. **Set Up a WebSocket Server**: Use services like AWS API Gateway with WebSocket support or Google Cloud's Cloud Run to create a WebSocket server.
2. **Integrate with Lambda or Cloud Functions**: Connect your WebSocket server with AWS Lambda or Google Cloud Functions to handle events such as user messages, notifications, or data updates.

Example: Using AWS API Gateway and Lambda, you can create a WebSocket API that sends messages to connected clients when data changes in a DynamoDB table.

7.5.3 Leveraging Change Data Capture (CDC)

Change Data Capture (CDC) is a technique used to identify and capture changes made to data in a database. This is particularly useful for real-time updates in serverless applications:

- **Using DynamoDB Streams**: For AWS, you can enable DynamoDB Streams to capture changes to your DynamoDB tables. These streams can then trigger AWS Lambda functions to process changes and push updates to clients.

Example:
javascript

```javascript
exports.handler = async (event) => {
  for (const record of event.Records) {
  const newValue = record.dynamodb.NewImage;
  // Logic to send update to clients, e.g., via WebSocket
  }
};
```

- **Firestore Triggers**: In Google Cloud, Firestore offers triggers that allow you to run Cloud Functions in response to changes in your Firestore database (e.g., document creation, updates).

7.5.4 Using Serverless Pub/Sub Messaging Systems

Message brokers can facilitate real-time data processing in serverless applications. Using a pub/sub messaging model, you can decouple data producers from consumers, allowing for scalable and responsive systems:

- **AWS SNS/SQS**: Utilize Amazon Simple Notification Service (SNS) for publishing messages to multiple subscribers and Amazon Simple Queue Service (SQS) for message queuing.
- **Google Cloud Pub/Sub**: This managed service allows you to create topics for publishing messages and subscriptions for consumers to receive them.

Example: When a new data entry is created, publish a message to a topic. Subscribers (e.g., Lambda functions or Cloud Functions) can process the message and update clients in real-time.

7.5.5 Implementing Real-Time Data with Serverless Databases

Integrating real-time data capabilities into your serverless architecture typically involves a combination of the above techniques:

1. **Data Modification**: Data changes are captured using CDC mechanisms like DynamoDB Streams or Firestore triggers.
2. **Processing Events**: Use serverless functions (Lambda or Cloud Functions) to process these changes and publish updates to clients.
3. **Client Updates**: Utilize WebSockets or other real-time communication methods to push updates to users.

Summary

In this section, we explored the management of databases in serverless applications, focusing on connecting AWS Lambda and Google Cloud Functions with various database services. We covered transaction management, best practices, design considerations, and techniques for implementing real-time data solutions.

By understanding how to leverage serverless databases for real-time capabilities, you can create highly responsive applications that meet modern user demands.

7.6 Migrating Databases for Serverless Architectures

Migrating databases to a serverless architecture can be a complex process, but it is often necessary to take full advantage of the scalability, flexibility, and cost-effectiveness of serverless computing. This section outlines the key steps and considerations for successfully migrating your databases to a serverless environment.

7.6.1 Assessing Current Database Systems

Before migration, conduct a thorough assessment of your current database systems:

- **Inventory Existing Databases**: Identify all databases in use, including their types (SQL, NoSQL) and any dependencies.
- **Evaluate Usage Patterns**: Analyze how data is currently accessed and modified. Understanding usage patterns will help determine the best serverless database options.

7.6.2 Choosing the Right Serverless Database

Select a serverless database that meets your application needs. Consider factors such as:

- **Data Model Compatibility**: Ensure the new database supports the data structures and access patterns required by your application.
- **Performance and Scalability**: Evaluate the database's ability to scale with your application's needs.
- **Cost Considerations**: Analyze the pricing model to avoid unexpected costs post-migration.

Examples:

- For applications heavily reliant on document storage and retrieval, consider migrating to AWS DynamoDB or Google Firestore.
- For applications requiring relational data structures, consider AWS Aurora Serverless or Google Cloud SQL with appropriate configuration for serverless environments.

7.6.3 Planning the Migration Process

Create a detailed migration plan that outlines the steps involved, including:

- **Data Migration Strategy**: Decide on a strategy for transferring data, such as:
  - **Lift and Shift**: Moving the entire database to the serverless environment with minimal changes.
  - **Refactoring**: Modifying data models and access patterns to optimize for serverless.
  - **Downtime Considerations**: Plan for any potential downtime and communicate with stakeholders to minimize disruptions.

7.6.4 Executing the Migration

Carry out the migration according to your plan:

1. **Data Transfer**: Use tools like AWS Database Migration Service (DMS) or Google Cloud Database Migration Service to transfer data securely and efficiently.
2. **Testing**: After migration, conduct thorough testing to ensure data integrity and application functionality.
3. **Optimization**: Fine-tune the new database configuration and access patterns to enhance performance and reduce costs.

7.6.5 Post-Migration Monitoring and Optimization

Once the migration is complete, ongoing monitoring is essential:

- **Performance Monitoring**: Use cloud monitoring tools (e.g., AWS CloudWatch, Google Cloud Monitoring) to track database performance and identify potential issues.
- **Cost Analysis**: Regularly review your usage and costs to optimize configurations and prevent overspending.
- **Iterative Improvements**: Continuously iterate on your database design and access patterns to adapt to changing application needs.

Conclusion

In this chapter, we explored the management of databases in serverless applications, emphasizing connections between AWS Lambda and Google Cloud Functions with various database services. We discussed transaction management, real-time data capabilities, and the critical steps for migrating databases to a serverless architecture.

By carefully planning your migration and utilizing the strengths of serverless databases, you can enhance the scalability, performance, and reliability of your applications.

CHAPTER 8: EVENT-DRIVEN ARCHITECTURES IN SERVERLESS

8.1 What is an Event-Driven Architecture?

Event-Driven Architecture (EDA) is a software architecture paradigm that promotes the production, detection, consumption, and reaction to events. In a serverless context, this architecture enables applications to respond to real-time events and triggers without the need for continuous server management. This section explores the key components, benefits, and use cases of event-driven architectures.

8.1.1 Key Components of Event-Driven Architecture

1. **Events**: Events are state changes or actions that occur in a system. They can be generated by user interactions, changes in data, or system triggers. Examples include a user submitting a form, a file being uploaded, or an order being placed.
2. **Event Producers**: These are the components that generate events. In a serverless architecture, this could be a front-end application, a scheduled job, or another service that emits events when certain conditions are met.
3. **Event Consumers**: These components listen for and react to events. In serverless applications, event consumers are typically serverless functions (like AWS Lambda or Google Cloud Functions) that execute specific logic in response to an event.
4. **Event Brokers**: Event brokers are intermediaries that route events from

producers to consumers. They facilitate communication between disparate systems and can enhance decoupling in architectures. Common tools include AWS EventBridge, AWS SNS, Google Cloud Pub/Sub, and Apache Kafka.

8.1.2 Benefits of Event-Driven Architectures

1. **Scalability**: EDA allows applications to scale efficiently, as services can react to events independently without direct dependencies.
2. **Responsiveness**: Applications can respond to events in real-time, enhancing user experiences with immediate feedback and actions.
3. **Decoupling**: Components in an event-driven system are loosely coupled, allowing for easier updates and maintenance without impacting other parts of the system.
4. **Cost Efficiency**: Serverless architectures can be more cost-effective since resources are used only when events occur, reducing idle compute time.
5. **Flexibility**: EDA enables the integration of various services and components, allowing for a more flexible architecture that can adapt to changing business needs.

8.1.3 Use Cases for Event-Driven Architectures

1. **Microservices Communication**: In microservices architectures, EDA facilitates communication between services, allowing them to operate independently while responding to events.
2. **Real-Time Data Processing**: Applications that require real-time analytics, such as monitoring IoT devices or processing user-generated content, benefit greatly from event-driven architectures.
3. **User Interactions**: Websites and applications can provide real-time feedback and updates to users, such as notifications, alerts, or live updates on data changes.
4. **Asynchronous Workflows**: EDA is ideal for handling long-running

processes or workflows that require multiple steps and can operate asynchronously, such as order processing and payment workflows.
5. **Data Pipeline Integrations**: Event-driven architectures can facilitate the integration of various data sources and sinks, enabling streamlined data flows and processing across systems.

Summary

Event-Driven Architecture provides a powerful paradigm for building responsive, scalable, and loosely coupled applications in serverless environments. By leveraging events as a core mechanism for communication, developers can create flexible systems that respond dynamically to changes in state and user interactions. In the next section, **8.2: Key Concepts of Event-Driven Architectures**, we will dive deeper into the fundamental concepts and patterns that define effective event-driven systems.

8.2 Working with AWS EventBridge and Lambda Triggers

AWS EventBridge is a serverless event bus service that makes it easy to connect applications using events from various sources. It enables event-driven architectures by facilitating the creation, routing, and processing of events between AWS services and custom applications. This section explores how to work with AWS EventBridge and Lambda triggers, detailing their roles in building event-driven applications.

8.2.1 Understanding AWS EventBridge

AWS EventBridge simplifies event-driven architecture by allowing you to ingest and process events from various sources:

1. **Event Sources**: These can include AWS services (like S3, DynamoDB, and API Gateway), custom applications, or even third-party services that emit events.
2. **Event Buses**: An event bus is a central hub that receives and routes events. EventBridge provides a default event bus for AWS services and allows you to create custom event buses for your applications.
3. **Event Rules**: Event rules define the filtering criteria for the events that will be sent to targets. You can create rules to match specific event

patterns and determine which events should trigger specific actions.

4. **Targets**: Targets are the AWS resources that will respond to the events. This can include AWS Lambda functions, SNS topics, SQS queues, and more.

8.2.2 Setting Up AWS EventBridge

To get started with AWS EventBridge, follow these steps:

1. **Create an Event Bus**:

- Log into the AWS Management Console.
- Navigate to the EventBridge service.
- Click on "Create event bus" and give your bus a unique name.

1. **Create Event Rules**:

- Once the event bus is created, you can set up event rules by selecting your event bus and clicking on "Create rule."
- Define a name, description, and event pattern that specifies the events of interest (e.g., events from an S3 bucket).

1. **Specify Targets**:

- Choose AWS Lambda as your target. When setting up the target, select the Lambda function that should be triggered by the matching events.
- Configure any additional settings, such as input transformations if needed.

8.2.3 Integrating AWS Lambda with EventBridge

AWS Lambda functions can be easily integrated with EventBridge to create a seamless event-driven architecture. Here's how to set up an AWS Lambda function to respond to events from EventBridge:

1. **Create an AWS Lambda Function**:

- Go to the Lambda service in the AWS Management Console.
- Click on "Create function" and choose "Author from scratch."
- Provide a name, choose a runtime (e.g., Node.js), and set up permissions.

1. **Add EventBridge as a Trigger**:

- In the Lambda function configuration, click on "Add trigger."
- Select "EventBridge (CloudWatch Events)" and choose the event bus and rule you created earlier.

1. **Handle Incoming Events**:

- In your Lambda function code, handle the incoming event. The event payload will include details about the event, which you can use to trigger specific logic in your application.

javascript

```
exports.handler = async (event) => {
  console.log("Received event: ", JSON.stringify(event, null, 2));
  // Your logic here
};
```

8.2.4 Monitoring and Troubleshooting EventBridge and Lambda

To ensure that your event-driven architecture runs smoothly, it's important to monitor and troubleshoot any issues:

1. **CloudWatch Logs**: AWS Lambda automatically integrates with CloudWatch, allowing you to view logs generated by your function. This is essential for debugging and understanding how events are processed.
2. **EventBridge Metrics**: You can monitor the performance of your EventBridge event buses and rules through AWS CloudWatch metrics.

This will help you track the number of events received, matched, and sent to targets.

3. **Error Handling**: Implement error handling in your Lambda functions to catch and manage exceptions. You can also configure DLQs (Dead Letter Queues) to capture failed event invocations for further investigation.

Summary

AWS EventBridge provides a powerful way to implement event-driven architectures in serverless applications. By integrating EventBridge with AWS Lambda, developers can create responsive applications that react to a wide range of events from multiple sources. This architecture enhances scalability, flexibility, and maintainability, allowing teams to build sophisticated applications with ease. In the next section, **8.3: Working with Google Cloud Pub/Sub and Cloud Functions**, we will explore how to implement a similar architecture using Google Cloud's event-driven services.

8.3 Using Google Cloud Pub/Sub for Event-Driven Applications

Google Cloud Pub/Sub is a fully managed messaging service that allows you to asynchronously send and receive messages between independent applications. It is designed for high-throughput and low-latency communication, making it an ideal choice for building event-driven architectures in serverless environments. This section covers how to leverage Google Cloud Pub/Sub in conjunction with Google Cloud Functions to create responsive and scalable applications.

8.3.1 Understanding Google Cloud Pub/Sub

Google Cloud Pub/Sub consists of several key components that work together to facilitate event-driven communication:

1. **Topics**: A topic is a named resource to which messages are sent by publishers. Topics are the entry point for event messages that need to be distributed to subscribers.
2. **Publishers**: Publishers are applications or services that send messages to a topic. They can send messages in various formats, including JSON,

binary data, and plain text.
3. **Subscriptions**: A subscription is a named resource that represents the connection between a topic and a subscriber. Subscribers receive messages from a topic through a subscription, enabling them to process events asynchronously.
4. **Subscribers**: Subscribers are applications or services that listen for messages on a subscription. They can either pull messages (retrieve them from the subscription) or have messages pushed to them via webhooks.

8.3.2 Setting Up Google Cloud Pub/Sub

To get started with Google Cloud Pub/Sub, follow these steps:

1. **Create a Pub/Sub Topic**:

- Go to the Google Cloud Console.
- Navigate to the Pub/Sub section.
- Click on "Create Topic" and give your topic a unique name.

1. **Create a Subscription**:

- After creating the topic, you can set up a subscription by selecting your topic and clicking "Create Subscription."
- Choose a name for the subscription and select the delivery type (pull or push).

1. **Publish Messages to the Topic**:

- Use the Google Cloud client libraries or REST API to publish messages to your topic. Here's an example using Node.js:

javascript

```javascript
const { PubSub } = require('@google-cloud/pubsub');
```

```javascript
const pubsub = new PubSub();
const topicName = 'your-topic-name';

async function publishMessage(data) {
  const dataBuffer = Buffer.from(JSON.stringify(data));
  await pubsub.topic(topicName).publish(dataBuffer);
  console.log(`Message ${data} published to ${topicName}`);
}
```

8.3.3 Integrating Google Cloud Functions with Pub/Sub

Google Cloud Functions can be easily integrated with Google Cloud Pub/Sub to create event-driven applications. Here's how to set it up:

1. **Create a Google Cloud Function**:

- In the Google Cloud Console, navigate to the Cloud Functions section.
- Click on "Create Function" and configure the settings, including the name, runtime (e.g., Node.js), and trigger type.

1. **Set the Trigger to Pub/Sub**:

- Under "Trigger," select "Pub/Sub" and choose the topic you created earlier.
- This will automatically link your Cloud Function to the Pub/Sub topic.

1. **Handle Incoming Messages**:

- In your Cloud Function code, implement the logic to handle incoming messages. The message payload will be available in the function's data parameter:

javascript

```
exports.yourFunctionName = (data, context) => {
```

```
const message = Buffer.from(data.data, 'base64').toString();
console.log('Received message: ${message}');
// Your logic here
};
```

8.3.4 Monitoring and Troubleshooting Google Cloud Pub/Sub and Functions

To maintain the performance and reliability of your event-driven applications, it's essential to monitor and troubleshoot Google Cloud Pub/Sub and Cloud Functions:

1. **Logging**: Google Cloud Functions automatically integrate with Cloud Logging. You can view logs for each function execution to diagnose issues and understand message processing.
2. **Metrics**: Google Cloud provides metrics for Pub/Sub topics and subscriptions through Cloud Monitoring. Key metrics include message published, message acknowledged, and subscription backlog.
3. **Error Handling**: Implement error handling within your Cloud Functions to manage failures when processing messages. You can configure dead-letter topics to capture messages that cannot be processed after several attempts.

Summary

Google Cloud Pub/Sub provides a robust mechanism for building event-driven applications in serverless architectures. By integrating Pub/Sub with Google Cloud Functions, developers can create responsive systems that react to events in real-time. This architecture enhances scalability and flexibility while minimizing operational overhead. In the next section, **8.4: Designing Event-Driven Workflows with Cloud Services**, we will explore how to design comprehensive workflows using event-driven principles across different cloud services.

8.4 Queueing Systems with AWS SQS and Google Cloud Tasks

Queueing systems are vital for decoupling components in event-driven architectures, ensuring that messages are processed reliably and efficiently.

AWS Simple Queue Service (SQS) and Google Cloud Tasks are two powerful queueing solutions that enable developers to manage workloads in a serverless environment. This section will discuss how to use these queueing systems to enhance the scalability and resilience of serverless applications.

8.4.1 Understanding AWS SQS

AWS Simple Queue Service (SQS) is a fully managed message queuing service that enables you to decouple and scale microservices, distributed systems, and serverless applications. SQS offers two types of queues:

1. **Standard Queues**: These provide maximum throughput and at-least-once delivery, allowing messages to be delivered in any order. Standard queues are suitable for scenarios where message order is not critical.
2. **FIFO Queues**: First-In-First-Out (FIFO) queues guarantee that messages are processed in the exact order they are sent. This type of queue is ideal for applications where the order of operations is crucial.

8.4.2 Setting Up AWS SQS

To set up AWS SQS, follow these steps:

1. **Create a Queue**:

- Log into the AWS Management Console.
- Navigate to the SQS service.
- Click on "Create Queue" and choose between Standard and FIFO.
- Configure the queue settings, such as visibility timeout, message retention period, and access permissions.

1. **Send Messages to the Queue**:

- You can send messages to your SQS queue using the AWS SDK for JavaScript. Here's an example:

javascript

```javascript
const AWS = require('aws-sdk');
const sqs = new AWS.SQS();
const queueUrl = 'https://sqs.us-east-1.amazonaws.com/123456789012/MyQueue';

const params = {
  MessageBody: JSON.stringify({ key: 'value' }),
  QueueUrl: queueUrl,
};

sqs.sendMessage(params, (err, data) => {
  if (err) {
    console.error('Error sending message:', err);
  } else {
    console.log('Message sent successfully:', data.MessageId);
  }
});
```

1. **Receive Messages from the Queue**:

- You can retrieve messages from the queue and process them using a Lambda function or another application. Here's how to receive messages:

javascript

```javascript
const params = {
  QueueUrl: queueUrl,
  MaxNumberOfMessages: 10,
  WaitTimeSeconds: 20, // Long polling
};

sqs.receiveMessage(params, (err, data) => {
  if (err) {
```

```
console.error('Error receiving messages:', err);
} else {
console.log('Messages received:', data.Messages);
// Process messages here
}
});
```

8.4.3 Understanding Google Cloud Tasks

Google Cloud Tasks is a fully managed service that allows you to manage the execution of background tasks. It enables you to asynchronously execute tasks and decouple components in your applications. Cloud Tasks is designed to handle a large volume of tasks while providing reliable task delivery and scheduling.

8.4.4 Setting Up Google Cloud Tasks

To set up Google Cloud Tasks, follow these steps:

1. **Create a Queue**:

- Go to the Google Cloud Console.
- Navigate to the Cloud Tasks section.
- Click on "Create Queue" and provide a name and optional configuration settings.

1. **Enqueue Tasks**:

- You can enqueue tasks by sending HTTP requests to your Cloud Tasks queue. Here's an example using Node.js:

javascript

```javascript
const { CloudTasksClient } = require('@google-cloud/tasks');
  const client = new CloudTasksClient();
  const project = 'your-project-id';
  const queue = 'your-queue-name';
```

```
const location = 'us-central1';
const url = 'https://your-service-url'; // The endpoint to handle the task
const payload = JSON.stringify({ key: 'value' });

async function createTask() {
  const task = {
  httpRequest: {
  httpMethod: 'POST',
  url: url,
  body: Buffer.from(payload).toString('base64'),
  headers: {
  'Content-Type': 'application/json',
  },
  },
  };

  const [response] = await client.createTask({
    parent: client.queuePath(project, location, queue),
    task: task,
  });
  console.log(`Task created: ${response.name}`);
}
```

8.4.5 Processing Tasks in Queueing Systems

After you have set up your queueing systems, you can implement the logic to process the messages or tasks:

1. **AWS SQS**:

- Use AWS Lambda functions or EC2 instances to poll the SQS queue and process messages. Ensure that you delete messages from the queue after successful processing to prevent reprocessing.

1. **Google Cloud Tasks**:

- Implement an HTTP endpoint (such as a Cloud Function) to handle incoming tasks. When a task is triggered, your function will receive the request, process the data, and respond accordingly.

8.4.6 Monitoring and Troubleshooting Queueing Systems

Monitoring is essential for ensuring that your queueing systems operate smoothly:

1. **AWS SQS Monitoring**:

- Use CloudWatch to monitor SQS metrics such as the number of messages sent, received, and deleted. Set up alarms to notify you of any issues.

1. **Google Cloud Tasks Monitoring**:

- Monitor task execution using Cloud Monitoring. Track metrics like task creation rate, execution time, and error rates.

1. **Error Handling**:

- Implement error handling strategies in your application to manage failed tasks. For AWS SQS, consider using Dead Letter Queues (DLQs) to capture messages that cannot be processed. For Google Cloud Tasks, configure retry settings for tasks that fail.

Summary

AWS SQS and Google Cloud Tasks are powerful queueing solutions that enhance the reliability and scalability of serverless applications. By decoupling components and managing asynchronous workloads, these services allow developers to build resilient systems that can handle varying loads efficiently. In the next section, **8.5: Implementing Serverless Workflows with AWS Step Functions and Google Cloud Workflows**, we will explore how to design complex workflows in serverless environments.

8.5 Stream Processing with AWS Kinesis and Google Dataflow

Stream processing is an essential component of modern applications that need to handle continuous data streams in real-time. With the rise of serverless architectures, services like AWS Kinesis and Google Cloud Dataflow provide powerful tools for ingesting, processing, and analyzing real-time data without the need to manage underlying infrastructure. In this section, we will explore the fundamentals of stream processing and how to leverage these cloud services for serverless data streams.

8.5.1 What is Stream Processing?

Stream processing involves continuously ingesting and processing data as it arrives in real-time, rather than storing it for batch processing later. This is useful in scenarios such as monitoring sensor data, analyzing clickstreams, processing financial transactions, or real-time analytics for social media.

Unlike batch processing, where data is collected over time and processed in chunks, stream processing enables real-time insights, decision-making, and actions based on incoming data.

8.5.2 Introduction to AWS Kinesis

AWS Kinesis is a suite of services designed for real-time data streaming and processing. It includes three key components:

1. **Kinesis Data Streams**: Allows you to ingest large volumes of real-time data, split into shards for parallel processing.
2. **Kinesis Data Firehose**: Automatically loads streaming data into storage services like S3, Redshift, or Elasticsearch.
3. **Kinesis Data Analytics**: Enables real-time analytics on data streams using SQL queries.

8.5.3 Setting Up AWS Kinesis for Stream Processing

To set up AWS Kinesis, follow these steps:

1. **Create a Kinesis Data Stream**:

   - In the AWS Management Console, navigate to the Kinesis service.

CHAPTER 8: EVENT-DRIVEN ARCHITECTURES IN SERVERLESS

- Create a new Data Stream and define the number of shards based on the expected data throughput. Each shard supports up to 1 MB/sec of data input and 2 MB/sec of data output.

1. **Ingest Data into the Stream**:

- You can use the AWS SDK to ingest data into Kinesis. Here's an example in JavaScript:

javascript

```javascript
const AWS = require('aws-sdk');
  const kinesis = new AWS.Kinesis();
  const streamName = 'my-data-stream';

const data = JSON.stringify({ key: 'value', timestamp: Date.now() });

const params = {
  Data: data,
  PartitionKey: 'partitionKey1',
  StreamName: streamName,
};

kinesis.putRecord(params, (err, data) => {
  if (err) console.error(err);
  else console.log('Data successfully sent to Kinesis stream:', data);
});
```

1. **Processing Data with AWS Lambda**:

- Lambda can be triggered by Kinesis to process each new record in real-time. In the Lambda function, you can process the incoming records and take action, such as storing them in a database or analyzing trends.

8.5.4 Introduction to Google Cloud Dataflow

Google Cloud Dataflow is a fully managed service for stream and batch processing of data. It supports real-time analytics and provides built-in integration with Google Cloud services. Dataflow is based on the Apache Beam programming model, allowing you to write data processing pipelines in a unified way for both batch and streaming data.

Key features of Google Cloud Dataflow:

- **Unified Batch and Stream Processing**: Develop once, run anywhere.
- **Real-Time Processing**: Handle high-velocity, low-latency data streams.
- **Auto-Scaling**: Automatically adjusts the number of resources based on load.

8.5.5 Setting Up Google Cloud Dataflow

To set up Google Cloud Dataflow for stream processing, follow these steps:

1. **Create a Dataflow Pipeline**:

- Using the Google Cloud Console, create a new Dataflow job. You can write your Dataflow pipeline using the Apache Beam SDK in Java, Python, or Go.

1. **Define Data Sources and Sinks**:

- A typical Dataflow pipeline includes a source (e.g., Pub/Sub, BigQuery) and a sink (e.g., Google Cloud Storage, Bigtable). Here's an example pipeline using the Python SDK:

python

```python
import apache_beam as beam
from apache_beam.options.pipeline_options import PipelineOptions
```

CHAPTER 8: EVENT-DRIVEN ARCHITECTURES IN SERVERLESS

```
def process_record(record):
  # Process the record (e.g., extract fields, transform data)
  return record

options = PipelineOptions(
  streaming=True, # Enable streaming mode
  project='your-project-id',
  region='us-central1',
)

with beam.Pipeline(options=options) as pipeline:
  (pipeline
  | 'ReadFromPubSub' » beam.io.ReadFromPubSub(topic='projects/your-project-id/topics/your-topic')
  | 'ProcessRecord' » beam.Map(process_record)
  | 'WriteToStorage' » beam.io.WriteToText('gs://your-bucket/output.txt'))
```

1. **Monitoring Dataflow Jobs**:

- Dataflow provides a real-time dashboard where you can monitor your pipeline's progress, errors, and performance metrics. It also integrates with Google Cloud Monitoring for setting up alerts.

8.5.6 Key Differences Between AWS Kinesis and Google Cloud Dataflow
8.5.7 Use Cases for Stream Processing in Serverless Applications

1. **Real-Time Analytics**:

- Track website clicks, IoT sensor data, or user interactions in real-time.

1. **Log Aggregation**:

- Collect and process logs from multiple services, allowing for real-time alerting and insights.

1. **Fraud Detection**:

- Monitor financial transactions and detect anomalies as they happen.

1. **Social Media Monitoring**:

- Analyze social media data streams to track trends, sentiment, and engagement.

Summary

Stream processing plays a crucial role in serverless applications, allowing for real-time insights and action on continuous data flows. AWS Kinesis and Google Cloud Dataflow provide powerful stream processing capabilities in their respective cloud ecosystems, each suited for different use cases. By leveraging these services, developers can build scalable, event-driven applications that handle high-velocity data streams with minimal infrastructure management.

8.6 Building Real-Time Event-Driven Applications

Real-time event-driven applications respond to events as they occur, triggering workflows or functions immediately upon detecting those events. This approach is central to modern serverless architectures, where applications are designed to handle unpredictable traffic, minimize latency, and react dynamically to changes in data or user actions.

In this section, we will explore how to build real-time event-driven applications using serverless technologies like AWS Lambda, Google Cloud Functions, and event-triggering services such as AWS EventBridge and Google Pub/Sub.

8.6.1 Characteristics of Real-Time Event-Driven Applications

Real-time event-driven applications typically exhibit the following characteristics:

- **Asynchronous Processing**: Events are processed independently without blocking other operations.
- **Low Latency**: Responses to events are near-instantaneous.
- **Scalability**: Applications can handle spikes in traffic by automatically scaling up or down.
- **Loose Coupling**: Components of the application are loosely coupled, allowing for modular and maintainable design.
- **Resilience**: Event-driven systems can fail gracefully by retrying or rerouting events in case of errors.

8.6.2 Real-Time Data Ingestion with AWS Lambda and Google Cloud Functions

In real-time event-driven applications, data ingestion is a critical first step. Whether it's incoming data from IoT devices, user interactions, or external webhooks, serverless functions like AWS Lambda and Google Cloud Functions can be triggered to handle these events instantly.

For example:

- **AWS Lambda + EventBridge**: AWS EventBridge can trigger Lambda functions when it detects specific patterns in the event stream. These Lambda functions can then process the incoming data, store it, or trigger additional workflows.
- **Google Cloud Functions + Pub/Sub**: Google Cloud Pub/Sub acts as the event bus, sending messages to Google Cloud Functions, which process the data in real time and trigger other services as needed.

Here's an example of a simple Lambda function triggered by EventBridge:
javascript

```javascript
exports.handler = async (event) => {
  console.log("Event received:", JSON.stringify(event));
  // Process event data here
  return {
```

statusCode: 200,
body: JSON.stringify('Event processed successfully!'),
};
};

8.6.3 Designing Event-Driven Workflows

A key part of building event-driven applications is designing workflows that react to events in a structured manner. Services like AWS Step Functions and Google Cloud Workflows help orchestrate these workflows by connecting different serverless functions, API calls, and services.

For example:

- **AWS Step Functions** can create workflows where each step is triggered by the successful completion of the previous one. This is useful for building multi-step processes such as processing e-commerce orders, where different functions handle inventory checks, payment, and shipping.
- **Google Cloud Workflows** provides a similar orchestration service, allowing you to define complex workflows across different Google Cloud services.

8.6.4 Handling Real-Time Data Streams

Real-time data streaming is an essential feature for event-driven applications, especially those that need to react immediately to large volumes of data. AWS Kinesis and Google Cloud Dataflow allow you to process and analyze continuous data streams in real-time.

For example:

- **E-commerce**: Process orders as they come in and trigger follow-up actions like inventory updates and shipment scheduling.
- **IoT Monitoring**: Continuously ingest sensor data and trigger alerts when thresholds are exceeded.
- **Real-Time Analytics**: Analyze clickstream data on a website in real-time and update recommendations or marketing campaigns instantly.

8.6.5 Real-World Use Cases of Event-Driven Architectures

1. **Financial Trading**: In financial markets, real-time event-driven systems monitor trades and trigger automatic actions based on predefined criteria, such as buying or selling stocks.
2. **Fraud Detection**: Payment systems often use event-driven architectures to detect anomalies in real-time and trigger alerts or block transactions if necessary.
3. **Content Delivery**: Social media platforms use real-time event-driven processing to deliver notifications, update feeds, or adjust content recommendations based on user activity.
4. **Healthcare**: Event-driven architectures can monitor patient data in real-time and trigger alerts for healthcare providers when critical thresholds are crossed.

Conclusion

Event-driven architectures are a foundational element of serverless computing, enabling applications to respond dynamically to events with minimal latency. In this chapter, we explored how AWS EventBridge and Google Cloud Pub/Sub allow us to trigger serverless functions and workflows, process real-time data streams with AWS Kinesis and Google Cloud Dataflow, and orchestrate multi-step workflows using AWS Step Functions and Google Cloud Workflows.

By embracing event-driven designs, developers can build applications that are more resilient, scalable, and responsive to changes in the environment.

CHAPTER 9: AUTHENTICATION AND AUTHORIZATION IN SERVERLESS APPLICATIONS

Authentication and authorization are critical components in serverless applications, as they determine how users interact with your services, which resources they can access, and under what conditions. In this chapter, we explore how to implement secure and scalable authentication and authorization mechanisms in serverless architectures, with a focus on AWS and Google Cloud services.

9.1 Implementing User Authentication in AWS Lambda with Cognito

AWS Cognito is a managed service that simplifies user authentication and identity management in serverless applications. It allows developers to quickly implement user sign-up, sign-in, and access control for their applications without managing a custom authentication system.

9.1.1 What is AWS Cognito?

AWS Cognito provides two main components:

- **User Pools**: A user directory for managing user registration and authentication. It supports sign-up, sign-in, multi-factor authentication (MFA), and social identity providers (Google, Facebook, etc.).
- **Identity Pools**: Allow you to grant temporary access to AWS services (e.g., S3, DynamoDB) based on user identities, whether from a Cognito user pool or an external provider (OAuth).

9.1.2 Setting Up AWS Cognito with Lambda

To implement authentication in a serverless application using AWS Lambda and Cognito, you need to follow these steps:

1. **Create a Cognito User Pool**:

- Go to the AWS Management Console, navigate to **Cognito**, and create a new user pool.
- Customize user attributes (e.g., email, phone number) and configure security policies such as MFA or password complexity.

1. **Configure Lambda Triggers**:

- Cognito provides several triggers (pre-signup, post-confirmation, etc.) that allow you to invoke AWS Lambda functions at various points in the user lifecycle.
- For example, you can use a Lambda trigger for **pre-signup validation** to enforce custom rules, or for **post-confirmation** actions like sending a welcome email.

1. **Integrate Cognito with Your Front-End**:

- Use the **AWS Amplify** library to easily connect your JavaScript front-end (e.g., React, Vue) with the Cognito user pool.
- Amplify provides pre-built authentication components for sign-up, sign-in, and password reset flows.

Example: Using AWS Amplify in a React App for Cognito Integration:
javascript

import { Amplify, Auth } from 'aws-amplify';
  import awsconfig from './aws-exports';

Amplify.configure(awsconfig);

```
function signIn(username, password) {
  Auth.signIn(username, password)
  .then(user => console.log(user))
  .catch(err => console.log(err));
}
```

1. **Grant Access to AWS Resources**:

- Using **Cognito Identity Pools**, you can map authenticated users to specific roles with appropriate permissions to AWS resources. This enables users to securely access resources like S3 and DynamoDB from the front end.

9.1.3 Securing Your Serverless APIs with AWS Cognito

Once Cognito is set up, you can use it to secure APIs exposed via API Gateway. Cognito's JWT tokens can be passed in the Authorization header of API requests, and API Gateway can verify these tokens to restrict access to authenticated users only.

1. **Set Up API Gateway with Cognito**:

- In the API Gateway console, go to your API and configure **Cognito User Pool Authorizer**.
- Select your user pool and enable authorization on specific routes of your API.

1. **Use JWT Tokens for API Calls**:

- When users sign in via Cognito, they receive an ID token (JWT) which they can include in API requests.
- API Gateway validates the token before forwarding the request to AWS

CHAPTER 9: AUTHENTICATION AND AUTHORIZATION IN SERVERLESS...

Lambda.

Example: Attaching a Cognito JWT Token to API Requests:

javascript

```
fetch('https://your-api-endpoint', {
  method: 'GET',
  headers: {
    'Authorization': 'Bearer ${idToken}'
  }
})
.then(response => response.json())
.then(data => console.log(data));
```

9.1.4 Advanced Features: MFA, Social Sign-On, and Custom Authentication Flows

- **Multi-Factor Authentication (MFA)**: Cognito supports MFA, enhancing security by requiring users to provide a second authentication factor (SMS, TOTP) in addition to their password.
- **Social Identity Providers**: Cognito integrates with external providers (Google, Facebook, etc.) for social sign-on. You can configure these providers in the Cognito console and allow users to authenticate via their existing accounts.
- **Custom Authentication Flows**: If the built-in authentication flows don't meet your needs, you can implement custom flows using **Lambda Triggers**.

Summary

In this section, we focused on the implementation of user authentication and authorization in a serverless environment. We explored how AWS Cognito simplifies user management, how it integrates seamlessly with AWS Lambda and API Gateway, and how it can secure your serverless applications through features like JWT tokens, MFA, and social sign-on. Properly securing serverless applications is critical, especially when handling sensitive data or enabling public-facing services.

9.2 Google Cloud Identity and Access Management for Serverless Apps

In serverless applications, managing access to resources and ensuring secure authentication is paramount. Google Cloud provides **Identity and Access Management (IAM)** as a unified system for securely controlling access to resources across its platform. In serverless architectures, such as those using **Google Cloud Functions**, IAM plays a critical role in defining which users or services can invoke functions, access cloud storage, or interact with databases.

9.2.1 Overview of Google Cloud IAM

Google Cloud IAM provides fine-grained access control, allowing you to assign permissions based on roles to users, groups, or service accounts. It follows the principle of **least privilege**, meaning you can assign the minimum necessary permissions required for users or services to perform specific actions.

Key components of IAM in Google Cloud include:

- **IAM Roles**: Predefined roles (e.g., roles/cloudfunctions.invoker) or custom roles that bundle specific permissions.
- **Service Accounts**: Special accounts used by serverless services or other cloud resources to authenticate and access resources on your behalf.
- **IAM Policies**: Attach roles to users or service accounts, and define conditions under which access is granted.

9.2.2 Setting Up IAM for Google Cloud Functions

When deploying serverless functions with Google Cloud Functions, you need to set up appropriate permissions to control who can trigger your functions and what resources the functions can access.

Step 1: Granting Invoker Permissions

By default, Google Cloud Functions are private and can only be invoked by authenticated users or services. To grant specific users or services the ability

CHAPTER 9: AUTHENTICATION AND AUTHORIZATION IN SERVERLESS...

to invoke a function, you assign the **Cloud Functions Invoker** role to them.

- In the **Google Cloud Console**, navigate to your function's **Permissions** tab.
- Click on **Add** and assign the roles/cloudfunctions.invoker role to a user, service account, or group.

Example:
bash

gcloud functions add-iam-policy-binding my-function \
 —member=user:alice@example.com \
 —role=roles/cloudfunctions.invoker

Step 2: Using Service Accounts with Functions

For internal services or applications running on Google Cloud, you can use **service accounts** to authenticate and call functions. Each function runs under a service account that you can customize to grant it specific permissions.

- You can create a service account via the **IAM & Admin** page and then associate that account with the function during its deployment:

bash

gcloud functions deploy my-function —runtime nodejs16 \
 —service-account my-service-account@my-project.iam.gserviceaccount.com

Step 3: Assigning Roles to Functions for Resource Access

In many cases, your function will need to interact with other Google Cloud services like Firestore, Cloud Storage, or Pub/Sub. You can grant specific roles to the function's service account to allow it to access these resources.

- For example, to allow a function to write to a Firestore database, you would grant the service account the **Cloud Firestore User** role:

bash

gcloud projects add-iam-policy-binding my-project \
—member serviceAccount:my-service-account@my-project.iam.gserviceaccount.com \
—role roles/datastore.user

9.2.3 Enabling Authentication in Google Cloud Functions

Google Cloud Functions can be integrated with authentication systems like **Google Identity Platform, Firebase Authentication,** or **OAuth 2.0** to restrict access and provide secure authentication for APIs or back-end services.

Option 1: Firebase Authentication

Firebase Authentication is a common choice for web and mobile applications hosted on Google Cloud. It allows you to authenticate users with email/password, phone numbers, or third-party identity providers (Google, Facebook, etc.).

- To enable Firebase Authentication with Google Cloud Functions:

1. Set up Firebase in your project and add Firebase Authentication.
2. Use Firebase Admin SDK in your functions to verify user identity from the front end.

Example:
javascript

```
const admin = require('firebase-admin');
  admin.initializeApp();

exports.myFunction = (req, res) => {
  const token = req.headers.authorization.split('Bearer ')[1];
```

CHAPTER 9: AUTHENTICATION AND AUTHORIZATION IN SERVERLESS...

```
admin.auth().verifyIdToken(token)
.then((decodedToken) => {
const uid = decodedToken.uid;
// Proceed with business logic
res.status(200).send('User is authenticated');
})
.catch((error) => {
res.status(401).send('Unauthorized');
});
};
```

Option 2: OAuth 2.0 and Google Identity

For advanced use cases, especially involving third-party applications, you can use **OAuth 2.0** to manage authorization. Google Cloud provides OAuth 2.0 as part of the Google Identity Platform to authenticate users, applications, or services.

You can use the Google APIs Client Libraries to authenticate and authorize requests, or configure **OAuth 2.0 policies** in the Google API Gateway to secure your Google Cloud Functions.

Example:

javascript

```
const {google} = require('googleapis');
const oauth2Client = new google.auth.OAuth2(CLIENT_ID, CLIENT_SECRET, REDIRECT_URI);

// After user signs in and provides consent, use the token to make API requests
oauth2Client.setCredentials({ access_token: 'ACCESS_TOKEN' });

google.people('v1').people.get({
  resourceName: 'people/me',
  auth: oauth2Client,
}, (err, res) => {
if (err) return console.error(err);
```

```
console.log('User data:', res.data);
});
```

9.2.4 Securing APIs with IAM in Google Cloud

When using **Google API Gateway** to expose Google Cloud Functions, you can configure IAM policies to ensure only authorized users or services can access your APIs.

- **IAM Policies for API Gateway**: You can set IAM permissions on specific API routes to control who can invoke them. This ensures that sensitive API endpoints are protected from unauthorized access.
- **OAuth Scopes**: When integrating with Google services, you can specify the required OAuth scopes that a user or application must possess to access the APIs.

Example of securing an API route:
bash

```
gcloud api-gateway apis update my-api \
  —set-iam-policy "{
  'bindings': [
  {'role': 'roles/apigateway.invoke', 'members': ['user:alice@example.com']}
  ]
  }"
```

Summary

Google Cloud Identity and Access Management (IAM) offers robust tools for managing authentication and authorization in serverless applications. Whether securing Google Cloud Functions, integrating service accounts for resource access, or implementing authentication with Firebase or OAuth 2.0, IAM provides flexible and secure solutions for serverless environments. Understanding how to properly configure IAM roles, policies, and service accounts is essential for building secure, scalable serverless applications in Google Cloud.

9.3 Securing Serverless APIs with JWT and OAuth2

Security is one of the most critical concerns when developing serverless APIs. Since serverless applications often handle sensitive data or perform essential services, they need robust authentication and authorization mechanisms to ensure that only authorized users or services can access them. Two widely adopted standards for securing APIs are **JSON Web Tokens (JWT)** and **OAuth 2.0**. Both can be implemented in a serverless context to protect APIs from unauthorized access.

9.3.1 What is OAuth 2.0?

OAuth 2.0 is an open standard for authorization that allows third-party services to access resources on behalf of users without exposing their credentials. It's widely used for authenticating users on platforms such as Google, Facebook, and GitHub. OAuth 2.0 works by issuing an **access token** that the client can use to authenticate API requests.

- **Authorization Grant Types**: OAuth 2.0 defines multiple flows, such as:
- **Authorization Code Grant**: Typically used for web and mobile apps where the user needs to authorize the application to access resources.
- **Client Credentials Grant**: Used for service-to-service communication without user involvement.
- **Implicit Grant**: Suitable for browser-based applications but not recommended for most modern applications due to security concerns.
- **Resource Owner Password Grant**: Should be used sparingly, as it involves sharing user credentials with the client application.

9.3.2 Understanding JWT (JSON Web Tokens)

JSON Web Tokens (JWT) is a compact, URL-safe method for representing claims to be transferred between two parties. JWTs are used for securely transmitting information, such as user authentication data, between systems. JWT consists of three parts:

1. **Header**: Contains metadata about the type of token and the algorithm used (e.g., HMAC, RSA).
2. **Payload**: Holds the claims, such as user information (e.g., sub, email) or

the roles of a user.

3. **Signature**: A cryptographic signature that ensures the token's authenticity and integrity.

JWT tokens are self-contained, meaning all the information required for authorization is encoded within the token itself, eliminating the need for server-side sessions.

Example of a decoded JWT:

json

```
{
  "header": {
    "alg": "HS256",
    "typ": "JWT"
  },
  "payload": {
    "sub": "1234567890",
    "name": "John Doe",
    "admin": true,
    "iat": 1516239022
  },
  "signature": "SflKxwRJSMeKKF2QT4fwpMeJf36POk6yJV_adQssw5c"
}
```

9.3.3 Implementing OAuth 2.0 in Serverless Applications

To secure serverless APIs with OAuth 2.0, the serverless function must verify the access token before processing any request. Typically, the access token is issued by an **authorization server** (e.g., Google, Auth0, AWS Cognito) and passed in the **Authorization** header as a Bearer token.

Step 1: Setting Up OAuth 2.0 Authorization

1. **Choose an Authorization Server**: For serverless applications, you can use an external OAuth provider (e.g., Google Identity, Auth0) or set up your own authorization server using AWS Cognito or Firebase

Authentication.

2. **Configure Client Application**: For example, in Auth0, register your serverless API as a client, and configure redirect URIs and allowed grant types (e.g., Authorization Code, Client Credentials).
3. **Generate Access Tokens**: When users authenticate with OAuth, an access token is generated. The serverless API will use this token to verify the user's identity and permissions.

Step 2: Verifying OAuth Tokens in Serverless Functions

Once an access token is received, your serverless API needs to validate the token to authenticate and authorize the user.

Example of validating an OAuth token in **Google Cloud Functions**:
javascript

```javascript
const {google} = require('googleapis');
  const oauth2 = google.oauth2('v2');
  const OAuth2Client = new google.auth.OAuth2();

exports.verifyToken = async (req, res) => {
  const token = req.headers.authorization.split('Bearer ')[1];
  OAuth2Client.verifyIdToken({
  idToken: token,
  audience: CLIENT_ID, // Specify your client ID
  })
  .then((ticket) => {
  const payload = ticket.getPayload();
  const userId = payload['sub'];
  // Token is valid, proceed with request
  res.status(200).send('User authenticated');
  })
  .catch((err) => {
  res.status(401).send('Unauthorized');
  });
```

};

9.3.4 Securing APIs with JWT in Serverless Functions

JWT is a common choice for token-based authentication in serverless APIs. In this approach, the client sends a JWT token along with each request, and the serverless function validates the token before granting access.

Step 1: Issuing JWT Tokens

1. **Use a JWT Provider**: You can generate JWT tokens using libraries like **jsonwebtoken** in Node.js or use identity providers like AWS Cognito, Firebase Authentication, or Auth0, which handle the JWT lifecycle.
2. **Encode User Information in JWT**: The payload can contain relevant information such as the user's ID (sub), email, and roles.

Step 2: Verifying JWT Tokens

When a request is made to your serverless API, it should validate the token's signature and claims.

Example of validating a JWT token in **AWS Lambda**:

javascript

```javascript
const jwt = require('jsonwebtoken');
  const secret = 'your-256-bit-secret'; // Ensure your secret is stored securely

exports.handler = (event, context, callback) => {
  const token = event.headers.Authorization.split('Bearer ')[1];

jwt.verify(token, secret, (err, decoded) => {
  if (err) {
  callback(null, {
  statusCode: 401,
  body: JSON.stringify({ message: 'Unauthorized' }),
  });
  } else {
  // Proceed with the request, user is authenticated
```

```
callback(null, {
statusCode: 200,
body: JSON.stringify({ message: 'User authenticated', user: decoded }),
});
}
});
};
```

Step 3: Expiring and Refreshing Tokens

JWT tokens typically have an expiration time (exp claim), after which the token becomes invalid. You can use refresh tokens to allow users to request new tokens without having to re-authenticate.

9.3.5 Combining OAuth 2.0 and JWT in Serverless Applications

In many serverless applications, OAuth 2.0 is used for the initial authorization flow, and the authorization server issues JWTs for subsequent API requests. This combination leverages the strengths of both systems:

- OAuth 2.0 provides a flexible way for third-party services or users to obtain access tokens.
- JWT provides a stateless, lightweight token that can be validated without querying a database.

9.3.6 Best Practices for Securing Serverless APIs

- **Use HTTPS**: Always use HTTPS to encrypt the communication between clients and serverless APIs, especially when sending access tokens.
- **Token Expiration**: Implement short-lived access tokens with expiration times and refresh tokens to maintain security.
- **Scopes and Permissions**: Assign granular scopes to tokens to ensure they only grant access to the resources needed for the operation.
- **Rate Limiting and Throttling**: Implement rate limiting to prevent abuse and DoS attacks on your serverless APIs.
- **Audit and Monitor**: Use logging and monitoring tools like AWS CloudWatch or Google Stackdriver to track access and detect suspicious

activities in real time.

Summary

Securing serverless APIs with **JWT** and **OAuth 2.0** ensures that only authorized users or services can access your serverless functions. OAuth 2.0 provides a robust framework for managing access tokens, while JWT offers a lightweight, stateless approach to handle authentication. When implemented correctly, these techniques provide the necessary security layers to protect your serverless APIs, ensuring both performance and safety.

9.4 Managing Permissions and Roles in Serverless Architectures

In a serverless architecture, managing permissions and roles is critical to ensuring security, controlling access to resources, and preventing unauthorized actions. Serverless functions often interact with multiple cloud services, databases, APIs, and other resources, making it necessary to enforce the principle of least privilege — ensuring that each component only has the permissions it needs to operate.

This section will discuss how to manage roles and permissions in serverless architectures, with a focus on **AWS Lambda, Google Cloud Functions,** and their respective Identity and Access Management (IAM) frameworks.

9.4.1 AWS Identity and Access Management (IAM)

In AWS, **IAM** allows administrators to control who can access which resources and what actions they can perform. Every AWS resource, including Lambda functions, API Gateway, S3 buckets, and DynamoDB tables, can be restricted based on IAM policies.

IAM Roles for AWS Lambda

When setting up a Lambda function, it is assigned an **IAM role** that defines what AWS services and actions the function is allowed to access. For example, a Lambda function may need to access an S3 bucket, write logs to CloudWatch, or query a DynamoDB table.

- **Step 1: Creating an IAM Role for Lambda**

1. Navigate to the **IAM Console**.

2. Create a new **role** for AWS Lambda.
3. Attach policies such as AmazonS3ReadOnlyAccess, CloudWatchLogsFullAccess, or any custom policies needed.

- **Step 2: Attaching the Role to a Lambda Function** After creating the role, attach it to the Lambda function. This can be done through the **AWS Lambda Console** when setting up the function or by modifying the function's configuration.

Example Policy for S3 Access:
json

```
{
  "Version": "2012-10-17",
  "Statement": [
    {
      "Effect": "Allow",
      "Action": "s3:GetObject",
      "Resource": "arn:aws:s3:::my-bucket/*"
    }
  ]
}
```

This policy allows the Lambda function to read objects from a specific S3 bucket.

IAM Policies for Fine-Grained Access Control

In addition to roles, **IAM policies** allow administrators to define fine-grained permissions. Policies can be attached to users, groups, or roles, and they can either allow or deny actions based on specified conditions.

- **Actions**: Define the permitted actions (e.g., s3:PutObject, dynamodb:Scan).
- **Resources**: Specify the resources to which the action applies (e.g., an S3 bucket or DynamoDB table).

- **Conditions**: Use conditions to define when and how the policy applies (e.g., time-based access or IP address restrictions).

9.4.2 Google Cloud Identity and Access Management (IAM)

Similar to AWS, **Google Cloud IAM** provides a unified system for managing access to Google Cloud resources. Permissions in Google Cloud are handled by assigning **IAM roles** to users, groups, or service accounts.

IAM Roles for Google Cloud Functions

Google Cloud Functions also operate under the principle of least privilege. Each function is assigned a **service account** that defines its permissions. Service accounts are Google Cloud identities that can be assigned roles to allow access to specific resources (e.g., Google Cloud Storage, Firestore, Pub/Sub).

- **Step 1: Creating a Service Account**

1. Navigate to the **IAM & Admin** section in the Google Cloud Console.
2. Create a new **service account** and assign it the necessary roles (e.g., Storage Object Viewer, Cloud Functions Invoker).

- **Step 2: Attaching the Service Account to a Cloud Function** When deploying a Cloud Function, you can specify the service account it should use. This service account will define what resources the function can access.

Example Role for Google Cloud Storage:

json

```
{
  "role": "roles/storage.objectViewer",
  "members": [
    "serviceAccount:my-service-account@my-project.iam.gserviceaccount.com"
```

]
}

This role grants the service account read access to objects in Cloud Storage.

Custom Roles in Google Cloud

Google Cloud IAM allows you to create **custom roles** that can provide more granular control over resources. For example, you might create a custom role that allows a function to only write logs to Stackdriver Logging without giving it access to other services.

9.4.3 Managing Permissions with Azure Functions

For serverless applications running in **Azure Functions**, permissions are managed using **Azure Active Directory (AAD)** and **Role-Based Access Control (RBAC)**.

Azure RBAC for Functions

Azure RBAC allows administrators to assign specific roles to users, groups, or services. Azure Functions can interact with other Azure resources, such as **Blob Storage, Cosmos DB**, and **Event Grid**, by assigning roles to function apps.

- **Step 1: Assigning Roles**

1. Navigate to the **Azure Portal** and find the function app.
2. Assign roles like Storage Blob Data Contributor or Cosmos DB Account Reader to the function app.

- **Step 2: Using Managed Identities** Azure Functions can use **Managed Identities**, which are AAD accounts automatically managed by Azure, to access resources without the need for explicit credentials.

Example Role Assignment in Azure:

json

{
  "roleDefinitionName": "Storage Blob Data Contributor",

"principalId": "function-app-principal-id"
}

This assigns the Storage Blob Data Contributor role to the function app, allowing it to write to Azure Blob Storage.

9.4.4 Best Practices for Managing Permissions in Serverless Architectures

1. **Principle of Least Privilege**: Always grant the minimum permissions required for a function to operate. This reduces the risk of unauthorized access if a function is compromised.
2. **Use Role-Based Access Control (RBAC)**: Assign roles at the resource level (e.g., for specific databases, storage buckets, or queues) instead of granting blanket permissions across the entire cloud account.
3. **Limit Access Time**: Where possible, set time-bound access policies to limit how long a role or permission is active.
4. **Audit and Monitor Access**: Use monitoring tools such as AWS CloudTrail, Google Cloud Audit Logs, or Azure Monitor to keep track of which identities are accessing your resources.
5. **Use Separate Roles for Different Functions**: Don't reuse roles across multiple functions. Assign specific roles based on each function's needs to avoid over-permissioning.
6. **Rotate Secrets and Keys**: Use managed services like AWS Secrets Manager, Google Secret Manager, or Azure Key Vault to store and rotate API keys, database credentials, and other secrets.

Summary

Managing permissions and roles in a serverless architecture is critical to ensuring the security and efficiency of your applications. By leveraging cloud provider-specific tools such as **AWS IAM, Google Cloud IAM**, and **Azure RBAC**, you can define granular access controls that limit what your functions can do, reducing the attack surface and preventing accidental or malicious misuse of resources. Always adhere to the principle of least privilege, and ensure that your permissions model is aligned with your application's security requirements.

9.5 Integrating Third-Party Authentication Services (e.g., Auth0, Okta)

In serverless applications, integrating third-party authentication services like **Auth0** and **Okta** provides an efficient way to manage user authentication, authorization, and identity management without building complex authentication systems from scratch. These services offer features such as **OAuth2, OpenID Connect (OIDC), Single Sign-On (SSO),** and **Multi-Factor Authentication (MFA),** which are critical for securing serverless applications.

In this section, we will discuss the process of integrating third-party authentication services, focusing on **Auth0** and **Okta**, with serverless environments like **AWS Lambda** and **Google Cloud Functions**.

9.5.1 Why Use Third-Party Authentication Services?

Third-party authentication providers simplify the process of adding secure user authentication to serverless applications by offering:

- **Scalability**: They handle millions of authentication requests while you focus on application logic.
- **Security**: Built-in security features like MFA, anomaly detection, and passwordless authentication.
- **Ease of Use**: Pre-built libraries and SDKs for easy integration with various programming languages, including JavaScript.
- **Standards Compliance**: Support for industry standards such as **OAuth2, OIDC,** and **SAML**.
- **Customizability**: Options for customizing login flows, user management, and user experience (e.g., custom branding).

9.5.2 Integrating Auth0 with Serverless Applications

Auth0 is a flexible authentication and authorization platform that offers features like passwordless authentication, SSO, and social logins. You can easily integrate Auth0 with serverless applications running on platforms like AWS Lambda or Google Cloud Functions using its SDKs and APIs.

Step 1: Setting Up Auth0

1. **Create an Auth0 Account**: Go to Auth0 and sign up for a free account.
2. **Create an Application**:

- In the Auth0 dashboard, create a new **application**. Choose the type of application (Single Page App, Native App, or Regular Web App) depending on your use case.
- Under settings, note the **Client ID**, **Client Secret**, and **Domain**, as you'll need them for your serverless application.

1. **Configure Authentication**:

- Choose the identity providers you want to support (e.g., Google, Facebook, GitHub).
- Enable **OAuth2** and **OIDC** for secure communication between Auth0 and your serverless app.

Step 2: Integrating with AWS Lambda

1. **Install the Auth0 SDK**: If you are using Node.js in AWS Lambda, install the Auth0 SDK for Node.js.

bash

npm install jsonwebtoken jwks-rsa

1. **Verify Access Tokens in Lambda**: In your Lambda function, verify the JWT token issued by Auth0 to ensure the request is authenticated.

javascript

const jwt = require('jsonwebtoken');

CHAPTER 9: AUTHENTICATION AND AUTHORIZATION IN SERVERLESS...

```
const jwksClient = require('jwks-rsa');

const client = jwksClient({
  jwksUri: 'https://YOUR_AUTH0_DOMAIN/.well-known/jwks.json'
});

function getKey(header, callback) {
  client.getSigningKey(header.kid, function(err, key) {
  var signingKey = key.publicKey || key.rsaPublicKey;
  callback(null, signingKey);
  });
}

const token = event.headers.Authorization.split(' ')[1];
  jwt.verify(token, getKey, (err, decoded) => {
  if (err) {
  return callback('Unauthorized');
  }
  // Proceed with authenticated request
});
```

1. **Handle Authentication and Roles**: Based on the decoded JWT token, you can enforce user roles and permissions in your Lambda function.

Step 3: Integrating with Google Cloud Functions

1. **Verify Access Tokens**: Similar to AWS Lambda, you can use the Auth0 SDK to verify JWT tokens in Google Cloud Functions. Install the jsonwebtoken and jwks-rsa packages, and use the same approach to verify tokens in your Cloud Function.
2. **Protecting Endpoints**: You can restrict access to Google Cloud Functions based on the roles or claims included in the JWT.

9.5.3 Integrating Okta with Serverless Applications

Okta is another popular identity management service that provides user authentication, SSO, and MFA capabilities. It is widely used in enterprise environments and offers robust integrations with serverless platforms like AWS Lambda and Google Cloud Functions.

Step 1: Setting Up Okta

1. **Create an Okta Developer Account**: Go to Okta and create a developer account.
2. **Create an Application**:

- In the Okta dashboard, create a new **OAuth2** or **OIDC** application.
- Configure your application's settings, including **Redirect URIs** and **Allowed Web Origins**.
- Note down the **Client ID, Client Secret**, and **Issuer URI**.

Step 2: Integrating with AWS Lambda

1. **Install the Okta SDK**: If using Node.js, install the jsonwebtoken and jwks-rsa libraries.

bash

```
npm install jsonwebtoken jwks-rsa
```

1. **Verify Okta Access Tokens**: Similar to Auth0, verify the Okta-issued JWT tokens in your AWS Lambda function.

javascript

```
const jwt = require('jsonwebtoken');
  const jwksClient = require('jwks-rsa');
```

CHAPTER 9: AUTHENTICATION AND AUTHORIZATION IN SERVERLESS...

```
const client = jwksClient({
  jwksUri: 'https://YOUR_OKTA_DOMAIN/oauth2/default/v1/keys'
});

function getKey(header, callback) {
  client.getSigningKey(header.kid, function(err, key) {
  var signingKey = key.publicKey || key.rsaPublicKey;
  callback(null, signingKey);
  });
}

const token = event.headers.Authorization.split(' ')[1];
  jwt.verify(token, getKey, (err, decoded) => {
  if (err) {
  return callback('Unauthorized');
  }
  // Proceed with authenticated request
});
```

Step 3: Integrating with Google Cloud Functions

1. **Verify JWT Tokens**: Similar to AWS Lambda, use the jsonwebtoken and jwks-rsa libraries to verify Okta-issued JWT tokens in Google Cloud Functions.
2. **Manage Roles and Permissions**: Based on the claims or roles embedded in the JWT, you can enforce access control in your Google Cloud Function.

9.5.4 Best Practices for Third-Party Authentication Integration

1. **Use HTTPS**: Always ensure that your serverless functions communicate with third-party services over HTTPS to avoid man-in-the-middle attacks.
2. **Short-Lived Tokens**: Use short-lived access tokens with refresh tokens

to minimize the risk of token hijacking.
3. **Role-Based Access Control (RBAC)**: Use roles and scopes in the JWT to control access to different parts of your serverless application.
4. **MFA**: Implement multi-factor authentication (MFA) to add an additional layer of security for sensitive operations.
5. **Token Rotation**: Rotate your OAuth2 tokens and ensure that the refresh tokens have an expiration policy in place.
6. **Audit and Logging**: Enable auditing and logging to track authentication and authorization events for security and compliance purposes.

Summary

Integrating third-party authentication services like **Auth0** and **Okta** in serverless architectures simplifies user authentication, authorization, and identity management. These services provide secure, scalable solutions that support industry standards such as **OAuth2** and **OIDC**, making them ideal for use in serverless environments like **AWS Lambda** and **Google Cloud Functions**. Following best practices, such as using HTTPS, implementing MFA, and enforcing short-lived tokens, ensures the security and efficiency of the authentication process in your serverless applications.

9.6 Best Practices for Secure Serverless Applications

Securing serverless applications requires a multi-layered approach to ensure that your APIs, data, and infrastructure are protected from vulnerabilities. Serverless architectures introduce unique security challenges, as developers often have less control over the underlying infrastructure. In this section, we will explore some best practices to follow when building secure serverless applications.

9.6.1 Principle of Least Privilege

The **Principle of Least Privilege** (PoLP) states that each component in your system (e.g., Lambda functions, APIs, or microservices) should only have the minimum necessary permissions to perform its task. This reduces the risk of accidental or intentional misuse of permissions.

- **AWS Lambda**: Ensure your Lambda functions only have the necessary permissions to access the specific AWS services they require (e.g., S3, DynamoDB).

- **Google Cloud Functions**: Similarly, ensure your Google Cloud Functions are restricted to the minimal set of permissions needed, using **Cloud IAM roles** and **policies**.

9.6.2 Securing API Gateways

Your serverless APIs are often the entry point to your serverless architecture, and securing them is paramount.

- **Use Authentication**: Implement authentication mechanisms such as **OAuth2**, **JWT**, or API keys to secure your API endpoints.
- **Implement Rate Limiting**: Protect your APIs from abuse by limiting the number of requests that can be made in a given period.
- **Enable HTTPS**: Ensure that all communication with your API gateway happens over HTTPS to protect sensitive data in transit.

9.6.3 Encrypting Data

Encryption should be applied to both data at rest and data in transit to prevent unauthorized access.

- **At Rest**: Use cloud-native encryption tools to encrypt sensitive data stored in services like **AWS S3**, **Google Cloud Storage**, **DynamoDB**, and **Firestore**.
- **In Transit**: Use HTTPS and secure connections (e.g., **TLS**) when transferring data between your serverless components and external services or clients.

9.6.4 Securing Event-Driven Architectures

Serverless applications often rely on event-driven architectures, where services like **AWS S3**, **AWS EventBridge**, **Google Cloud Pub/Sub**, and **Google Cloud Functions** trigger functions based on events. Securing these event triggers is critical to ensuring the integrity of your serverless application.

- **Validate Events**: Ensure that the events triggering your serverless functions are coming from trusted sources.
- **Encrypt Messages**: Use message encryption (e.g., AWS KMS, Google KMS) when passing sensitive data between services in event-driven workflows.
- **Audit Event Sources**: Regularly audit and monitor the sources of events that trigger your serverless functions.

9.6.5 Monitoring and Logging

Implement logging and monitoring across your serverless application to detect anomalies and respond to potential security threats.

- **CloudWatch and Cloud Logging**: Use services like **AWS CloudWatch** and **Google Cloud Logging** to log function invocations, track errors, and monitor performance.
- **Centralized Logging**: Consider centralizing your logs for easier monitoring and analysis, enabling quick responses to potential security incidents.
- **Auditing Access Logs**: Regularly audit access logs to ensure that no unauthorized access has occurred.

9.6.6 Automatic Security Patching

Serverless platforms automatically handle infrastructure-level security patching, but developers are still responsible for managing application-level security updates.

- **Third-Party Libraries**: Keep third-party libraries and dependencies up to date to prevent vulnerabilities from being exploited in your application.
- **Container Security**: For serverless environments using containers (e.g., AWS Fargate), ensure that your container images are kept up to date with security patches.

- **Vulnerability Scanning**: Use automated vulnerability scanning tools (e.g., **Snyk, AWS Inspector**) to continuously monitor your serverless application for security issues.

9.6.7 Protecting Serverless from DDoS Attacks

Distributed Denial of Service (DDoS) attacks can overwhelm your serverless application with a flood of requests, causing slowdowns or even outages.

- **AWS Shield and AWS WAF**: Use **AWS Shield** and **AWS Web Application Firewall (WAF)** to protect your serverless APIs from DDoS attacks.
- **Google Cloud Armor**: For Google Cloud Functions, enable **Google Cloud Armor** to mitigate DDoS attacks and apply security policies at the edge.
- **Rate Limiting**: As mentioned, rate limiting can help mitigate the effects of DDoS by preventing too many requests from overwhelming your serverless functions.

Conclusion

Securing serverless applications requires a comprehensive approach that covers both authentication and authorization, as well as general security best practices. In this chapter, we explored how to implement user authentication using services like **AWS Cognito** and **Google Cloud IAM**, and how to integrate third-party identity providers like **Auth0** and **Okta**. We also discussed securing serverless APIs with **JWT**, **OAuth2**, and managing permissions through role-based access controls.

Best practices for secure serverless applications include following the **Principle of Least Privilege**, encrypting data, monitoring and logging for anomalies, and ensuring automated patching of security vulnerabilities. As serverless architecture continues to gain popularity, understanding and implementing strong security measures is critical to protect your applications from modern security threats, such as DDoS attacks and unauthorized access.

With a focus on both platform-specific security tools and general best practices, this chapter equips you with the knowledge to build secure, scalable, and reliable serverless applications.

CHAPTER 10: SERVERLESS MICROSERVICES ARCHITECTURE

Microservices architecture has become a popular pattern for building scalable, maintainable, and resilient applications. When combined with serverless technologies, it offers even greater flexibility by allowing individual services to scale independently while reducing operational overhead. In this chapter, we'll dive into how serverless platforms can be used to implement microservices architecture and explore the benefits and challenges of building microservices in a serverless environment.

10.1 Introduction to Microservices in Serverless

Microservices are an architectural style in which applications are built as a collection of loosely coupled, independently deployable services. Each microservice is focused on a specific business capability, and they communicate with each other through well-defined APIs. The key advantage of microservices is their ability to allow rapid development and scaling of different parts of an application without affecting the entire system.

With serverless computing, microservices take on a new dimension. Traditional microservices architectures require managing servers and infrastructure for each service, but with serverless platforms like AWS Lambda and Google Cloud Functions, you only focus on writing the business logic of your microservices, leaving the infrastructure management to the cloud provider.

Benefits of Serverless Microservices

- **Automatic Scaling**: Each serverless microservice scales independently based on the number of requests. This means there's no need to provision or manage servers manually, and your services scale automatically to handle increased load.
- **Reduced Costs**: With serverless, you only pay for the resources consumed during execution, making it cost-efficient, especially for unpredictable workloads. Since microservices can vary significantly in usage, this model fits perfectly.
- **Decoupled Services**: Microservices naturally promote loose coupling, and serverless functions take this further by ensuring that services are independent and only activated when necessary.
- **Faster Time to Market**: Serverless platforms eliminate the need to manage infrastructure, allowing developers to focus solely on building and deploying services faster.

Challenges of Serverless Microservices

While serverless microservices offer significant advantages, there are also challenges to be mindful of:

- **Cold Start Latency**: Serverless functions can experience cold start delays, particularly in microservices architectures where multiple services may be invoked in sequence.
- **Distributed Complexity**: Managing the interactions between several microservices, especially when they're serverless, adds complexity in terms of debugging, monitoring, and coordination.
- **State Management**: Serverless functions are stateless, so managing application state can be challenging in microservices architectures where persistence and consistency are critical.
- **Inter-Service Communication**: Serverless microservices require efficient and reliable communication channels. Depending on the architecture, this may involve REST APIs, message queues, or event-driven mechanisms, all of which need to be monitored and secured.

Key Concepts in Serverless Microservices

To understand how to build microservices in serverless architectures, there are several foundational concepts:

1. **Service Independence**: Each microservice should be independent in terms of deployment and scaling. In serverless, this means each service is a separate Lambda function or Cloud Function.
2. **Event-Driven Design**: Serverless architectures excel in event-driven applications where services respond to events (e.g., HTTP requests, file uploads, message queues). AWS EventBridge, Google Pub/Sub, and AWS SQS are common tools for managing these events.
3. **Statelessness**: Serverless functions are stateless by design. For microservices, state management typically involves using external databases (e.g., DynamoDB, Firestore) or caching services (e.g., AWS ElastiCache).

10.2 Breaking Down Monoliths into Serverless Microservices

One of the most common use cases for microservices, especially in serverless architectures, is to break down monolithic applications into smaller, more manageable services. Monolithic applications are characterized by a single, large codebase where all the functionality is tightly integrated and dependent on a central architecture. While this structure can be easier to develop initially, it often becomes difficult to maintain, scale, and update as the application grows.

In this section, we'll explore the process of breaking a monolithic application into serverless microservices, highlighting the benefits and challenges, as well as practical steps for the migration.

Why Migrate from Monoliths to Microservices?

There are several compelling reasons for migrating from a monolithic architecture to microservices, particularly when using a serverless approach:

- **Scalability**: Monolithic applications often struggle with scaling efficiently since the entire application must scale together. Microservices, on the other hand, can scale independently based on specific workloads,

optimizing resources.
- **Faster Development Cycles**: Microservices allow for independent development, testing, and deployment of services. This accelerates the development cycle, enabling teams to focus on specific components without worrying about breaking the entire system.
- **Flexibility in Technology Choices**: Microservices enable different services to use different languages, frameworks, or cloud services depending on the specific needs. With serverless platforms like AWS Lambda, each microservice can be written in JavaScript (Node.js), Python, or any other supported language.
- **Improved Fault Isolation**: In a monolithic system, a failure in one component can cause the entire application to crash. Microservices isolate failures to specific services, reducing the impact on the rest of the system.

Steps to Break Down a Monolith into Serverless Microservices

Breaking a monolith into microservices is a complex process that requires careful planning and execution. Here are the main steps:

1. Identify the Core Components

Start by identifying the main components or domains in your monolithic application. These could be functional areas like user authentication, payment processing, or product catalog. The goal is to isolate these components into separate services that can be independently deployed.

- **Example**: If you have an e-commerce application, consider breaking it down into services such as "User Service" for authentication, "Product Service" for handling product listings, and "Order Service" for processing transactions.

2. Define Service Boundaries

Once you've identified the core components, define the boundaries between these services. Each service should have a specific responsibility and communicate with other services through well-defined APIs (such as REST or GraphQL). In a serverless environment, these services could be individual Lambda functions or Cloud Functions.

- **Example**: In the "Order Service," the service might expose a set of APIs (e.g., /createOrder, /getOrderDetails) that other services can consume.

3. Decouple Data Storage

One of the biggest challenges in breaking apart a monolith is handling the database. In a monolithic architecture, a single database might be shared across all components. With microservices, each service should have its own data store to ensure independence. In a serverless architecture, you can use services like DynamoDB, Google Cloud Firestore, or SQL databases like AWS Aurora.

- **Example**: The "Product Service" could have its own DynamoDB table for storing product information, while the "User Service" uses an entirely separate database for managing user profiles.

4. Move Business Logic to Microservices

Once the service boundaries and data stores are defined, begin migrating the business logic of each component from the monolithic application into the newly created serverless microservices. This process involves refactoring code and ensuring that each microservice handles only the tasks relevant to its domain.

- **Example**: The logic for user registration, login, and authentication, which might have been part of the monolith, should now reside solely in the "User Service."

5. Set Up Event-Driven Communication

In a serverless architecture, microservices often communicate via event-driven mechanisms. AWS Lambda and Google Cloud Functions are perfect for building event-driven applications. AWS EventBridge, Google Pub/Sub, and SQS queues are common tools for managing inter-service communication.

- **Example**: When a user places an order, the "Order Service" could publish an event (e.g., "order created") to an event bus (like AWS EventBridge), which triggers other services, such as a notification service to send a confirmation email.

6. Use API Gateways for External Access

When transitioning to microservices, external clients (such as mobile apps or web browsers) need a consistent way to interact with the services. This is where API gateways like AWS API Gateway and Google Cloud API Gateway come in. These gateways allow you to expose multiple microservices as a single unified API while managing routing, security, rate-limiting, and other concerns.

- **Example**: The API Gateway can route a /login request to the "User Service" Lambda function and a /createOrder request to the "Order Service."

7. Gradual Migration and Testing

Instead of refactoring the entire application at once, consider migrating one component at a time. This gradual migration allows you to test each microservice independently and ensure that it integrates well with the remaining parts of the monolith until the migration is complete.

- **Example**: Start with the "User Service" migration. Once it works independently, move to the "Product Service" and so on.

Challenges in Migrating to Serverless Microservices

- **Complexity of Refactoring**: Breaking down a large monolithic application can be complex and time-consuming. Refactoring must be done with

care to ensure that dependencies are properly handled and performance is not impacted.
- **Inter-Service Communication Overhead**: While serverless functions are independent, they must communicate through APIs or message queues, which can introduce latency and complexity.
- **Data Consistency**: Managing data consistency across multiple services with different databases can be challenging, especially if transactional consistency is required.

10.3 Deploying and Managing Serverless Microservices on AWS and Google Cloud

Deploying and managing serverless microservices on platforms like AWS and Google Cloud involves several steps to ensure seamless operation, scalability, and efficient resource usage. Both cloud providers offer comprehensive tools to build, deploy, monitor, and manage microservices in a serverless architecture.

This section covers the deployment process on AWS and Google Cloud, along with management best practices for serverless microservices.

Deploying Serverless Microservices on AWS

Amazon Web Services (AWS) provides a suite of tools to deploy and manage serverless microservices. The core services involved in deployment are AWS Lambda, API Gateway, and AWS Step Functions. Here's a step-by-step guide on how to deploy a serverless microservice on AWS:

1. Develop and Package Microservices

Each microservice can be developed as an independent AWS Lambda function. For example, in a microservice architecture, you might have different Lambda functions handling user authentication, product management, and order processing.

- Use AWS SDKs or AWS CLI to package and deploy the Lambda functions. You can package the function code into a .zip file or use container images if your code exceeds the size limits for Lambda packages.

2. Set Up API Gateway

Use Amazon API Gateway to expose your Lambda functions as RESTful APIs. API Gateway allows you to map HTTP requests to specific Lambda functions.

- For instance, a /createOrder endpoint could route incoming POST requests to an "Order Service" Lambda function.
- API Gateway also handles authentication, rate limiting, and CORS (Cross-Origin Resource Sharing) issues.

3. Use Infrastructure as Code (IaC) for Deployment

AWS provides tools like AWS CloudFormation and AWS Serverless Application Model (SAM) for defining and deploying your infrastructure as code. This enables you to automate the deployment of microservices.

- **AWS CloudFormation**: Allows you to define the infrastructure (Lambda functions, API Gateway, DynamoDB tables, etc.) in a JSON or YAML file, which can then be deployed as a stack.
- **AWS SAM**: A framework specifically for serverless applications, making it easy to define and deploy serverless microservices. With SAM, you can define APIs, functions, and permissions in a template file.

Example SAM template for a Lambda function and API Gateway:
yaml

```yaml
Resources:
  OrderFunction:
    Type: AWS::Serverless::Function
    Properties:
      Handler: order.create
      Runtime: nodejs14.x
      Events:
        ApiGateway:
```

Type: Api
Properties:
Path: /createOrder
Method: post

4. Monitoring with CloudWatch

AWS CloudWatch provides real-time monitoring of your Lambda functions and APIs. You can track metrics like function invocations, errors, and latency, and set up alarms for specific thresholds.

- Use **CloudWatch Logs** to capture detailed logs from each Lambda invocation for debugging and analysis.
- You can also use **CloudWatch Alarms** to trigger alerts when metrics such as errors or execution time exceed predefined limits.

5. Managing Permissions with IAM

AWS Identity and Access Management (IAM) helps manage permissions and roles for your microservices. Each Lambda function should have an IAM role that grants it permission to access other AWS resources such as DynamoDB or S3.

- Example: The "Order Service" Lambda function might need access to a DynamoDB table to store order details. You would define an IAM role with specific permissions for this task.

Deploying Serverless Microservices on Google Cloud

Google Cloud offers a similar set of tools for building, deploying, and managing serverless microservices. Key services include Google Cloud Functions, API Gateway, and Google Cloud Pub/Sub. Below are the steps for deploying microservices on Google Cloud:

1. Develop and Package Microservices

Each microservice can be implemented as a Google Cloud Function. Cloud Functions are triggered by events such as HTTP requests or messages from Pub/Sub.

- Example: The "Order Service" microservice can be written as a function that processes incoming HTTP POST requests to create new orders.

2. Set Up API Gateway

Google API Gateway is used to expose Cloud Functions as RESTful APIs. Similar to AWS API Gateway, it manages routing, security, and rate limiting.

- You can create an API Gateway that routes HTTP requests to specific Cloud Functions. For instance, the /createOrder endpoint can trigger the "Order Service" Cloud Function.
- API Gateway also integrates with Identity and Access Management (IAM) to secure your APIs with OAuth2 and custom authentication.

3. Use Cloud Deployment Manager or Terraform for IaC

Google Cloud Deployment Manager allows you to define and deploy your infrastructure using configuration files. Alternatively, you can use Terraform, which is cloud-agnostic, to manage your Google Cloud resources.

- With Deployment Manager, you can define resources like Cloud Functions, API Gateway routes, and Pub/Sub topics in YAML or Jinja2 templates.
- Example YAML snippet for deploying a Cloud Function:

yaml

```
resources:
  - name: order-service-function
    type: cloudfunctions.v1beta2.function
    properties:
      location: us-central1
      entryPoint: createOrder
      runtime: nodejs14
```

4. Monitoring with Google Cloud Monitoring

Google Cloud Monitoring (formerly Stackdriver) provides metrics and logs for Cloud Functions and API Gateway. You can monitor execution times, error rates, and memory usage.

- **Cloud Logging** captures logs for each function invocation, which can be useful for debugging.
- Set up **Alert Policies** in Google Cloud Monitoring to trigger notifications when metrics exceed predefined thresholds.

5. Managing Permissions with IAM

Google Cloud IAM is used to manage permissions for Cloud Functions and other services. Each Cloud Function should have a service account with the appropriate permissions to access Google Cloud resources, such as Firestore or Cloud Storage.

- Example: The "Order Service" function may require a service account with permission to read and write to Firestore. You can create and assign this service account when deploying the function.

Key Differences Between AWS and Google Cloud for Serverless Microservices

1. **Cold Starts**: AWS Lambda and Google Cloud Functions both experience "cold starts" when a function is invoked after being idle for some time. However, AWS provides more options, such as **Provisioned Concurrency**, to mitigate this issue.
2. **Event Sources**: AWS Lambda supports a broader range of event sources (S3, DynamoDB streams, API Gateway, etc.), while Google Cloud Functions primarily rely on Pub/Sub and HTTP triggers.
3. **Tooling**: AWS offers more mature tools for serverless architectures (SAM, CloudFormation, and Step Functions), while Google Cloud relies more on open-source tools like Terraform and Pub/Sub for event-driven microservices.

Managing Serverless Microservices

Managing serverless microservices involves ensuring efficient resource usage, debugging, and scaling. Both AWS and Google Cloud offer services and best practices for managing microservices.

1. Scaling

- AWS Lambda and Google Cloud Functions automatically scale based on the number of requests or events.
- Use **API Gateway rate limiting** and quotas to manage high-traffic scenarios.

2. Debugging and Monitoring

- **CloudWatch Logs** and **Google Cloud Logging** capture detailed execution logs.
- Set up **alarms** in AWS CloudWatch or Google Cloud Monitoring to monitor performance metrics and set up notifications for errors or high latency.

3. Security and Permissions

- Manage fine-grained access control using **IAM roles** (AWS) or **service accounts** (Google Cloud).
- Use **API Gateway** to authenticate and authorize requests with OAuth, JWT, or custom authentication mechanisms.

10.4 Communication Between Microservices in a Serverless Environment

In a serverless architecture, microservices often need to communicate with one another to perform complex tasks and deliver integrated functionality. This communication can be synchronous or asynchronous, depending on the requirements of the application. Understanding the various communication patterns and technologies available is essential for designing robust serverless microservices.

1. Communication Patterns

1.1 Synchronous Communication

Synchronous communication occurs when a microservice sends a request to another service and waits for a response before continuing its processing. This pattern is commonly used for APIs, where one microservice acts as a client that calls another microservice's API.

- **Examples**:
- AWS Lambda functions can be invoked directly by Amazon API Gateway or AWS AppSync to respond to client requests.
- Google Cloud Functions can be triggered via HTTP requests through Google Cloud Endpoints.

Pros:

- Easy to implement and understand.
- Immediate feedback on the success or failure of a request.

Cons:

- Can lead to increased latency, as the calling service must wait for a response.
- More challenging to scale due to potential bottlenecks.

1.2 Asynchronous Communication

Asynchronous communication allows microservices to send messages to one another without waiting for an immediate response. This is often done using message queues or event streams.

- **Examples**:
- AWS SQS (Simple Queue Service) for queuing messages between services.
- Google Pub/Sub for event-driven messaging.

Pros:

- Improved decoupling between services, enhancing scalability and fault tolerance.
- Can handle spikes in traffic by queuing requests for later processing.

Cons:

- Complexity in managing message delivery, retries, and error handling.
- Potential for eventual consistency, where data across services may not be immediately synchronized.

2. Communication Mechanisms
2.1 API Gateway

API Gateway acts as a front door for your microservices, enabling them to communicate over HTTP/HTTPS. Both AWS API Gateway and Google Cloud Endpoints provide the necessary infrastructure to manage APIs.

- **Use Cases**:
- For synchronous requests, an API Gateway can route incoming requests to the appropriate Lambda function or Cloud Function.
- API Gateway also supports throttling, caching, and versioning of APIs.

2.2 Message Queues

Message queues enable asynchronous communication between microservices. AWS SQS and Google Cloud Pub/Sub are popular solutions for handling messages.

- **Use Cases**:
- For a user registration microservice, a message can be placed in a queue to notify a separate email service to send a welcome email after user registration.
- Microservices can push messages onto a queue that other services

consume at their own pace.

2.3 Event Streaming

Event streaming technologies like AWS Kinesis and Google Cloud Dataflow allow microservices to process and respond to streams of events in real time.

- **Use Cases**:
- For processing logs or real-time analytics, microservices can consume events from a stream and react accordingly.
- Useful for building real-time dashboards or data processing pipelines.

3. Design Considerations

When designing communication between microservices in a serverless architecture, consider the following:

3.1 Latency and Performance

- Synchronous communications may introduce latency; thus, use asynchronous patterns where possible to improve responsiveness.
- Consider the performance implications of the chosen communication method, especially under load.

3.2 Fault Tolerance and Reliability

- Implement retries and dead-letter queues (DLQs) for message-based systems to handle failures gracefully.
- Ensure that your services can recover from transient errors without losing data.

3.3 Security

- Use API Gateway features to secure APIs with authentication and authorization mechanisms.
- For message queues and event streams, use encryption in transit and at

rest to protect sensitive data.

3.4 Monitoring and Logging

- Implement monitoring for both synchronous and asynchronous communications to track performance and detect issues.
- Use logging to provide visibility into the interactions between microservices, which is crucial for debugging.

Effective communication between microservices is a cornerstone of a successful serverless architecture. By choosing the right communication patterns and mechanisms, developers can build scalable, resilient, and efficient serverless applications. Synchronous communication is straightforward but can introduce latency, while asynchronous communication improves scalability and fault tolerance at the cost of added complexity.

10.5 Ensuring Scalability and Fault Tolerance in Serverless Microservices

Scalability and fault tolerance are critical considerations when designing serverless microservices architectures. Since serverless environments automatically manage resource allocation, understanding how to effectively leverage this capability is key to building robust applications that can handle varying loads and recover gracefully from failures.

1. Scalability in Serverless Microservices

1.1 Automatic Scaling

One of the significant advantages of serverless architecture is its inherent ability to scale automatically. Both AWS Lambda and Google Cloud Functions can automatically allocate resources based on the incoming request load.

- **How It Works**:
- When demand increases, the cloud provider automatically spins up new instances of your function to handle the increased load, without any manual intervention required from the developer.
- **Use Cases**:

- A retail application experiencing sudden spikes during a sale can seamlessly handle increased traffic without service degradation.
- A data processing application that processes events from IoT devices can scale to accommodate fluctuating message rates.

1.2 Concurrency Limits

While serverless functions can scale automatically, they may be subject to concurrency limits imposed by the cloud provider. Understanding and managing these limits is crucial to ensure consistent performance.

- **AWS Lambda** has a default limit of 1,000 concurrent executions per account per region, which can be increased by request.
- **Google Cloud Functions** also has limits based on the project and can scale up to a certain number of instances depending on the configuration.

1.3 Scaling Strategies

To optimize scaling, consider the following strategies:

- **Decoupling Services**: Use message queues or event-driven architectures to decouple microservices, allowing them to scale independently based on their load.
- **Load Testing**: Regularly perform load testing to understand how your system behaves under different traffic patterns and adjust configurations accordingly.

2. Fault Tolerance in Serverless Microservices

2.1 Error Handling

Fault tolerance involves designing your microservices to gracefully handle failures. This can be accomplished through effective error handling mechanisms:

- **Retries**: Implement retry logic for transient errors, allowing your services to automatically attempt to execute a failed operation a defined

number of times before giving up.
- **Fallback Mechanisms**: Use fallback strategies to provide alternative responses or degrade gracefully when a service is unavailable.

2.2 Using Dead-Letter Queues (DLQs)

For asynchronous operations, dead-letter queues are an essential component for fault tolerance. DLQs store messages that fail to be processed after a certain number of attempts.

- **How It Works**:
- When a message fails processing, it is automatically moved to a DLQ, allowing developers to analyze and retry the failed messages without losing them.
- **Implementation**:
- Both AWS SQS and Google Cloud Pub/Sub support DLQs, providing a way to manage failed processing attempts.

2.3 Circuit Breaker Pattern

The circuit breaker pattern is a robust design strategy that helps prevent cascading failures in a microservices architecture. It temporarily blocks calls to a service that is experiencing failures, allowing it time to recover.

- **Implementation**:
- Integrate a circuit breaker library that monitors service health and automatically opens the circuit (i.e., stops calls) when the failure threshold is reached.
- **Benefits**:
- This pattern helps maintain overall system stability by preventing additional requests from overwhelming a failing service.

3. Monitoring and Observability

To ensure both scalability and fault tolerance, implementing robust monitoring and observability is essential:

3.1 Performance Metrics

Monitor key performance metrics, such as:

- **Invocation Count**: Track the number of times functions are invoked to assess load patterns.
- **Latency**: Measure the time taken for functions to execute, allowing for identification of performance bottlenecks.
- **Error Rates**: Monitor the percentage of failed invocations to catch issues early.

3.2 Logging and Tracing

Use structured logging and distributed tracing tools to gain insights into the behavior of your microservices:

- **AWS CloudWatch**: For AWS Lambda, use CloudWatch Logs to capture logs and monitor function performance.
- **Google Stackdriver**: For Google Cloud Functions, Stackdriver provides monitoring and logging capabilities to track performance and troubleshoot issues.

3.3 Alerts and Notifications

Set up alerts based on the metrics and logs collected to notify the development team when certain thresholds are breached, allowing for proactive maintenance.

Ensuring scalability and fault tolerance in serverless microservices requires a thoughtful approach to design, implementation, and monitoring. By leveraging the automatic scaling features of cloud providers, implementing effective error handling strategies, and utilizing monitoring tools, developers can create resilient applications that can handle varying loads and recover from failures gracefully.

10.6 Monitoring and Logging in Serverless Microservices

Effective monitoring and logging are crucial components of maintaining serverless microservices architecture. They provide insights into application performance, help identify issues, and facilitate debugging. In a serverless environment, where components are highly distributed and ephemeral, robust monitoring and logging practices are essential to ensure system reliability and efficiency.

1. Importance of Monitoring in Serverless Microservices

1.1 Understanding Application Health

Monitoring allows developers to gain visibility into how their microservices are performing in real-time. Key metrics to monitor include:

- **Invocation Counts**: Track the number of times each function is called to understand usage patterns.
- **Response Times**: Measure the time taken for functions to execute, helping identify performance bottlenecks.
- **Error Rates**: Monitor the percentage of failed invocations, which can indicate underlying issues in the system.

1.2 Real-Time Alerts

Setting up alerts based on specific thresholds can help teams respond quickly to potential issues. For instance, if error rates exceed a certain limit or response times spike unexpectedly, alerts can trigger notifications to the development team, allowing for immediate investigation.

1.3 Resource Utilization

Monitoring resource utilization, such as memory and execution time, helps optimize performance and control costs. Cloud providers typically charge based on resource consumption, making it important to understand how resources are being used.

2. Logging in Serverless Applications

2.1 Structured Logging

Structured logging is essential for analyzing logs effectively. Instead of using plain text, structured logs use a consistent format (like JSON), making it easier to parse and analyze log data. This approach allows for better insights into application behavior and easier troubleshooting.

2.2 Centralized Logging Solutions

Utilizing centralized logging solutions can help aggregate logs from multiple microservices, making it easier to search and analyze log data. Popular options include:

- **AWS CloudWatch Logs**: For AWS Lambda, CloudWatch provides a way to store and analyze logs generated by your functions.
- **Google Cloud Logging**: For Google Cloud Functions, Cloud Logging captures logs, enabling developers to monitor applications effectively.

2.3 Log Retention and Management

Establish a log retention policy to manage the storage of logs efficiently. Determine how long logs should be kept based on compliance requirements and system needs. Older logs can be archived or deleted to save costs and maintain system performance.

3. Tracing in Serverless Microservices

3.1 Distributed Tracing

In a microservices architecture, requests often traverse multiple services. Distributed tracing provides visibility into these requests, helping to identify latency issues and performance bottlenecks across services.

- **AWS X-Ray**: AWS provides X-Ray to help visualize and analyze service requests, allowing developers to trace the path of requests through their serverless applications.
- **Google Cloud Trace**: Google Cloud offers Trace for monitoring latency, allowing you to pinpoint performance issues in your applications.

4. Best Practices for Monitoring and Logging

- **Automate Alerts**: Automate the alerting process based on predefined thresholds to ensure rapid response to issues.
- **Monitor End-to-End**: Implement monitoring across all layers of your application to gain a complete view of performance.
- **Use Tags and Metadata**: Tag logs with relevant metadata (like environ-

ment, version, etc.) to facilitate easier searching and analysis.
- **Regularly Review Logs and Metrics**: Set aside time for regular reviews of logs and performance metrics to identify trends and areas for improvement.

Conclusion

In this chapter, we explored the critical aspects of monitoring and logging in serverless microservices. Effective monitoring allows developers to understand application performance, while structured logging and centralized solutions enable easy analysis and troubleshooting. By implementing distributed tracing, teams can gain deeper insights into request flows and identify bottlenecks across services.

CHAPTER 11: DEVOPS AND CI/CD FOR SERVERLESS APPLICATIONS

11.1 Setting Up CI/CD Pipelines for AWS Lambda

Continuous Integration and Continuous Deployment (CI/CD) are essential practices in modern software development, enabling teams to deliver code changes more reliably and efficiently. In the context of serverless applications, particularly those built on AWS Lambda, setting up a CI/CD pipeline involves automating the processes of building, testing, and deploying Lambda functions and associated resources.

1. **Understanding CI/CD Concepts**

- **Continuous Integration (CI)**: This practice involves regularly merging code changes into a shared repository, followed by automated builds and tests to ensure code quality.
- **Continuous Deployment (CD)**: This extends CI by automatically deploying code changes to production after passing the automated tests, facilitating quick releases and feedback loops.

2. **Tools and Services for AWS Lambda CI/CD**

Several AWS services and third-party tools can help set up a CI/CD pipeline for AWS Lambda:

- **AWS CodePipeline**: A fully managed CI/CD service that automates the build, test, and deployment phases of application development. It

integrates seamlessly with other AWS services.
- **AWS CodeBuild**: A fully managed build service that compiles source code, runs tests, and produces artifacts ready for deployment.
- **AWS CodeDeploy**: A deployment service that automates the deployment of applications to various AWS services, including Lambda.

3. Steps to Set Up a CI/CD Pipeline for AWS Lambda
Step 1: Version Control System (VCS) Setup

- Use a version control system like Git to manage your codebase. Platforms such as GitHub, GitLab, or Bitbucket provide repository hosting and integration capabilities.

Step 2: Create a Build Specification File

- Define a build specification file (buildspec.yml) that AWS CodeBuild uses to run the build process. This file specifies the commands to install dependencies, run tests, and package the application.

Example buildspec.yml:
  yaml

version: 0.2

phases:
  install:
  runtime-versions:
  nodejs: 14
  commands:
  - npm install
  build:
  commands:
  - npm run build

```
post_build:
commands:
- echo Build completed on 'date'
artifacts:
files:
- '**/*'
```

Step 3: Configure AWS CodePipeline

- Create a new pipeline in AWS CodePipeline. Define the source stage (e.g., GitHub), the build stage (using CodeBuild), and the deployment stage (using CodeDeploy or direct Lambda deployment).

Step 4: Add Automated Testing

- Integrate automated tests in the pipeline to ensure code quality. Use testing frameworks such as Jest or Mocha for JavaScript applications. Configure your buildspec file to run these tests.

Step 5: Deploy to AWS Lambda

- After the build and tests pass, configure the pipeline to deploy the Lambda function automatically. You can deploy the entire stack using AWS CloudFormation or deploy just the Lambda function using the AWS CLI.

4. Monitoring CI/CD Pipelines

Monitoring your CI/CD pipeline is crucial to ensure smooth operation and quick identification of issues. Use AWS CloudWatch to track metrics such as build duration, error rates, and deployment statuses. Implement notifications via AWS SNS (Simple Notification Service) to alert your team about pipeline failures or issues.

5. Best Practices for CI/CD in Serverless Applications

- **Keep It Simple**: Start with a simple pipeline and iterate. Gradually add complexity (like integration tests) as needed.
- **Isolate Functionality**: Use microservices architecture to isolate functionality, allowing for independent deployments and updates.
- **Test in Isolation**: Write unit and integration tests to validate individual components without relying on other services.
- **Use Environment Variables**: Store configuration and secrets securely using AWS Systems Manager Parameter Store or AWS Secrets Manager.

Summary

Setting up CI/CD pipelines for AWS Lambda enables teams to streamline their development and deployment processes, fostering a culture of continuous improvement and rapid iteration. By automating testing and deployment, organizations can deliver high-quality serverless applications efficiently. In the next chapter, we will explore **Best Practices for Serverless Development**, focusing on strategies to enhance performance, security, and maintainability in serverless architectures.

11.2 Continuous Integration with Google Cloud Functions

Continuous Integration (CI) is a critical component of modern software development practices, allowing teams to automate the process of building, testing, and validating their code. For serverless applications built with Google Cloud Functions, establishing a robust CI pipeline ensures that code changes are continuously integrated and tested, leading to faster and more reliable deployments.

1. Understanding Google Cloud CI/CD Ecosystem

Google Cloud provides a suite of tools to facilitate CI/CD, including:

- **Google Cloud Build**: A fully managed CI/CD platform that automates the building and testing of applications.
- **Cloud Source Repositories**: A service for hosting Git repositories that can be integrated with Cloud Build.
- **Cloud Run**: While not directly part of Cloud Functions, it can be used for deploying containerized applications that might need to interact with

CHAPTER 11: DEVOPS AND CI/CD FOR SERVERLESS APPLICATIONS

serverless functions.

2. Setting Up Continuous Integration for Google Cloud Functions
Step 1: Source Code Management
Use a version control system (VCS) like Git, hosted on platforms such as GitHub, GitLab, or Bitbucket. Ensure your code is organized in a way that follows best practices for serverless applications, with separate directories for different functions if needed.

Step 2: Creating a Build Configuration File
Google Cloud Build uses a configuration file named cloudbuild.yaml to define the steps for building and testing your application. This file specifies the build steps, environment variables, and artifacts produced during the build process.

Example cloudbuild.yaml:

yaml

```
steps:
  - name: 'node'
    entrypoint: 'bash'
    args:
    - '-c'
    - |
    npm install
    npm run test
  - name: 'gcr.io/cloud-builders/gcloud'
    args: ['functions', 'deploy', 'YOUR_FUNCTION_NAME', '—runtime', 'nodejs14', '—trigger-http', '—allow-unauthenticated']
```

Step 3: Configuring Google Cloud Build Triggers
Set up triggers in Google Cloud Build to automatically start a build when changes are pushed to your repository. This can be configured for specific branches or pull requests, ensuring that your CI process is responsive to code changes.

- Navigate to Google Cloud Console.
- Go to Cloud Build > Triggers.
- Click "Create Trigger" and configure the necessary settings (repository, branch, etc.).

Step 4: Running Automated Tests

Integrate automated testing into your build process to validate the functionality of your Cloud Functions. Use testing frameworks like Jest or Mocha for JavaScript applications. Ensure your test scripts are defined in your package.json and that the cloudbuild.yaml file includes steps to run these tests.

Step 5: Build and Deploy

Once your CI pipeline is set up, it will automatically build and test your Google Cloud Functions whenever changes are made. If all tests pass, the pipeline will deploy the function to Google Cloud.

3. Monitoring CI Processes

To ensure the CI process is running smoothly, monitor build logs and outcomes using Google Cloud Console. Google Cloud Build provides detailed logs for each build, which can help diagnose issues quickly.

- Access Cloud Build from the Google Cloud Console.
- Review build history and logs to identify any failures or warnings.

4. Best Practices for CI with Google Cloud Functions

- **Small, Focused Functions**: Break down your application into small functions that perform single tasks, making it easier to test and deploy.
- **Consistent Testing**: Ensure all functions have comprehensive unit tests and integration tests, enabling confidence in code changes.
- **Environment Variables**: Use Google Cloud's Secret Manager to manage sensitive data and configuration securely.
- **Code Quality Checks**: Integrate tools like ESLint for code quality checks in your CI pipeline to maintain code standards.

Summary

Implementing Continuous Integration for Google Cloud Functions enables teams to automate testing and deployment, leading to more efficient workflows and higher-quality code. By leveraging Google Cloud Build and integrating automated tests, developers can ensure that their serverless applications are consistently reliable and ready for production. In the next section, we will explore **Continuous Deployment Strategies for Google Cloud Functions**, detailing how to automate the deployment process and manage versioning effectively.

11.3 Automating Deployments with AWS CodePipeline and Google Cloud Build

Automating deployments is a crucial aspect of DevOps practices, especially in serverless architectures where rapid iteration and frequent updates are common. Both AWS and Google Cloud offer powerful tools to facilitate the automation of deployment processes. In this section, we will explore how to use AWS CodePipeline and Google Cloud Build to automate deployments for serverless applications.

1. Overview of AWS CodePipeline

AWS CodePipeline is a continuous integration and continuous delivery (CI/CD) service for fast and reliable application updates. It allows you to define your release process as a series of stages, including building, testing, and deploying your application.

Key Features of AWS CodePipeline:

- **Integration with Other AWS Services**: CodePipeline integrates seamlessly with services like AWS Lambda, Amazon S3, and AWS CodeBuild.
- **Customizable Workflows**: You can define custom workflows tailored to your application's deployment requirements.
- **Support for Third-Party Tools**: Integrates with popular third-party tools for source control, build automation, and testing.

2. Setting Up AWS CodePipeline for Serverless Applications
Step 1: Create an S3 Bucket for Source Code

1. Log in to the AWS Management Console.
2. Navigate to S3 and create a new bucket to store your application code.

Step 2: Create a CodePipeline

1. Go to the AWS CodePipeline console.
2. Click "Create pipeline" and enter a name for your pipeline.
3. Choose the source provider (e.g., S3, GitHub) and specify the location of your source code.
4. Configure the build provider (e.g., AWS CodeBuild) to compile your application.

Step 3: Add Stages to Your Pipeline

- **Build Stage**: Use AWS CodeBuild to compile your application and run tests. Define the build specification in a buildspec.yml file.

Example buildspec.yml:
yaml

```
version: 0.2
  phases:
  install:
  runtime-versions:
  nodejs: 14
  build:
  commands:
  - npm install
  - npm run test
  artifacts:
  files:
  - '**/*'
```

CHAPTER 11: DEVOPS AND CI/CD FOR SERVERLESS APPLICATIONS

- **Deploy Stage**: Choose AWS Lambda as the deployment provider and specify the function name and related settings.

3. Overview of Google Cloud Build

Google Cloud Build is a fully managed CI/CD platform that automates the build, test, and deployment of applications. It allows developers to define their CI/CD workflows in a simple configuration file.

Key Features of Google Cloud Build:

- **Fast and Scalable**: Automatically scales to match your build and deployment needs.
- **Extensive Integration**: Works well with various Google Cloud services and third-party tools.
- **Build Triggers**: Automatically builds and deploys applications in response to code changes.

4. Setting Up Google Cloud Build for Serverless Applications
Step 1: Configure Cloud Build

1. Go to the Google Cloud Console and navigate to Cloud Build.
2. Set up a cloudbuild.yaml configuration file that defines the build and deployment steps.

Example cloudbuild.yaml:
yaml

steps:
  - name: 'node'
  entrypoint: 'bash'
  args:
  - '-c'
  - |
  npm install

npm run test
- name: 'gcr.io/cloud-builders/gcloud'
args: ['functions', 'deploy', 'YOUR_FUNCTION_NAME', '—runtime', 'nodejs14', '—trigger-http', '—allow-unauthenticated']

Step 2: Set Up Build Triggers

1. In the Google Cloud Console, navigate to Cloud Build > Triggers.
2. Create a new trigger that starts the build process whenever changes are pushed to your source code repository.

5. Best Practices for Automating Deployments

- **Use Infrastructure as Code (IaC)**: Tools like AWS CloudFormation or Google Cloud Deployment Manager help define and manage infrastructure through code, enabling version control and automation.
- **Environment Segregation**: Implement separate pipelines for different environments (development, staging, production) to reduce the risk of deploying untested code.
- **Monitoring and Alerts**: Set up monitoring and alerts for your deployment pipelines to detect and respond to failures quickly.

Summary

Automating deployments with AWS CodePipeline and Google Cloud Build streamlines the release process for serverless applications, enabling teams to deliver updates quickly and reliably. By setting up these CI/CD pipelines, developers can focus more on writing code and less on the intricacies of deployment processes. In the next section, we will explore **Monitoring and Logging in Serverless Applications**, focusing on best practices and tools for ensuring application reliability and performance.

11.4 Versioning and Rollbacks in Serverless Deployments

Versioning and rollback strategies are essential components of serverless deployments, enabling teams to manage application updates effectively while ensuring stability and reliability. In this section, we will discuss the importance of versioning, how to implement it in AWS Lambda and Google Cloud Functions, and how to perform rollbacks when necessary.

1. Understanding Versioning in Serverless Architectures

Versioning allows you to maintain multiple iterations of your serverless functions or applications, making it possible to manage changes over time. This is especially useful for:

- **Testing New Features**: Developers can deploy new features as separate versions and test them without disrupting the existing functionality.
- **A/B Testing**: You can run different versions of a function concurrently to determine which performs better based on user interactions or metrics.
- **Stability**: If a new version introduces bugs or performance issues, versioning allows you to revert to a stable release quickly.

2. Implementing Versioning in AWS Lambda

AWS Lambda provides built-in support for versioning, enabling you to publish and manage different versions of your Lambda functions.

Step 1: Create a New Version

1. After deploying a new function or updating an existing one, navigate to the AWS Lambda console.
2. Select your function and click on the "Publish new version" button.
3. Provide a description for the new version and publish it.

Step 2: Accessing Versions

- Each published version is assigned a unique ARN (Amazon Resource Name) that you can use to invoke it. You can also create aliases for different versions, allowing you to manage them more easily.

Example of Invoking a Specific Version:
javascript

```javascript
const AWS = require('aws-sdk');
const lambda = new AWS.Lambda();

const params = {
  FunctionName: 'yourFunctionName:1', // Invokes version 1
  Payload: JSON.stringify({ /* your payload */ })
};

lambda.invoke(params, function(err, data) {
  if (err) console.log(err, err.stack);
  else console.log(data);
});
```

Step 3: Managing Aliases

You can create aliases that point to specific versions of your function. This allows you to switch between versions easily and create staged deployments (e.g., development, production).

javascript

```javascript
const params = {
  FunctionName: 'yourFunctionName',
  Name: 'production',
  FunctionVersion: '1' // Points alias 'production' to version 1
};

lambda.putAlias(params, function(err, data) {
  if (err) console.log(err, err.stack);
  else console.log(data);
});
```

3. Implementing Versioning in Google Cloud Functions

Google Cloud Functions also supports versioning through deployments. However, it manages versioning automatically with each deployment, and you can specify the version to use.

Step 1: Deploy a Function with a Version Tag

When deploying a function, you can specify a version tag to keep track of deployments.

bash

```
gcloud functions deploy YOUR_FUNCTION_NAME \
  --entry-point YOUR_ENTRY_POINT \
  --runtime nodejs14 \
  --trigger-http \
  --update-labels version=1.0
```

Step 2: Listing Function Versions

To see all versions of a function, you can use the following command:

bash

```
gcloud functions describe YOUR_FUNCTION_NAME
```

This command will list the details of all versions, including their labels.

4. Rollback Strategies

Rollback strategies are crucial for maintaining application stability in the event of deployment failures or issues. Here are approaches for rolling back deployments in both AWS Lambda and Google Cloud Functions:

AWS Lambda Rollbacks:

- **Using Aliases**: If a new version causes issues, you can update an alias to point back to the last known stable version. For example, if version 2 introduces problems, you can update the production alias to point to version 1.

javascript

```javascript
const params = {
  FunctionName: 'yourFunctionName',
  Name: 'production',
  FunctionVersion: '1' // Rollback to version 1
};
```

```
lambda.putAlias(params, function(err, data) {
  if (err) console.log(err, err.stack);
  else console.log(data);
});
```

- **Manual Invocation**: You can also invoke the previous version directly if aliases are not used.

Google Cloud Functions Rollbacks:

- **Re-deploying the Previous Version**: To roll back a Google Cloud Function, you can redeploy a previous version using the —version flag.

bash

```
gcloud functions deploy YOUR_FUNCTION_NAME \
  —entry-point YOUR_ENTRY_POINT \
  —runtime nodejs14 \
  —trigger-http \
  —version PREVIOUS_VERSION_TAG
```

Summary

Versioning and rollback strategies are vital for maintaining stability and facilitating rapid development in serverless architectures. By leveraging built-in versioning features in AWS Lambda and Google Cloud Functions, teams can deploy updates confidently, test new features, and swiftly revert to stable versions when needed.

11.5 Using Infrastructure as Code (IaC) for Serverless Applications

Infrastructure as Code (IaC) is a modern approach that allows developers to manage and provision their cloud infrastructure through code, rather than manual configuration. This practice is especially beneficial for serverless applications, as it enhances consistency, reduces errors, and streamlines deployment processes. In this section, we will explore the fundamentals of IaC, its benefits for serverless architectures, and how to implement it using popular tools such as AWS CloudFormation, AWS SAM (Serverless Application Model), and the Serverless Framework.

1. Understanding Infrastructure as Code (IaC)

IaC enables you to define your infrastructure in code and manage it through version control systems. Instead of manually setting up cloud resources through a web console, you write configuration files (in YAML or JSON format) that describe your desired state of infrastructure.

Key features of IaC include:

- **Declarative Syntax**: You specify what you want, and the IaC tool determines how to achieve that state.
- **Version Control**: Infrastructure definitions can be stored in Git repositories, allowing for collaborative development and change tracking.
- **Automated Provisioning**: Resources can be provisioned automatically, reducing the risk of human error during deployment.

2. Benefits of IaC for Serverless Applications

Using IaC for serverless applications provides several advantages:

- **Consistency and Reproducibility**: Infrastructure can be consistently deployed across multiple environments (development, staging, production) using the same codebase.
- **Scalability**: IaC allows you to quickly scale your infrastructure up or down by modifying the code and redeploying.
- **Easier Collaboration**: Teams can collaborate on infrastructure changes through code reviews and version control processes, leading to better communication and fewer misunderstandings.
- **Cost Efficiency**: By automating the provisioning and configuration of serverless resources, organizations can optimize their cloud usage and minimize costs.

3. Implementing IaC with AWS CloudFormation

AWS CloudFormation is a powerful IaC service that allows you to define your AWS resources in a declarative template.

Step 1: Create a CloudFormation Template

Here's a basic example of a CloudFormation template that creates an AWS Lambda function and an API Gateway:

yaml

```yaml
AWSTemplateFormatVersion: '2010-09-09'
  Resources:
  MyFunction:
  Type: AWS::Lambda::Function
  Properties:
  Handler: index.handler
  Role: arn:aws:iam::123456789012:role/service-role/MyLambdaRole
  Code:
  S3Bucket: my-bucket
  S3Key: my-function.zip
  Runtime: nodejs14.x
  Timeout: 30

MyApi:
  Type: AWS::ApiGateway::RestApi
  Properties:
  Name: My API
```

Step 2: Deploy the Template

You can deploy the CloudFormation template using the AWS Management Console, AWS CLI, or SDKs:

bash

```bash
aws cloudformation create-stack —stack-name my-stack —template-body file://template.yaml
```

4. Using AWS SAM for Serverless Applications

AWS SAM is an extension of CloudFormation tailored specifically for serverless applications. It simplifies the process of defining serverless resources and includes local testing capabilities.

Step 1: Create a SAM Template

An example SAM template might look like this:

yaml

```yaml
AWSTemplateFormatVersion: '2010-09-09'
  Transform: AWS::Serverless-2016-10-31
  Resources:
  MyFunction:
  Type: AWS::Serverless::Function
  Properties:
  Handler: index.handler
  Runtime: nodejs14.x
  CodeUri: ./src
  Events:
  Api:
  Type: Api
  Properties:
  Path: /my-endpoint
  Method: get
```

Step 2: Build and Deploy

To deploy your SAM application, use the SAM CLI:

bash

```bash
sam build
  sam deploy —guided
```

The guided option will prompt you for necessary parameters and help create a configuration file for future deployments.

5. Using the Serverless Framework

The Serverless Framework is another popular tool for managing serverless applications across different cloud providers, including AWS, Google Cloud, and Azure.

Step 1: Create a Serverless Configuration File

Here's an example serverless.yml file for an AWS Lambda function:
yaml

service: my-service

provider:
    name: aws
    runtime: nodejs14.x

functions:
    hello:
    handler: handler.hello
    events:
    - http:
    path: hello
    method: get

Step 2: Deploy Your Service

You can deploy the serverless service with a simple command:
bash

serverless deploy

This command provisions the defined resources, uploads your code, and configures the necessary permissions.

Conclusion

Using Infrastructure as Code (IaC) for serverless applications significantly enhances deployment processes by providing a consistent, repeatable, and error-resistant approach to managing cloud resources. By leveraging tools such as AWS CloudFormation, AWS SAM, and the Serverless Framework, developers can streamline the setup and management of their serverless environments.

CHAPTER 12: MONITORING AND DEBUGGING SERVERLESS APPLICATIONS

12.1 Monitoring AWS Lambda with CloudWatch and X-Ray

Monitoring is crucial for maintaining the health and performance of serverless applications. AWS Lambda provides built-in monitoring capabilities through Amazon CloudWatch and AWS X-Ray, enabling developers to gain insights into their functions' performance, troubleshoot issues, and optimize resource usage. In this section, we will explore how to leverage these tools effectively.

1. Amazon CloudWatch: Metrics and Alarms

Amazon CloudWatch is a monitoring and observability service that collects and tracks metrics, logs, and events. For AWS Lambda, CloudWatch provides several key metrics that are essential for monitoring function performance:

- **Invocation Count**: The number of times a function is invoked.
- **Duration**: The time taken for the function to execute, measured in milliseconds.
- **Error Count**: The number of failed invocations, which helps identify potential issues in the code.
- **Throttles**: The number of invocation requests that are throttled due to exceeding the concurrency limits.

Setting Up CloudWatch Alarms

You can create CloudWatch alarms to notify you of performance anomalies or errors. For example, you can set an alarm to trigger if the error count exceeds a certain threshold:

1. Go to the CloudWatch console.
2. Select "Alarms" and click "Create Alarm."
3. Choose the "Lambda" namespace and select the metric you want to monitor (e.g., "Errors").
4. Configure the conditions for the alarm, such as setting a threshold and evaluation period.
5. Choose actions, such as sending notifications via Amazon SNS.

2. AWS X-Ray: Tracing and Debugging

AWS X-Ray is a distributed tracing service that helps you analyze and debug applications in production. It provides insights into the behavior of your Lambda functions by tracking requests as they travel through your application.

Enabling X-Ray for AWS Lambda

To enable X-Ray tracing for a Lambda function:

1. Go to the AWS Lambda console.
2. Select your function and scroll down to the "Configuration" section.
3. Under "Monitoring and Operations tools," enable "Active tracing."
4. Deploy the function to apply the changes.

Using X-Ray to Analyze Requests

Once X-Ray is enabled, it will automatically trace incoming requests to your Lambda function. You can view traces in the X-Ray console:

- **Service Map**: Visualizes the interactions between different services, helping you identify bottlenecks and latencies.
- **Traces**: Shows detailed information about individual requests, including response times and errors.

- **Insights**: Provides aggregated views of performance metrics, such as average latency and error rates.

By using X-Ray, you can pinpoint performance issues and understand how different services interact in your serverless application.

12.2 Monitoring Google Cloud Functions with Stackdriver

Google Cloud Functions integrates with Google Cloud's operations suite (formerly known as Stackdriver) for monitoring and logging. This section covers how to effectively monitor your Google Cloud Functions.

Key Metrics for Cloud Functions

Similar to AWS Lambda, Google Cloud Functions provides key metrics, including:

- **Execution Count**: Total number of function invocations.
- **Execution Time**: Duration of function execution.
- **Errors**: Count of failed executions.

Setting Up Alerts in Stackdriver

You can create alerts based on specific metrics to keep track of the performance of your Cloud Functions:

1. Open the Google Cloud Console.
2. Navigate to "Monitoring" and select "Alerting."
3. Click "Create Policy" and choose the metric you want to monitor (e.g., "Function Execution Errors").
4. Set the conditions for the alert and specify notification channels (e.g., email, SMS).

12.3 Debugging Serverless Applications

Debugging serverless applications can be challenging due to their event-driven nature and the abstraction of underlying infrastructure. Here are some strategies to effectively debug AWS Lambda and Google Cloud Functions:

1. Using Logs for Debugging

Both AWS Lambda and Google Cloud Functions automatically log output and errors. You can use these logs to trace issues:

- **AWS Lambda**: Logs are sent to CloudWatch Logs. You can view logs by navigating to the CloudWatch console, selecting "Logs," and finding your function's log group.
- **Google Cloud Functions**: Logs are accessible through the Google Cloud Console under the "Logs" section.

Add logging statements in your code to track variable values, execution paths, and errors:
javascript

console.log("Starting function execution with input:", input);

2. Using Local Debugging Tools

For more complex debugging, you can use local debugging tools that simulate serverless environments:

- **AWS SAM CLI**: Allows you to run Lambda functions locally for testing. You can invoke functions and step through the code using a debugger.
- **Google Cloud Functions Emulator**: Provides a local environment for testing your functions before deployment.

Summary

Monitoring and debugging serverless applications are critical for ensuring performance, reliability, and user satisfaction. By leveraging tools like Amazon CloudWatch and AWS X-Ray for AWS Lambda, as well as Google Cloud's operations suite for Google Cloud Functions, developers can gain valuable insights into application behavior and performance. Effective logging and local debugging strategies further enhance the ability to identify and resolve issues quickly.

12.2 Monitoring Google Cloud Functions with Stackdriver

Google Cloud Functions seamlessly integrates with Google Cloud's operations suite, now known as **Cloud Monitoring and Cloud Logging** (formerly Stackdriver). This powerful combination allows developers to monitor the performance and reliability of their serverless applications, gaining insights into function executions and potential issues. In this section, we will explore the key metrics available for Google Cloud Functions and how to set up monitoring alerts.

Key Metrics for Cloud Functions

Google Cloud Functions provides various metrics that are essential for monitoring function performance and behavior. Here are some of the critical metrics you should keep an eye on:

- **Execution Count**: This metric indicates the total number of times a specific Cloud Function has been invoked. It helps you understand the function's usage over time.
- **Execution Time**: This is the duration of function execution, measured in milliseconds. Monitoring execution time is crucial for identifying performance bottlenecks.
- **Errors**: This metric counts the number of failed executions, allowing you to detect issues quickly. High error rates might indicate problems with your function's logic or external dependencies.
- **Memory Usage**: Tracking memory consumption helps ensure that your function runs efficiently and does not exceed allocated limits, which can lead to throttling.
- **Cold Starts**: This metric measures the time it takes for a function to start from a cold state (when no instances are available to handle requests). Minimizing cold start times can improve user experience.

Accessing Metrics in Google Cloud Console

To access metrics for your Google Cloud Functions:

1. **Open the Google Cloud Console**: Go to console.cloud.google.com.
2. **Navigate to Monitoring**: Select "Monitoring" from the navigation menu.

3. **View Dashboards**: Click on "Dashboards" to see pre-configured dashboards for your project, which display various metrics related to Cloud Functions.
4. **Create Custom Dashboards**: You can create custom dashboards tailored to your specific monitoring needs by selecting "Create Dashboard" and adding relevant metrics.

Setting Up Alerts in Cloud Monitoring

Setting up alerts in Cloud Monitoring allows you to proactively respond to performance issues and anomalies in your Cloud Functions. Here's how to create alerts based on specific metrics:

1. **Open the Monitoring Console**: In the Google Cloud Console, navigate to the Monitoring section.
2. **Create an Alerting Policy**:

- Click on "Alerting" in the left sidebar.
- Select "Create Policy."

1. **Choose a Metric**:

- Click on "Add Condition."
- Select the resource type as "Cloud Function" and choose the metric you want to monitor (e.g., "Function Execution Errors").

1. **Set Alert Conditions**:

- Define the threshold that will trigger the alert. For instance, you might want to receive alerts if the error count exceeds a certain number within a specific time frame.
- Configure the notification channels (e.g., email, SMS) to receive alerts.

1. **Add Documentation** (optional): You can add documentation to the

alerting policy to provide context for team members regarding what the alert signifies and what actions to take.
2. **Save the Policy**: Click "Save" to create the alerting policy.

Using Logs for Monitoring and Debugging

Google Cloud Functions automatically logs output and errors to Cloud Logging. You can access these logs to trace issues and gain insights into function executions:

- **Accessing Logs**: To view logs for your Cloud Functions, go to the Google Cloud Console, select "Logging" from the navigation menu, and then click on "Logs Explorer." Here, you can filter logs based on resource type and function name.
- **Log Entries**: Log entries typically include information about the function invocation, including request payloads, execution time, and any errors that occurred during execution.
- **Structured Logging**: To enhance log quality, consider using structured logging by logging data in JSON format. This approach allows for better querying and filtering within the logs.

Example of structured logging:

```javascript
const { CloudLogging } = require('@google-cloud/logging');

const logging = new CloudLogging();
const log = logging.log('my-log');

const metadata = {
  resource: { type: 'cloud_function', labels: { function_name: 'myFunction' } },
};

const entry = log.entry(metadata, { message: 'Function executed successfully',
```

input: inputData });

log.write(entry)
  .then(() => {
  console.log('Logged: ', entry);
})
  .catch(err => {
  console.error('Error writing log: ', err);
});

Summary

Monitoring Google Cloud Functions through Cloud Monitoring and Cloud Logging is crucial for maintaining application performance and quickly identifying issues. By utilizing key metrics, setting up alerts, and employing effective logging strategies, developers can gain valuable insights into their serverless applications and ensure smooth operations.

12.3 Debugging Serverless Applications: Common Pitfalls

Debugging serverless applications presents unique challenges that differ significantly from traditional server-based environments. Understanding these common pitfalls can help developers proactively avoid issues and streamline the debugging process. In this section, we'll explore some of the most frequent challenges encountered in serverless debugging and provide strategies to overcome them.

1. Cold Start Delays

Description: Serverless functions can experience cold starts, which occur when a function is invoked after a period of inactivity. This delay can impact performance and user experience.

Pitfalls:

- Misunderstanding the impact of cold starts can lead to unnecessary performance complaints from users.
- Relying solely on average execution time metrics may mask the influence of cold starts.

Strategies:

- **Minimize Cold Starts**: Keep function code lightweight, utilize lighter dependencies, and consider using provisioned concurrency in AWS Lambda to reduce cold start frequency.
- **Monitoring**: Use monitoring tools to track cold start occurrences and their impact on execution times, allowing for better assessment and adjustments.

2. Lack of Local Debugging Tools

Description: Debugging serverless applications locally can be challenging due to the lack of available emulators that accurately replicate the serverless environment.

Pitfalls:

- Developers may assume that functions will behave the same way locally as they do in the cloud, leading to missed errors that only manifest in production.

Strategies:

- **Use Local Emulators**: Leverage tools like the AWS SAM CLI or Google Cloud Functions Emulator to run functions locally and test their behavior in a simulated environment.
- **Mock External Services**: Use libraries like moxios or nock to mock external API calls during local testing, ensuring that functions behave as expected without relying on actual services.

3. Poor Error Handling

Description: Failing to implement proper error handling can result in untraceable errors, making debugging difficult.

Pitfalls:

- Lack of specific error messages can make it challenging to pinpoint issues, especially in complex serverless applications.

Strategies:

- **Implement Comprehensive Error Handling**: Use try-catch blocks and proper error logging to capture exceptions and provide meaningful error messages.
- **Structured Logging**: Log detailed error information, including input parameters and stack traces, to facilitate easier debugging.

Example of error handling in a Lambda function:
javascript

```
exports.handler = async (event) => {
  try {
  // Your function logic here
  } catch (error) {
  console.error('Error occurred:', error);
  throw new Error('Function failed to execute');
  }
};
```

4. Dependencies and Versioning Issues

Description: Managing dependencies in serverless applications can lead to version conflicts and compatibility issues, particularly when multiple services are involved.

Pitfalls:

- Deployments might work perfectly in development but fail in production due to dependency mismatches.

Strategies:

- **Lock Dependencies**: Use package managers like npm or Yarn to lock dependency versions and ensure consistency across environments.
- **Separate Environments**: Maintain separate staging and production environments to test changes before deploying them to production.

5. Insufficient Monitoring and Logging

Description: Without proper monitoring and logging, it becomes challenging to diagnose issues in serverless applications.

Pitfalls:

- Inadequate logging can lead to blind spots, making it difficult to trace the execution flow and identify where errors occur.

Strategies:

- **Enhance Logging**: Implement structured logging to capture detailed execution paths, making it easier to track the flow of data through your functions.
- **Use Monitoring Tools**: Leverage tools like AWS CloudWatch, Google Cloud Monitoring, or third-party solutions like Datadog to gain insights into function performance and errors.

6. Overlooking Resource Limits

Description: Serverless platforms impose limits on resources like memory, execution time, and concurrent executions, which can lead to unexpected failures.

Pitfalls:

- Developers may underestimate resource requirements, leading to function timeouts or throttling.

Strategies:

- **Understand Limits**: Familiarize yourself with the resource limits of your chosen serverless platform (e.g., AWS Lambda has a maximum execution time of 15 minutes).
- **Optimize Resource Usage**: Optimize code for performance and ensure that functions are designed to execute within the imposed limits.

Summary

Debugging serverless applications requires an understanding of the unique challenges that arise from their architecture. By being aware of common pitfalls such as cold start delays, local debugging limitations, and resource constraints, developers can adopt strategies to mitigate these issues effectively. Implementing comprehensive logging, error handling, and monitoring will further enhance the debugging process, making it easier to identify and resolve problems in serverless applications.

12.4 Setting Up Alerts for Serverless Performance Issues

Effective monitoring in serverless applications involves not only tracking metrics but also proactively identifying and responding to potential performance issues. Setting up alerts can help developers catch issues before they affect end users. In this section, we will explore how to configure alerts for various performance issues in serverless applications, focusing on AWS Lambda and Google Cloud Functions.

1. Key Performance Metrics to Monitor

Before setting up alerts, it's essential to identify which metrics are critical for assessing the performance of your serverless functions. Here are some key metrics to monitor:

- **Invocation Count**: The number of times a function is invoked, which can help track usage patterns.
- **Error Rate**: The percentage of invocations that result in errors. A sudden spike could indicate an underlying issue.
- **Duration**: The amount of time it takes for a function to execute. Long execution times can affect user experience.
- **Cold Start Time**: The duration of cold starts. Monitoring this metric is

CHAPTER 12: MONITORING AND DEBUGGING SERVERLESS APPLICATIONS

crucial for performance-sensitive applications.
- **Concurrent Executions**: The number of concurrent instances of a function running. High values may indicate the need for scaling adjustments.

2. Setting Up Alerts in AWS Lambda

AWS CloudWatch provides robust monitoring capabilities, allowing you to set up alerts based on various metrics. Here's how to configure alerts for AWS Lambda functions:

Step 1: Create a CloudWatch Alarm

- Navigate to the **CloudWatch** console in AWS Management Console.
- Choose **Alarms** and then click on **Create Alarm**.
- Select the **Lambda Metrics** namespace and choose the metric you want to monitor (e.g., Error Count, Duration).

Step 2: Define Alarm Conditions

- Set the threshold for when the alarm should trigger. For example, if you want to be alerted when the error rate exceeds 5% over a 5-minute period, set this condition accordingly.

Step 3: Configure Notification Actions

- Specify the actions that should be taken when the alarm is triggered. You can send notifications via Amazon SNS (Simple Notification Service), which can deliver alerts through email, SMS, or other endpoints.

Example of a CloudWatch Alarm for Error Rate:
plaintext

Alarm Name: High Error Rate for MyFunction
  Metric: Errors

Threshold: Greater than 5 errors in the last 5 minutes
Notification: Send to my-email@example.com via SNS

3. Setting Up Alerts in Google Cloud Functions

Google Cloud Monitoring (formerly Stackdriver) offers similar capabilities for monitoring and alerting on Google Cloud Functions.

Step 1: Create an Alerting Policy

- Navigate to the **Google Cloud Console** and select **Monitoring**.
- Click on **Alerting** and then **Create Policy**.

Step 2: Configure Conditions

- Add a condition to monitor a specific metric, such as **function execution count** or **error count**.
- Define the threshold that should trigger the alert (e.g., alert if the error count exceeds a specified number in a defined time frame).

Step 3: Set Up Notification Channels

- Choose how you want to be notified when the alert is triggered. Options include email notifications, SMS, or integration with other services (e.g., Slack, PagerDuty).

Example of an Alerting Policy for Execution Errors:

plaintext

Alert Policy Name: High Execution Errors for MyFunction
  Metric: Cloud Functions Execution Errors
  Threshold: Greater than 5 errors in a 5-minute window
  Notification: Send to my-email@example.com

4. Best Practices for Alerts

To ensure that your alerting system is effective and not overwhelming, consider the following best practices:

CHAPTER 12: MONITORING AND DEBUGGING SERVERLESS APPLICATIONS

- **Set Meaningful Thresholds**: Define thresholds that reflect genuine issues rather than routine fluctuations in metrics. For example, avoid alerting on low error counts that are typical for your application.
- **Avoid Alert Fatigue**: Limit the number of alerts to prevent overwhelming developers with notifications. Group related alerts where possible and prioritize critical issues.
- **Document Alerting Policies**: Maintain clear documentation on what each alert signifies and the appropriate response actions. This will help your team respond quickly and effectively.
- **Test Alerts**: Periodically test your alerting mechanisms to ensure they are functioning correctly and that notifications reach the intended recipients.

Summary

Setting up alerts for serverless performance issues is a crucial step in maintaining the health and reliability of your applications. By monitoring key metrics and configuring alerts in AWS Lambda and Google Cloud Functions, developers can catch potential issues before they escalate and impact users. Employing best practices for alerting will further enhance the effectiveness of your monitoring efforts.

12.5 Analyzing Logs in AWS and Google Cloud

Logging is a fundamental aspect of monitoring and debugging serverless applications. It provides visibility into the internal workings of your functions and helps identify issues, understand user behavior, and improve application performance. This section will cover how to analyze logs for AWS Lambda and Google Cloud Functions effectively.

1. Understanding Logs in Serverless Architectures

In serverless architectures, logs capture critical information about function executions, including:

- **Invocation details**: The time of invocation, the event payload, and the function's execution context.
- **Execution results**: Success and failure messages, along with error details when applicable.

- **Performance metrics**: Duration, cold start times, and resource utilization information.

Both AWS and Google Cloud provide logging services that facilitate the collection, storage, and analysis of logs.

2. Analyzing Logs in AWS Lambda with CloudWatch Logs

AWS Lambda automatically generates logs for each function invocation and stores them in **Amazon CloudWatch Logs**. Here's how to access and analyze these logs:

Step 1: Accessing CloudWatch Logs

- Go to the **AWS Management Console** and open **CloudWatch**.
- Click on **Logs** in the navigation pane, then find the log group associated with your Lambda function (typically named /aws/lambda/YourFunctionName).

Step 2: Viewing Log Streams

- Click on the log group to view its log streams, which are generated for each execution of your function.
- Each log stream corresponds to a specific invocation, allowing you to inspect detailed output for that execution.

Step 3: Searching and Filtering Logs

- Use the search bar to filter logs based on keywords or specific error messages.
- You can also apply metrics filters to monitor specific patterns or thresholds in your logs, generating CloudWatch metrics from those patterns.

Example of a Log Entry in AWS Lambda:
plaintext

CHAPTER 12: MONITORING AND DEBUGGING SERVERLESS APPLICATIONS

START RequestId: abc123-xyz-456
  INFO: Event received: {"key1":"value1","key2":"value2"}
  ERROR: Failed to process the event: Invalid input format
  END RequestId: abc123-xyz-456
  REPORT RequestId: abc123-xyz-456 Duration: 150ms Billed Duration: 200ms Memory Size: 128MB Max Memory Used: 45MB

3. Analyzing Logs in Google Cloud Functions with Stackdriver Logging

Google Cloud Functions logs are integrated with **Google Cloud Logging** (formerly Stackdriver Logging). This allows for seamless logging and analysis of function executions.

Step 1: Accessing Cloud Logging

- Navigate to the **Google Cloud Console** and select **Logging** under the **Operations** menu.
- Choose **Logs Explorer** to view logs from all your cloud services, including Google Cloud Functions.

Step 2: Filtering Logs

- Use the query builder to filter logs specifically for your Google Cloud Functions. You can filter by resource type (Cloud Function) and specify function names.
- For example, to filter logs for a specific function, you might use the following query:

plaintext

resource.type="cloud_function"
  resource.labels.function_name="YourFunctionName"

Step 3: Viewing Log Entries

- Each log entry provides details about the invocation, including execution

time, payload, and any error messages.
- You can also use the **Logs Viewer** to analyze logs in real-time, set up alerts based on log entries, and create log-based metrics.

Example of a Log Entry in Google Cloud Functions:

plaintext

2024-10-11T12:34:56.789Z info YourFunctionName: Event received: {"data":"sample"}

2024-10-11T12:34:57.789Z error YourFunctionName: Error processing data: TypeError: Cannot read property 'foo' of undefined

4. Best Practices for Logging in Serverless Applications

To ensure that your logging strategy is effective and manageable, consider these best practices:

- **Use Structured Logging**: Format logs as structured data (e.g., JSON) to make parsing and querying easier. This allows for better integration with log analysis tools and automated processing.
- **Log Meaningful Information**: Capture essential details such as invocation context, event data, and relevant metadata (e.g., user ID). Avoid logging sensitive information, especially in production environments.
- **Implement Log Rotation and Retention Policies**: To avoid excessive storage costs, implement log rotation and set retention policies. Configure your logging service to retain logs only for a necessary period (e.g., 30 days).
- **Leverage Centralized Logging**: For applications spanning multiple functions and cloud services, consider using a centralized logging solution. This approach simplifies monitoring and correlating logs across services.
- **Analyze Logs Regularly**: Schedule regular log analysis sessions to identify patterns, recurring errors, or areas for optimization. Use automated tools to alert you to significant anomalies in your logs.

CHAPTER 12: MONITORING AND DEBUGGING SERVERLESS APPLICATIONS

Summary

Analyzing logs is vital for the successful operation of serverless applications. By effectively utilizing AWS CloudWatch Logs and Google Cloud Logging, developers can gain insights into function performance, troubleshoot issues, and enhance overall application reliability. Implementing best practices in logging will facilitate better monitoring, improve response times to incidents, and support continuous improvement in serverless architectures.

12.6 Handling Failures and Retries in Serverless Applications

In a serverless architecture, failures can occur due to various reasons, including timeout issues, dependency failures, or transient network problems. Understanding how to effectively handle failures and implement retry mechanisms is crucial for building resilient serverless applications. This section discusses best practices for failure handling and retry strategies in AWS Lambda and Google Cloud Functions.

1. Understanding Failure Types

Failures in serverless applications can be categorized into three main types:

- **Transient Failures**: Temporary issues that resolve themselves, such as network interruptions or external service unavailability.
- **Permanent Failures**: Errors that occur due to incorrect data or code logic, which require investigation and remediation.
- **Timeout Failures**: Occur when a function exceeds its execution time limit, resulting in an abrupt termination.

2. Implementing Retry Strategies

Both AWS Lambda and Google Cloud Functions provide built-in mechanisms to handle retries for asynchronous invocations. Here's how to implement these strategies effectively:

AWS Lambda:

- **Automatic Retries**: AWS Lambda automatically retries asynchronous invocations (like those from S3 or SNS) twice by default. You can customize the retry behavior in the event source mapping.

- **Dead Letter Queues (DLQ)**: For events that fail after retries, configure a DLQ (either SQS or SNS) to capture failed events for later analysis and reprocessing. This helps ensure no events are lost.

Example Configuration for DLQ in AWS:

json

```
{
    "FunctionName": "YourFunctionName",
    "DeadLetterConfig": {
        "TargetArn": "arn:aws:sqs:region:account-id:your-queue"
    }
}
```

Google Cloud Functions:

- **Automatic Retries**: Google Cloud Functions also retries asynchronous invocations automatically. The default behavior is to retry failed functions until they succeed or until a maximum retry time is reached.
- **Error Reporting and Notification**: Utilize Google Cloud Monitoring and Error Reporting to track function failures and receive alerts when issues arise.

3. Custom Retry Logic

In addition to built-in retries, you may want to implement custom retry logic within your function code for more granular control. This can include:

- **Exponential Backoff**: Introduce delays between retries that increase exponentially, which can reduce the load on services experiencing issues.

Example of Exponential Backoff in JavaScript:

javascript

```
async function retryWithBackoff(fn, retries = 3, delay = 1000) {
```

```
for (let i = 0; i < retries; i++) {
try {
return await fn();
} catch (error) {
if (i === retries - 1) throw error; // Rethrow if out of retries
await new Promise((resolve) => setTimeout(resolve, delay));
delay *= 2; // Double the delay for the next retry
}
}
}
```

- **Circuit Breaker Pattern**: Implement a circuit breaker to prevent your application from making calls to services that are failing consistently. This can reduce strain on services and allow them to recover.

4. Logging and Monitoring Failures

Effective logging is essential for identifying and diagnosing failures. Implement structured logging to capture relevant information such as:

- **Error Codes**: Capture and log error codes returned by external services or APIs.
- **Invocation Context**: Include details like request IDs, timestamps, and payloads to understand the context of failures.
- **User Notifications**: Implement mechanisms to notify users or administrators about critical failures that require immediate attention.

Utilizing tools like AWS CloudWatch or Google Cloud Logging helps you track failures and alerts you to potential issues proactively.

Summary

Handling failures and implementing retry mechanisms are crucial components of building resilient serverless applications. By leveraging built-in retry features, configuring dead letter queues, and implementing custom retry logic, developers can ensure that their applications can gracefully handle transient issues while minimizing data loss. Logging and monitoring provide the necessary visibility to diagnose problems quickly, allowing for prompt resolution and continuous improvement.

CHAPTER 13: SCALING SERVERLESS APPLICATIONS

13.1 Horizontal vs. Vertical Scaling in Serverless

Scaling is a fundamental aspect of application architecture, especially in serverless environments where workloads can fluctuate significantly. Understanding the differences between horizontal and vertical scaling is crucial for optimizing the performance and cost-effectiveness of serverless applications.

1. Horizontal Scaling

Horizontal scaling involves adding more instances of a service to handle increased load. In serverless architectures, this means deploying additional function instances to process requests concurrently.

Benefits of Horizontal Scaling:

- **Increased Concurrency**: Serverless platforms automatically manage the scaling of function instances based on the incoming request volume. This allows for handling multiple requests simultaneously without manual intervention.
- **Cost-Effectiveness**: You pay only for the compute resources consumed during the execution of your functions, making it economical for workloads with variable demand.
- **Fault Tolerance**: If one instance fails, others can continue to handle requests, enhancing the overall reliability of the application.

Example Scenario: Imagine a serverless e-commerce application that experiences a surge in traffic during a holiday sale. The serverless platform (e.g., AWS Lambda or Google Cloud Functions) automatically scales out by creating multiple instances of the function to handle the increased number of customer requests, ensuring that users experience minimal latency.

2. Vertical Scaling

Vertical scaling, also known as "scaling up," involves increasing the resources (CPU, memory) allocated to a single instance of a service. While vertical scaling can enhance performance, it is often limited by the maximum resource capacities of the serverless platform.

Considerations for Vertical Scaling:

- **Resource Limits**: Serverless platforms impose limits on the maximum memory and execution time for functions. For example, AWS Lambda has a memory limit ranging from 128 MB to 10 GB. If your application requires more resources than allowed, vertical scaling may not be an option.
- **Single Point of Failure**: In a vertically scaled environment, if the single instance encounters an issue, it can impact the entire service's availability.

Example Scenario: If a serverless function is processing large datasets and experiences performance issues, you might choose to increase the memory allocation of that function. While this can improve processing speed, it may not be as effective as horizontal scaling if demand significantly increases.

3. Best Practices for Scaling Serverless Applications

To effectively scale serverless applications, consider the following best practices:

- **Leverage Built-In Scaling**: Take advantage of the automatic scaling features provided by serverless platforms. Ensure that your functions are stateless and can be executed concurrently.
- **Optimize Function Execution Time**: Analyze and optimize the execution time of your functions. Reducing execution time not only

improves performance but also lowers costs.
- **Use Async Processing**: For tasks that do not require immediate responses, consider using asynchronous processing techniques, such as event-driven architectures with message queues (e.g., AWS SQS, Google Pub/Sub) to manage workloads efficiently.
- **Monitor Performance Metrics**: Regularly monitor performance metrics and application logs. Utilize tools like AWS CloudWatch or Google Cloud Monitoring to track function performance and make data-driven decisions for scaling.
- **Configure Timeout Settings**: Ensure that timeout settings for functions are appropriate for the expected workload. Adjusting these settings can prevent unnecessary failures during high-demand periods.

Summary

Scaling serverless applications effectively requires a solid understanding of horizontal and vertical scaling principles. While horizontal scaling offers significant benefits in terms of concurrency and fault tolerance, vertical scaling can be useful in specific scenarios where resource allocation is necessary. By following best practices and leveraging the capabilities of serverless platforms, developers can create responsive, resilient, and cost-effective applications that can handle varying workloads with ease.

13.2 Auto-Scaling with AWS Lambda and Google Cloud Functions

Auto-scaling is one of the most significant advantages of serverless architectures, enabling applications to adapt automatically to varying workloads without manual intervention. Both AWS Lambda and Google Cloud Functions are designed to automatically scale in response to incoming requests, but they have distinct mechanisms and features for handling auto-scaling.

1. Auto-Scaling in AWS Lambda

AWS Lambda is inherently designed for auto-scaling. When an event triggers a Lambda function, AWS provisions and manages the required infrastructure to run that function. Here's how it works:

- **Concurrency Limits**: AWS Lambda can handle multiple instances of a function running concurrently. Each function can scale to meet demand, but there is a default limit on the number of concurrent executions (typically 1,000 concurrent executions per region). If you expect higher traffic, you can request an increase in this limit.
- **Event Sources**: AWS Lambda integrates with various event sources, such as S3, DynamoDB, Kinesis, and API Gateway. Each of these services can trigger Lambda functions, allowing them to scale based on incoming events. For example, if a high volume of files is uploaded to an S3 bucket, multiple instances of a Lambda function can be invoked concurrently to process those files.
- **Provisioned Concurrency**: AWS Lambda offers an option called "Provisioned Concurrency," allowing you to pre-warm a specific number of function instances. This reduces cold start times for critical applications, ensuring that instances are available to handle requests immediately.
- **Cold Starts**: It's essential to consider the concept of cold starts, which occur when a function is invoked for the first time or after a period of inactivity. Cold starts can introduce latency, so employing strategies like Provisioned Concurrency can help mitigate this issue.

2. Auto-Scaling in Google Cloud Functions

Google Cloud Functions also provides robust auto-scaling capabilities, designed to handle varying workloads efficiently. Here's how Google Cloud achieves auto-scaling:

- **Dynamic Scaling**: Google Cloud Functions automatically scales in response to incoming traffic without needing configuration. Each function can scale up to the maximum allowed instances based on demand.
- **Concurrency Controls**: Each Cloud Function can handle multiple requests concurrently. By default, each function can handle up to 60 concurrent requests, but you can adjust this based on your needs. If the load exceeds the concurrency limit, Google Cloud Functions

automatically provisions new instances to handle the additional requests.

- **Integration with Other Google Cloud Services**: Similar to AWS Lambda, Google Cloud Functions integrates seamlessly with various Google Cloud services, such as Pub/Sub, Cloud Storage, and Firestore. These integrations facilitate event-driven architectures that can auto-scale based on the rate of incoming events.
- **Cold Start Management**: Google Cloud Functions also experience cold starts, especially for infrequently invoked functions. Google provides various techniques to mitigate cold starts, such as optimizing function size and using regional deployments.

3. Best Practices for Auto-Scaling in Serverless Applications

To effectively leverage auto-scaling in AWS Lambda and Google Cloud Functions, consider the following best practices:

- **Design for Concurrency**: Structure your functions to be stateless and capable of handling multiple concurrent executions. This design is essential for taking full advantage of the auto-scaling capabilities.
- **Use Efficient Event Sources**: Choose event sources that provide reliable triggers and allow for efficient scaling. For example, use SQS or Pub/Sub to queue tasks, ensuring that your functions can process them at a manageable pace.
- **Monitor and Optimize**: Utilize monitoring tools such as AWS CloudWatch and Google Cloud Monitoring to track function performance. Identify bottlenecks and optimize function code to improve response times and reduce costs.
- **Handle Failure Gracefully**: Implement error handling and retries to ensure that your functions can manage transient failures without impacting user experience.
- **Test Under Load**: Conduct load testing to understand how your application behaves under different traffic conditions. This testing helps identify limits and allows for adjustments to concurrency settings.

Summary

Auto-scaling is a powerful feature of serverless architectures, enabling applications to respond dynamically to varying workloads. Both AWS Lambda and Google Cloud Functions offer robust auto-scaling capabilities, allowing developers to focus on building applications without worrying about managing infrastructure. By understanding how auto-scaling works in each platform and following best practices, you can create responsive and efficient serverless applications.

13.3 Handling High Traffic and Load Balancing

Handling high traffic and ensuring that applications remain responsive during peak loads are critical components of building scalable serverless applications. Serverless architectures, such as AWS Lambda and Google Cloud Functions, offer built-in mechanisms for dealing with sudden spikes in traffic, but it's essential to understand how these systems manage load balancing and traffic distribution effectively.

1. Understanding Load Balancing in Serverless

Load balancing is the process of distributing incoming application traffic across multiple instances of a service to ensure no single instance is overwhelmed. In a serverless environment, this concept is inherently integrated, as the cloud provider manages the underlying infrastructure. Here's how it works:

- **Dynamic Provisioning**: When a serverless function is invoked, the cloud provider automatically provisions resources based on the incoming request volume. This dynamic provisioning allows multiple instances of a function to run simultaneously, effectively distributing the load.
- **Automatic Scaling**: Both AWS Lambda and Google Cloud Functions automatically scale to handle increased traffic. If multiple requests come in at once, the cloud provider will spin up additional instances of the function to manage the load, ensuring that users experience minimal latency.
- **Traffic Routing**: The cloud provider's infrastructure intelligently routes requests to the available instances of the function. This routing minimizes

response times and balances the load across all running instances.

2. Strategies for Handling High Traffic in AWS Lambda

AWS Lambda provides several strategies to ensure applications can handle high traffic efficiently:

- **API Gateway Throttling**: When using AWS API Gateway in front of Lambda functions, you can configure throttling settings to limit the number of requests per second. This setting helps prevent overwhelming your backend and provides a buffer during unexpected traffic spikes.
- **Provisioned Concurrency**: As mentioned earlier, Provisioned Concurrency allows you to pre-warm a specific number of function instances, ensuring they are ready to handle requests immediately. This feature is especially useful during known traffic spikes (e.g., product launches, marketing campaigns).
- **Amazon CloudFront**: Integrating AWS Lambda with Amazon CloudFront, a content delivery network (CDN), can enhance performance. CloudFront caches responses at edge locations, reducing latency and distributing the load more effectively.

3. Strategies for Handling High Traffic in Google Cloud Functions

Google Cloud Functions also provides robust strategies for managing high traffic:

- **Google Cloud Load Balancing**: When deploying functions behind Google Cloud Load Balancer, you can handle traffic routing efficiently. This setup allows for even distribution of traffic to various function instances, ensuring no single instance is overloaded.
- **Scaling Policies**: Google Cloud Functions allows you to configure scaling policies based on the average request load. This capability ensures that the number of function instances can adjust automatically based on real-time traffic conditions.
- **Integration with Firebase**: If your application involves real-time data or

mobile traffic, integrating Google Cloud Functions with Firebase can help manage high loads effectively. Firebase handles traffic spikes gracefully, allowing functions to respond to events without being overwhelmed.

4. Best Practices for Handling High Traffic

To effectively manage high traffic and ensure optimal performance in serverless applications, consider the following best practices:

- **Optimize Function Performance**: Write efficient code that executes quickly. Minimize cold starts by optimizing package size and leveraging warm-up techniques such as Provisioned Concurrency in AWS Lambda.
- **Implement Caching**: Use caching strategies to store frequently accessed data. This approach reduces the number of requests hitting your serverless functions and can significantly improve response times.
- **Utilize Asynchronous Processing**: Offload heavy processing tasks to asynchronous services (like AWS SQS, Google Pub/Sub) that can queue requests for later processing. This design allows your functions to remain responsive to incoming traffic while managing background tasks.
- **Monitor Performance Metrics**: Regularly monitor key performance metrics, such as response times and error rates, using tools like AWS CloudWatch and Google Cloud Monitoring. Analyzing these metrics can help identify bottlenecks and inform scaling decisions.
- **Load Testing**: Conduct load testing to simulate high traffic scenarios and understand how your serverless application performs under stress. This testing can help you identify weak points and optimize accordingly.

Summary

Handling high traffic and ensuring effective load balancing are essential for building scalable serverless applications. By leveraging the auto-scaling features of AWS Lambda and Google Cloud Functions, along with strategies such as caching, asynchronous processing, and performance monitoring, you can create resilient applications that deliver a consistent user experience, even during peak loads.

13.4 Managing Cold Starts in Serverless Environments

Cold starts are a common challenge in serverless architectures, particularly for platforms like AWS Lambda and Google Cloud Functions. A cold start occurs when a serverless function is invoked after being idle for a period of time, causing the cloud provider to provision the necessary resources and initialize the function environment. This process can introduce latency, which may affect the user experience, especially for applications requiring low response times.

1. Understanding Cold Starts

When a serverless function is triggered for the first time or after a period of inactivity, the cloud provider must allocate infrastructure resources, load the function's code, and set up the execution environment. This process can take anywhere from a few milliseconds to several seconds, depending on various factors, including:

- **The Size of the Deployment Package**: Larger packages take longer to load into memory.
- **The Initialization Code**: Any code that runs before the actual function logic can delay execution.
- **The Runtime Environment**: Different runtimes (e.g., Node.js, Python, Java) may have varying initialization times.

Cold starts are particularly problematic for latency-sensitive applications, such as real-time APIs or interactive user interfaces.

2. Strategies to Mitigate Cold Starts

While cold starts cannot be completely eliminated, several strategies can help minimize their impact:

- **Provisioned Concurrency (AWS Lambda)**: Provisioned Concurrency allows you to pre-warm a specified number of function instances, ensuring they are always available to handle requests. This feature is especially beneficial during predictable traffic spikes, as it eliminates cold starts for pre-warmed instances.

- **Keep Functions Warm**: Implement a strategy to keep functions warm by periodically invoking them using scheduled events (e.g., AWS CloudWatch Events or Google Cloud Scheduler). Regular invocations can prevent functions from going idle, reducing the likelihood of cold starts.
- **Optimize Initialization Code**: Minimize the amount of code that runs during the initialization phase. Avoid loading large libraries or performing complex calculations upfront. Instead, defer these operations until they are necessary, and consider lazy loading for infrequently used resources.
- **Reduce Package Size**: Optimize your deployment package by removing unnecessary dependencies and using smaller libraries. Tools like Webpack or Parcel can help bundle and minify code, reducing load times.
- **Use Lightweight Runtimes**: Choose runtimes that have faster startup times. For instance, Node.js is often faster to initialize than Java or .NET. If possible, evaluate the trade-offs of using different runtimes based on your application's requirements.

3. Measuring Cold Start Impact

To effectively manage cold starts, it is essential to measure their impact on your application. Monitoring tools can help you track metrics related to cold starts:

- **Monitoring with CloudWatch (AWS)**: Use AWS CloudWatch to monitor invocation metrics, including the duration of cold starts. Analyze the data to determine patterns and identify when cold starts occur most frequently.
- **Google Cloud Monitoring**: Similarly, use Google Cloud Monitoring to track latency and performance metrics related to function invocations. Set up alerts to notify you when cold start latency exceeds acceptable thresholds.
- **Logging**: Implement logging in your functions to capture detailed information about invocation times, including cold start durations. This data can help identify optimization opportunities.

4. Best Practices for Managing Cold Starts

To effectively manage cold starts in serverless applications, consider the following best practices:

- **Benchmark and Optimize**: Regularly benchmark your functions to measure cold start times and optimize based on findings. Make performance improvements a continuous part of your development process.
- **Test in Production**: Test your application under real-world conditions to understand how cold starts impact user experience. Use canary deployments to gradually roll out changes and monitor their effects on latency.
- **Educate Your Team**: Ensure that all team members are aware of the cold start issue and the strategies to mitigate it. Sharing knowledge can lead to more effective optimizations across the development lifecycle.

Summary

Managing cold starts is a critical aspect of building responsive serverless applications. By understanding the factors that contribute to cold starts and implementing effective strategies, such as Provisioned Concurrency, optimizing initialization code, and monitoring performance metrics, you can significantly reduce the impact of cold starts on your applications. This proactive approach will help maintain a seamless user experience, even in a serverless architecture.

13.5 Strategies for Cost Optimization in Serverless Scaling

Scaling in a serverless environment can lead to cost efficiency, but without proper management, it can also result in unexpected expenses. Understanding how to optimize costs while effectively scaling your applications is crucial for maintaining profitability. Here are several strategies to help you achieve cost optimization in serverless scaling.

1. Understanding Cost Structure of Serverless Services

Before diving into optimization strategies, it's essential to understand the cost structure of serverless services like AWS Lambda and Google Cloud

Functions:

- **Invocation Costs**: You are charged for the number of requests your functions handle. Each invocation has a fixed cost, which can accumulate quickly if your function is invoked frequently.
- **Duration Costs**: You pay for the compute time your function consumes. This is measured in milliseconds, so optimizing the execution time of your functions can lead to significant savings.
- **Provisioned Concurrency Costs**: If you use features like AWS Lambda's Provisioned Concurrency, you will incur additional costs for the provisioned instances, regardless of whether they are invoked.
- **Data Transfer Costs**: Charges for data transfer can also add up, especially if your functions interact with external APIs or databases.

2. Optimize Function Execution Time

Minimizing the duration of your function executions can lead to substantial cost savings:

- **Efficient Code**: Write efficient, optimized code to reduce execution time. Use performance profiling tools to identify bottlenecks and optimize critical sections of your code.
- **Use of Caching**: Implement caching strategies, such as storing frequently accessed data in memory or using services like AWS ElastiCache or Google Cloud Memorystore. Caching reduces the need to fetch data repeatedly from slower data sources.
- **Asynchronous Processing**: If your function performs tasks that can run independently, consider using asynchronous programming techniques. This can reduce the overall execution time and allow for better resource utilization.

3. Optimize Resource Allocation

Adjusting resource allocation can help you manage costs effectively:

- **Adjust Memory Allocation**: In serverless environments, you can configure the memory allocated to your functions. Higher memory allocation typically results in faster execution times, but it also increases costs. Experiment with different memory settings to find the optimal balance between performance and cost.
- **Optimize Concurrency Settings**: For services like AWS Lambda, where you can control concurrency limits, adjust the settings based on your application's load patterns. Setting appropriate concurrency limits can help prevent over-provisioning and unnecessary costs.

4. Use Scheduled Functions Wisely

Scheduled functions (using CloudWatch Events, Google Cloud Scheduler, etc.) can incur costs even when they are not heavily utilized:

- **Evaluate the Frequency of Scheduled Events**: Review the frequency of your scheduled invocations. Reducing the frequency can save costs, especially for functions that are not time-sensitive.
- **Implement Conditional Execution**: If possible, implement conditional logic within scheduled functions to skip execution unless specific criteria are met (e.g., based on data changes or user requests).

5. Monitor and Analyze Costs

Implement robust monitoring and analysis practices to track and optimize costs:

- **Cost Management Tools**: Utilize tools like AWS Cost Explorer or Google Cloud Billing Reports to visualize and analyze your serverless costs over time. These tools help identify cost trends and highlight areas for optimization.
- **Set Budgets and Alerts**: Establish budgets for your serverless functions and set up alerts to notify you when spending exceeds expected thresholds. This proactive approach can help you react before costs escalate.
- **Analyze Usage Patterns**: Regularly analyze usage patterns to identify

underutilized resources or functions that could be optimized. This analysis can reveal opportunities for reducing costs.

6. Leverage Free Tiers and Discounts

Take advantage of the free tiers and discounts offered by cloud providers:

- **Free Tier Usage**: Both AWS and Google Cloud offer generous free tiers for their serverless products. Make sure you are aware of these limits and optimize your usage to stay within the free tier whenever possible.
- **Savings Plans and Commitments**: For consistent workloads, consider committing to usage discounts or savings plans offered by cloud providers. This can lead to significant savings over time.

Summary

Cost optimization is an essential aspect of scaling serverless applications. By understanding the cost structure, optimizing function execution times, and leveraging resource allocation strategies, you can effectively manage costs while enjoying the benefits of serverless architecture. Regular monitoring and analysis of your costs will help you make informed decisions and adjustments, ensuring your serverless applications remain both efficient and economical.

13.6 Real-World Examples of Scaling Serverless Applications

Understanding theoretical concepts of scaling serverless applications is crucial, but seeing how they translate into real-world success stories can provide invaluable insights. Here are a few notable examples of organizations that have effectively scaled their serverless applications, illustrating diverse use cases and the strategies they employed.

1. Netflix

Overview: Netflix uses AWS Lambda for various functions within its streaming platform, including encoding and data processing tasks.

Scaling Strategy: To handle millions of concurrent users, Netflix leverages AWS Lambda's auto-scaling capabilities. By deploying Lambda functions to manage real-time data processing, they ensure that their system can scale dynamically with user demand. This means they can handle peak loads seamlessly while optimizing costs by only paying for the compute time they use.

2. Coca-Cola

Overview: Coca-Cola implemented serverless architecture for its internal systems to streamline operations.

Scaling Strategy: Coca-Cola utilizes AWS Lambda to manage its order processing system, which experiences varying loads based on seasonal demand. By using a serverless approach, they can quickly scale their processing capabilities without the overhead of managing server infrastructure. This flexibility allows Coca-Cola to respond to fluctuations in demand effectively, optimizing their operational costs.

3. iRobot

Overview: iRobot, the company behind the Roomba, employs AWS Lambda to process telemetry data from its devices.

Scaling Strategy: With millions of devices sending data concurrently, iRobot relies on AWS Lambda to process this information in real time. By leveraging event-driven architecture, they ensure that each data packet is handled efficiently, scaling their processing power automatically as needed. This allows them to maintain performance while keeping costs in check, as they only use resources during data processing events.

4. Serverless Framework

Overview: The Serverless Framework is an open-source framework that simplifies the development and deployment of serverless applications.

Scaling Strategy: The Serverless Framework team uses their own tool to deploy applications across various cloud providers. They demonstrate how to manage different serverless environments and scale applications by implementing CI/CD practices. This allows for quick deployments and updates, enabling them to respond to user feedback and improve their service without worrying about server management.

5. The Guardian

Overview: The Guardian, a UK-based news organization, has adopted serverless architecture to support its content delivery systems.

Scaling Strategy: The Guardian uses AWS Lambda and Google Cloud

Functions to handle spikes in traffic during major news events. By implementing serverless solutions, they can quickly scale their content delivery, ensuring that their website remains responsive during peak times. This capability has proven crucial for delivering breaking news, allowing them to provide timely information to their audience without incurring excessive infrastructure costs.

Conclusion

Scaling serverless applications presents unique opportunities and challenges. Real-world examples demonstrate that organizations across various sectors can effectively harness the power of serverless architecture to achieve significant scalability and cost efficiency. By employing strategies such as event-driven architecture, efficient resource management, and leveraging cloud provider capabilities, businesses can adapt to changing demands and maintain high performance.

CHAPTER 14: SECURITY IN SERVERLESS ARCHITECTURE

14.1 Best Practices for Securing AWS Lambda

Securing AWS Lambda functions is crucial for maintaining the integrity and confidentiality of serverless applications. Given that serverless architectures operate in a shared environment, implementing robust security practices is essential. Here are key best practices for securing AWS Lambda:

1. Implement Least Privilege Access

- **Use IAM Roles**: Assign AWS Identity and Access Management (IAM) roles with the minimum permissions necessary for Lambda functions. This principle of least privilege ensures that functions can only access the resources they need.
- **Refine Permissions**: Regularly review and refine permissions as the application evolves. Avoid broad permissions that could expose sensitive resources.

2. Validate Input Data

- **Input Validation**: Always validate and sanitize input data to prevent common attacks such as injection attacks and data corruption.
- **Use Schema Validation**: Implement JSON schema validation to ensure that incoming data conforms to expected formats and types.

3. Enable VPC Integration

- **Private Network**: If your Lambda functions need to access resources within a Virtual Private Cloud (VPC), configure them to run inside the VPC. This adds an additional layer of security, preventing direct access from the internet.
- **NAT Gateway**: Use a NAT Gateway to allow outbound internet access for functions in a VPC without exposing them to the public internet.

4. Secure Environment Variables

- **Use Encrypted Variables**: Store sensitive data, such as API keys and database credentials, in environment variables. Enable encryption for these variables using AWS Key Management Service (KMS).
- **Limit Access**: Control access to environment variables through IAM policies, ensuring only authorized entities can read them.

5. Monitor and Log Activities

- **Enable AWS CloudTrail**: Use AWS CloudTrail to log all API calls made to your AWS account, including those made by Lambda functions. This provides a comprehensive audit trail for security and compliance.
- **Use Amazon CloudWatch**: Monitor Lambda performance and security metrics through Amazon CloudWatch. Set up alerts for unusual activity that may indicate a security incident.

6. Implement API Gateway Security

- **Enable CORS**: Configure Cross-Origin Resource Sharing (CORS) to restrict which domains can access your API Gateway endpoints.
- **Throttle Requests**: Use API Gateway throttling features to protect your Lambda functions from excessive requests and potential denial-of-service attacks.

- **Require Authentication**: Implement authentication mechanisms, such as API keys or AWS Cognito, to restrict access to your APIs.

7. Perform Regular Security Audits

- **Conduct Audits**: Regularly audit your Lambda functions, IAM roles, and overall architecture for vulnerabilities. Use tools such as AWS Trusted Advisor and AWS Inspector to identify security gaps.
- **Penetration Testing**: Perform penetration testing to identify potential vulnerabilities and validate the effectiveness of your security controls.

8. Update and Patch Dependencies

- **Stay Current**: Regularly update and patch any dependencies your Lambda functions rely on to mitigate vulnerabilities. Use automated tools to identify outdated libraries and frameworks.
- **Use Dependency Scanners**: Incorporate tools like Snyk or npm audit to scan for vulnerabilities in your code dependencies.

Summary

Securing AWS Lambda functions requires a proactive and comprehensive approach. By implementing best practices such as least privilege access, input validation, VPC integration, and regular security audits, organizations can significantly reduce their risk of security breaches. As serverless architectures continue to gain popularity, understanding and addressing security concerns is paramount for maintaining trust and protecting sensitive data.

14.2 Google Cloud Functions Security Guidelines

Securing Google Cloud Functions is essential to ensure that your serverless applications remain robust against various security threats. Google Cloud provides several tools and best practices to help secure your functions. Here are key guidelines to follow:

1. Implement Principle of Least Privilege

- **IAM Roles**: Assign IAM roles to your Cloud Functions with the least amount of privilege necessary to perform their tasks. Ensure that each function has specific permissions tailored to its operations.
- **Custom Roles**: Utilize custom IAM roles to fine-tune permissions, granting access only to the services and resources required for each function.

2. Secure Your Code

- **Input Validation**: Always validate and sanitize input data to protect against SQL injection, cross-site scripting (XSS), and other forms of attacks. Ensure that inputs conform to expected formats and types.
- **Use Security Libraries**: Leverage established security libraries and frameworks to implement common security practices, such as authentication and input validation.

3. Enable VPC Service Controls

- **Private Access**: When applicable, run Cloud Functions in a Virtual Private Cloud (VPC) to control access to your function and its resources. This restricts access to only those within your VPC, enhancing security.
- **VPC Service Controls**: Use VPC Service Controls to create a security perimeter around your resources and restrict data exfiltration.

4. Protect Environment Variables

- **Encryption**: Store sensitive configuration data, such as API keys and database passwords, in environment variables. Ensure these variables are encrypted using Google Cloud's built-in encryption mechanisms.
- **Limited Access**: Restrict access to environment variables by applying IAM policies that control who can view or modify them.

5. Use Cloud Armor for API Security

CHAPTER 14: SECURITY IN SERVERLESS ARCHITECTURE

- **Application Security**: Implement Google Cloud Armor to provide a security layer for your APIs. This service protects against Distributed Denial of Service (DDoS) attacks and allows for traffic filtering based on predefined rules.
- **WAF Policies**: Use Web Application Firewall (WAF) policies to define rules that block specific traffic patterns that may indicate malicious activity.

6. Monitor and Log Activities

- **Cloud Audit Logs**: Enable Google Cloud Audit Logs to track API activity and changes to your functions and related resources. This helps in auditing and troubleshooting any security incidents.
- **Stackdriver Logging**: Use Stackdriver Logging to collect logs from your Cloud Functions, allowing you to monitor performance and security events in real-time.

7. API Security with Identity-Aware Proxy (IAP)

- **Access Control**: Utilize Identity-Aware Proxy to manage access to your Cloud Functions. This allows you to authenticate users and manage their permissions at a granular level.
- **OAuth 2.0**: Implement OAuth 2.0 for user authentication, ensuring that only authorized users can access your functions.

8. Conduct Regular Security Assessments

- **Vulnerability Scanning**: Regularly perform vulnerability assessments on your code and configurations using tools like Google Cloud Security Scanner to identify potential weaknesses.
- **Penetration Testing**: Engage in penetration testing to simulate attacks and assess the robustness of your security measures.

9. Update Dependencies Regularly

- **Dependency Management**: Keep your function's dependencies up to date to mitigate known vulnerabilities. Use tools like npm audit to identify outdated or vulnerable packages.
- **Automated Tools**: Leverage automated tools to monitor your dependencies for security issues and receive alerts when updates are necessary.

Summary

Securing Google Cloud Functions requires a multifaceted approach that encompasses best practices in access control, code security, network configurations, and monitoring. By implementing these security guidelines, organizations can enhance the security posture of their serverless applications, protect sensitive data, and reduce the risk of security incidents.

14.3 Securing Serverless Storage (S3, Google Cloud Storage)

In serverless architectures, data storage is a critical component, as it directly affects the security and integrity of your applications. Both AWS S3 (Simple Storage Service) and Google Cloud Storage offer robust storage solutions, but securing them requires following best practices to prevent unauthorized access and data breaches. Here are essential guidelines for securing serverless storage:

1. Implement Fine-Grained Access Control

- **Bucket Policies and IAM Roles**:
- For **AWS S3**, use bucket policies to define access permissions at the bucket level, and leverage IAM roles for granular control over who can access specific objects within your buckets.
- For **Google Cloud Storage**, use IAM roles and policies to grant permissions on a per-bucket or per-object basis, ensuring that only authorized users and services can access the data.
- **Principle of Least Privilege**:
- Always adhere to the principle of least privilege by granting only the permissions necessary for users and services to perform their functions.

2. Use Encryption for Data at Rest and in Transit

- **Encryption at Rest**:
- Both AWS S3 and Google Cloud Storage offer server-side encryption options. For S3, you can choose between SSE-S3 (Amazon-managed keys), SSE-KMS (customer-managed keys), or SSE-C (customer-provided keys). In Google Cloud Storage, use Google-managed encryption keys or customer-managed keys for additional control.
- **Encryption in Transit**:
- Ensure that data transmitted to and from your storage solutions is encrypted using HTTPS. This protects data from eavesdropping and man-in-the-middle attacks.

3. Enable Versioning and Object Locking

- **S3 Versioning**:
- Enable versioning in AWS S3 to preserve, retrieve, and restore every version of an object stored in a bucket. This feature is useful for recovering from accidental deletions or overwrites.
- **Object Locking**:
- Utilize S3 Object Locking to prevent objects from being deleted or overwritten for a specified retention period, helping protect sensitive data.
- **Google Cloud Storage Object Versioning**:
- Similar to S3, Google Cloud Storage allows you to enable object versioning to maintain previous versions of objects, offering an additional layer of data protection.

4. Monitor Access Logs and Use Alerts

- **AWS S3 Access Logs**:
- Enable access logging for S3 buckets to track requests made to your buckets. Analyze these logs for unusual access patterns or unauthorized

access attempts.
- **Google Cloud Storage Access Logs**:
- Activate access logs in Google Cloud Storage to monitor requests and identify potential security threats.
- **Set Up Alerts**:
- Use monitoring tools like AWS CloudWatch or Google Cloud Monitoring to create alerts for suspicious activities, such as unauthorized access attempts or unusual access patterns.

5. **Secure API Access to Storage Services**

- **Authentication and Authorization**:
- Always require authentication for accessing storage services via APIs. Use OAuth 2.0 for secure token-based authentication.
- Ensure that your serverless functions interacting with storage services authenticate properly and have the necessary permissions to perform actions.

6. **Implement Data Lifecycle Policies**

- **AWS S3 Lifecycle Policies**:
- Set lifecycle policies to automate the transition of objects to cheaper storage classes or delete objects after a specified period. This helps manage costs while ensuring data is retained only as long as necessary.
- **Google Cloud Storage Lifecycle Management**:
- Use lifecycle management policies in Google Cloud Storage to automatically manage your data based on predefined rules, ensuring efficient use of storage resources.

7. **Conduct Regular Security Audits**

- **Periodic Review**:
- Regularly review access policies, encryption settings, and logging config-

urations to ensure they align with best practices and your organization's security policies.

- **Vulnerability Assessments**:
- Perform vulnerability assessments to identify potential security weaknesses in your storage configurations and address them promptly.

Summary

Securing serverless storage solutions such as AWS S3 and Google Cloud Storage requires implementing a combination of access control, encryption, monitoring, and lifecycle management strategies. By following these best practices, organizations can ensure the integrity and confidentiality of their data, mitigate risks associated with unauthorized access, and maintain compliance with data protection regulations.

14.4 Protecting Serverless APIs with Firewalls and Authentication

In a serverless architecture, APIs serve as the primary interface for client applications to communicate with backend services. Given their accessibility and critical role, it is imperative to implement robust security measures to protect these APIs from unauthorized access, attacks, and data breaches. This section will discuss various strategies for securing serverless APIs using firewalls, authentication methods, and other best practices.

1. Implement Web Application Firewalls (WAF)

- **What is a WAF?**
- A Web Application Firewall (WAF) filters and monitors HTTP traffic between a web application and the Internet. WAFs help protect APIs from common threats, such as SQL injection, cross-site scripting (XSS), and other web application attacks.
- **Using AWS WAF with API Gateway**:
- AWS WAF can be easily integrated with Amazon API Gateway to provide an additional layer of security. You can create rules to allow, block, or count web requests based on specific conditions such as IP addresses, HTTP headers, or request body patterns.
- **Using Google Cloud Armor with Google Cloud Functions**:

- Google Cloud Armor provides WAF capabilities for Google Cloud Functions, allowing you to configure security policies that filter traffic to your APIs based on geographic location, request attributes, and more.

2. Enforce Authentication and Authorization

- **OAuth 2.0 and OpenID Connect**:
- Use OAuth 2.0 for authentication and authorization to control access to your APIs. This standard allows clients to securely access resources without exposing credentials.
- **JSON Web Tokens (JWT)**:
- Implement JWT for stateless authentication. When users log in, they receive a signed token that contains user information and can be used for subsequent API requests. This approach reduces the need for sessions and server-side storage.
- **API Keys**:
- For less sensitive APIs, consider using API keys for authentication. However, keep in mind that API keys should not be considered secure on their own and should be combined with other security measures, such as IP whitelisting or rate limiting.

3. Enable CORS (Cross-Origin Resource Sharing)

- **CORS Configuration**:
- CORS is a security feature implemented by web browsers that restricts web pages from making requests to a different domain than the one that served the web page. Properly configuring CORS for your APIs allows you to control which origins can access your resources.
- **CORS in API Gateway**:
- For AWS API Gateway, you can enable CORS by configuring the appropriate headers, such as Access-Control-Allow-Origin, to specify allowed origins. In Google Cloud Functions, you can manage CORS in your function code to handle preflight requests.

4. Rate Limiting and Throttling

- **Why Rate Limiting?**
- Rate limiting helps prevent abuse and denial-of-service (DoS) attacks by controlling the number of requests a user can make to your API within a specific timeframe.
- **Implementing Rate Limiting**:
- Use AWS API Gateway's built-in throttling capabilities to set limits on requests per second and burst capacity. Similarly, Google Cloud Functions can be configured with quotas to manage usage and prevent overload.

5. Input Validation and Sanitization

- **Validating Input**:
- Ensure that all inputs to your API endpoints are validated and sanitized to protect against injection attacks and other malicious inputs. Use libraries and frameworks that provide built-in validation features.
- **Schema Validation**:
- Implement schema validation to define the expected structure of incoming requests. This can be achieved using JSON Schema or similar libraries that can enforce rules on the data being processed.

6. Monitor and Audit API Activity

- **Logging API Requests**:
- Enable logging for your APIs to track all incoming requests and responses. Use AWS CloudWatch or Google Cloud Logging to collect and analyze logs for unusual activities.
- **Regular Security Audits**:
- Conduct regular audits of your API security configurations, authentication mechanisms, and access logs to identify potential vulnerabilities and remediate them promptly.

Summary

Protecting serverless APIs requires a comprehensive approach that includes implementing web application firewalls, enforcing authentication and authorization, managing CORS, rate limiting, input validation, and monitoring activity. By following these best practices, organizations can significantly enhance the security posture of their serverless applications and mitigate potential threats.

14.5 Managing Secrets in Serverless Applications (AWS Secrets Manager, Google Secret Manager)

In modern software development, managing sensitive information—such as API keys, database credentials, and other secret tokens—has become increasingly crucial. In a serverless architecture, where applications can scale dynamically, securely storing and retrieving these secrets is vital to maintaining security and ensuring operational integrity. This section will discuss best practices for managing secrets in serverless applications, focusing on AWS Secrets Manager and Google Secret Manager.

1. Importance of Secret Management

- **Preventing Data Breaches**:
- Hardcoding secrets directly into application code can lead to serious security vulnerabilities. If the code is exposed or shared inadvertently, sensitive information can be compromised. Using a dedicated secret management tool helps mitigate this risk.
- **Dynamic Configuration**:
- In a serverless environment, functions are ephemeral, meaning they may be created and destroyed frequently. Managing secrets centrally allows applications to retrieve configuration data dynamically at runtime, enhancing flexibility and security.

2. AWS Secrets Manager

- **Overview**:
- AWS Secrets Manager is a fully managed service that helps you protect

CHAPTER 14: SECURITY IN SERVERLESS ARCHITECTURE

access to your applications, services, and IT resources without the upfront investment and on-going maintenance costs of operating your own infrastructure.

- **Key Features**:
- **Secret Rotation**: Secrets Manager enables you to automatically rotate secrets for supported AWS services (like RDS) without requiring code changes.
- **Fine-Grained Access Control**: Use AWS Identity and Access Management (IAM) policies to define who can access which secrets.
- **Audit Logging**: Integration with AWS CloudTrail allows you to track and log all access and changes to secrets.
- **How to Use AWS Secrets Manager**:
- Create a new secret via the AWS Management Console, CLI, or SDK.
- Store your secret, such as a database password.
- Grant your Lambda functions permission to access the secret through IAM roles.
- Retrieve the secret programmatically in your Lambda function using the AWS SDK.

3. Google Secret Manager

- **Overview**:
- Google Secret Manager provides a secure and convenient way to store API keys, passwords, certificates, and other sensitive data. It allows developers to manage secrets centrally while providing fine-grained access control.
- **Key Features**:
- **Versioning**: Secret Manager keeps track of versions, allowing you to manage and revert changes easily.
- **IAM Integration**: Integrates with Google Cloud IAM to provide role-based access control over secrets.
- **Audit Logging**: Secret access and modifications are logged in Google Cloud's operations suite, ensuring accountability.

- **How to Use Google Secret Manager:**
- Create a new secret in the Google Cloud Console or using the gcloud command-line tool.
- Store your sensitive data securely.
- Grant access permissions to Cloud Functions or other Google Cloud services via IAM roles.
- Retrieve the secret using the Google Cloud Client Library for your application.

4. Best Practices for Managing Secrets

- **Use Managed Services:**
- Leverage AWS Secrets Manager or Google Secret Manager instead of rolling out your own secret management system.
- **Apply Principle of Least Privilege:**
- Grant the minimum permissions necessary for services to access secrets. This minimizes the potential impact of a compromised function.
- **Rotate Secrets Regularly:**
- Set up automatic rotation for secrets to minimize the risk of exposure over time. Ensure your application can handle secrets being rotated without downtime.
- **Audit Access:**
- Regularly review access logs to identify any unauthorized attempts to access secrets. Use CloudTrail (AWS) or Cloud Audit Logs (Google Cloud) to track changes and access patterns.
- **Secure Application Code:**
- Avoid hardcoding secrets in your application code. Instead, use environment variables or configuration files that reference secrets stored in a secret manager.

Summary

Effective secret management is crucial in serverless architectures to protect sensitive data from unauthorized access and breaches. By utilizing services like AWS Secrets Manager and Google Secret Manager, organizations can securely store, retrieve, and manage secrets while following best practices such as access control, regular rotation, and auditing. This approach ensures that serverless applications remain secure and resilient against threats.

14.6 Auditing and Compliance in Serverless Architectures

In an era where data privacy and security are paramount, maintaining compliance with industry standards and regulations is crucial for organizations adopting serverless architectures. This section discusses the auditing and compliance aspects in serverless environments, focusing on best practices and tools that can help organizations ensure adherence to security policies and regulatory requirements.

1. Understanding Auditing and Compliance

- **Definition**:
  - Auditing involves systematically examining and evaluating an organization's processes, systems, and controls to ensure they meet established standards and regulations. Compliance refers to adhering to laws, regulations, and industry standards relevant to data protection, privacy, and security.
- **Importance**:
  - Non-compliance can result in significant legal penalties, reputational damage, and loss of customer trust. Regular auditing helps organizations identify vulnerabilities and enforce security policies effectively.

2. Key Regulations and Standards

- **General Data Protection Regulation (GDPR)**:
  - GDPR mandates stringent data protection measures for personal data of EU citizens. Organizations must ensure they have clear policies for data access, retention, and deletion.
- **Health Insurance Portability and Accountability Act (HIPAA)**:
  - HIPAA requires healthcare organizations to protect sensitive patient data. Serverless applications handling health information must implement

appropriate safeguards and maintain detailed logs of access to sensitive information.
- **Payment Card Industry Data Security Standard (PCI DSS)**:
- Organizations handling credit card information must comply with PCI DSS, which outlines security measures to protect payment data. This includes regular audits of system access and data handling processes.

3. Implementing Auditing in Serverless Architectures

- **Use of Logging Services**:
- Leverage cloud-native logging services such as AWS CloudTrail, AWS CloudWatch, Google Cloud Audit Logs, and Google Cloud Logging to monitor and log API calls and access to resources.
- Ensure that all serverless functions log relevant events, including access to sensitive data and modifications to resources.
- **Setting Up Alerts**:
- Configure alerts for suspicious activities, such as unauthorized access attempts, excessive function invocations, or changes to IAM roles and policies.
- **Regular Review of Access Logs**:
- Conduct periodic reviews of access logs to identify anomalies and ensure that only authorized personnel have access to sensitive resources.
- **Conducting Security Audits**:
- Perform regular security audits of serverless applications to assess compliance with organizational policies and regulatory requirements.
- Utilize automated tools for vulnerability scanning and penetration testing to identify weaknesses in serverless architectures.

4. Tools for Compliance Management

- **AWS Config**:
- AWS Config enables you to assess, audit, and evaluate the configurations of AWS resources. It provides a detailed inventory of resources and their

configuration history, allowing you to monitor compliance with best practices and regulatory standards.

- **Google Cloud Security Command Center**:
- This service provides a comprehensive overview of security and compliance for Google Cloud resources, allowing organizations to detect vulnerabilities, assess risks, and manage security policies.
- **Third-Party Compliance Solutions**:
- Consider utilizing third-party tools and platforms designed to assist with compliance monitoring and management, such as Prisma Cloud, Snyk, or Qualys.

Conclusion

In a serverless architecture, where the infrastructure is abstracted away, ensuring auditing and compliance requires diligent attention to security policies and practices. By leveraging cloud-native services for logging, monitoring, and access management, organizations can effectively maintain compliance with regulations such as GDPR, HIPAA, and PCI DSS. Regular audits, combined with the use of automated tools for vulnerability scanning and compliance checks, can help organizations safeguard sensitive data and build trust with their customers.

In summary, as serverless architectures continue to evolve, so too must the strategies for securing and managing them.

CHAPTER 15: SERVERLESS ON OTHER CLOUD PLATFORMS

15.1 Serverless with Microsoft Azure Functions

Microsoft Azure Functions is a serverless compute service that allows users to run event-driven code without worrying about the underlying infrastructure. Azure Functions enables developers to create applications that can automatically scale based on demand and respond to events from various sources.

Key Features of Azure Functions

- **Event-Driven Architecture**: Azure Functions can be triggered by a variety of events, including HTTP requests, timer schedules, message queue entries, and events from Azure services (e.g., Blob Storage, Event Hubs).
- **Multi-Language Support**: Azure Functions supports several programming languages, including JavaScript, C#, Python, Java, and PowerShell, providing flexibility for developers to choose their preferred language.
- **Integration with Azure Services**: Azure Functions can easily integrate with other Azure services such as Azure Logic Apps, Azure Event Grid, Azure Cosmos DB, and Azure Storage, enabling developers to build complex workflows and applications.
- **Consumption-Based Pricing**: With Azure Functions, users are only charged for the compute resources consumed during the execution of functions, making it a cost-effective solution for building applications

CHAPTER 15: SERVERLESS ON OTHER CLOUD PLATFORMS

that experience variable workloads.

Creating Azure Functions

To get started with Azure Functions, follow these steps:

1. **Setting Up Your Azure Account**:

- Sign up for an Azure account if you don't have one. Microsoft offers a free tier that allows you to experiment with Azure Functions.

1. **Creating a Function App**:

- Use the Azure Portal, Azure CLI, or Azure PowerShell to create a Function App, which is a container for one or more functions. You can choose the hosting plan (Consumption or Premium) based on your requirements.

1. **Developing Your Function**:

- You can create functions directly in the Azure Portal using the built-in editor or develop them locally using tools like Visual Studio Code with the Azure Functions extension. Define the function's trigger, input, and output bindings, and write the business logic in your preferred language.

1. **Deploying Your Function**:

- Functions can be deployed using the Azure CLI, Azure DevOps, or directly from your local development environment. Continuous deployment can also be set up using GitHub Actions or Azure DevOps.

Best Practices for Azure Functions

- **Use Durable Functions for Long-Running Processes**:
- Azure Durable Functions allow you to manage long-running workflows

and stateful operations seamlessly. This is particularly useful for processes that require orchestration of multiple functions or when dealing with external systems.
- **Implement Proper Logging and Monitoring**:
- Use Azure Application Insights to monitor performance and diagnose issues. Set up logging within your functions to track execution times, errors, and other relevant metrics.
- **Manage Secrets Safely**:
- Use Azure Key Vault to manage sensitive information, such as connection strings and API keys, securely.
- **Optimize Function Performance**:
- Pay attention to cold start performance by minimizing the initialization time of your functions and using the Premium or Dedicated plans if necessary.

Summary

Microsoft Azure Functions provide a robust serverless platform that empowers developers to build event-driven applications with minimal operational overhead. By leveraging Azure's ecosystem of services and adhering to best practices, organizations can create scalable and efficient applications that meet the demands of modern business environments.

15.2 IBM Cloud Functions: A Serverless Approach

IBM Cloud Functions is a serverless compute platform that allows developers to execute code in response to events without managing the underlying infrastructure. Built on Apache OpenWhisk, IBM Cloud Functions enables developers to build applications that are scalable, flexible, and cost-effective. This platform emphasizes the ease of use and integration with other IBM Cloud services.

Key Features of IBM Cloud Functions

- **Event-Driven Execution**: Functions can be triggered by a variety of events, such as HTTP requests, messages from IBM Cloud Message Hub, or events from various IBM Cloud services. This enables developers to

respond quickly to changes in data or system states.
- **Multi-Language Support**: IBM Cloud Functions supports multiple programming languages, including JavaScript (Node.js), Python, Java, Swift, and more. This flexibility allows developers to use the tools and languages they are most comfortable with.
- **Integration with IBM Cloud Services**: The platform easily integrates with other IBM services such as IBM Cloud Object Storage, IBM Cloud Databases, and IBM Watson services, enabling the creation of sophisticated applications with minimal effort.
- **Auto-Scaling**: IBM Cloud Functions automatically scales based on the workload. Functions can be executed in parallel, allowing applications to handle varying levels of traffic efficiently.

Getting Started with IBM Cloud Functions

To start using IBM Cloud Functions, follow these steps:

1. **Create an IBM Cloud Account**:

- Sign up for an IBM Cloud account to access the cloud platform and its services. IBM offers a free tier with limited resources to explore its capabilities.

1. **Setting Up Your Environment**:

- Use the IBM Cloud Console, IBM Cloud CLI, or SDKs to configure your environment. Install the IBM Cloud CLI to manage functions and services through your command line.

1. **Creating Functions**:

- Functions can be created directly through the IBM Cloud Console or via the command line. Define the function's code and specify the trigger (e.g., HTTP request, Cloud Object Storage event).

1. **Deploying Functions**:

   - Deploy your functions using the IBM Cloud CLI or from the IBM Cloud Console. Functions can also be packaged into actions for easier management.

Best Practices for IBM Cloud Functions

- **Use Actions and Triggers Wisely**:
- Organize your code into actions and set up triggers effectively to ensure that your functions execute promptly and efficiently.
- **Leverage Composition**:
- Use sequences and workflows to compose multiple functions into a single process. This approach allows for better organization and handling of complex workflows.
- **Implement Logging and Monitoring**:
- Utilize IBM Cloud Monitoring and Logging services to track performance, errors, and other key metrics. This helps in diagnosing issues and optimizing function performance.
- **Manage Dependencies Carefully**:
- Ensure that your function code is lightweight and includes only necessary dependencies. Avoid packaging large libraries unless absolutely needed, as this can slow down cold starts.

Summary

IBM Cloud Functions provides a powerful serverless computing platform that simplifies application development and deployment. By enabling developers to focus on writing code rather than managing infrastructure, IBM Cloud Functions accelerates the development process and reduces costs. Integrating seamlessly with other IBM Cloud services, it offers a flexible solution for building scalable and event-driven applications.

15.3 Exploring Serverless Options on Alibaba Cloud

Alibaba Cloud offers a comprehensive suite of serverless computing

CHAPTER 15: SERVERLESS ON OTHER CLOUD PLATFORMS

services, with **Function Compute** being its primary serverless solution. Function Compute enables developers to run code in response to events without having to manage servers or infrastructure, allowing for rapid development and scalability. This service is designed to support a wide variety of workloads and integrates seamlessly with other Alibaba Cloud services.

Key Features of Alibaba Cloud Function Compute

- **Event-Driven Architecture**: Function Compute is inherently event-driven, allowing functions to be triggered by a variety of events such as HTTP requests, messages from message queues, file uploads to Object Storage Service (OSS), and more. This enables dynamic and responsive application behavior.
- **Language Support**: Function Compute supports multiple programming languages, including Node.js, Python, Java, PHP, and Go. This allows developers to choose the best language for their applications and leverage existing codebases.
- **Automatic Scaling**: Alibaba Cloud Function Compute automatically scales the number of function instances in response to incoming requests, ensuring applications can handle fluctuating workloads without manual intervention.
- **Integrated Security**: Function Compute includes built-in security features, such as Virtual Private Cloud (VPC) support, and IAM (Identity and Access Management) policies to control access and permissions for functions.

Getting Started with Alibaba Cloud Function Compute

To begin using Function Compute, follow these steps:

1. **Create an Alibaba Cloud Account**:

- Sign up for an Alibaba Cloud account to access its services. New users often receive credits to explore various features.

1. **Accessing the Function Compute Service**:

- Navigate to the Function Compute console within the Alibaba Cloud Management Console. Here, you can create and manage your functions.

1. **Creating a Function**:

- Define your function by selecting the desired runtime and providing the code. You can write your code directly in the console or upload it as a ZIP package or via code repository integrations.

1. **Setting Triggers**:

- Configure event triggers for your functions. You can set up triggers based on HTTP requests through API Gateway, message queues, or other Alibaba Cloud services.

1. **Deploying and Testing**:

- Deploy your function to make it live. Use built-in testing tools to verify that your function behaves as expected under various conditions.

Best Practices for Alibaba Cloud Function Compute

- **Efficient Code Packaging**:
- Keep your function code lightweight and include only essential libraries. This minimizes cold start times and improves performance.
- **Optimize Function Configuration**:
- Set appropriate timeout and memory settings for your functions based on the expected workload to optimize performance and costs.
- **Use API Gateway for HTTP Triggers**:
- For functions triggered by HTTP requests, leverage Alibaba Cloud API Gateway for enhanced security, rate limiting, and traffic management.

- **Monitor and Log Function Performance**:
- Utilize Alibaba Cloud's logging and monitoring services to track function executions, performance metrics, and error logging. This helps in diagnosing issues and optimizing function behavior.

Summary

Alibaba Cloud Function Compute provides a robust serverless platform that enables developers to build and deploy applications efficiently. By abstracting the infrastructure layer and allowing for seamless scaling, it empowers developers to focus on writing code and delivering value to users. The service's integration with other Alibaba Cloud offerings enhances its capabilities, making it suitable for a wide range of applications, from web services to data processing pipelines.

15.4 Open-Source Serverless Platforms (OpenFaaS, Knative)

As the serverless computing paradigm gains traction, open-source platforms are emerging as powerful alternatives to proprietary cloud services. These platforms allow developers to leverage serverless architectures while retaining control over their infrastructure. Two notable open-source serverless frameworks are **OpenFaaS** and **Knative**. Each offers unique features and benefits for developers looking to implement serverless solutions.

OpenFaaS

OpenFaaS (Function as a Service) is an open-source framework that allows users to build and deploy serverless functions quickly. It is designed to simplify the process of creating and managing functions, enabling developers to focus on writing code rather than worrying about infrastructure management.

Key Features of OpenFaaS:

- **Simplicity and Ease of Use**: OpenFaaS provides a user-friendly interface and CLI (Command Line Interface) that simplifies the deployment and management of functions. Developers can write functions in their preferred language, package them in Docker containers, and deploy them effortlessly.

- **Multi-Cloud and On-Premises Support**: OpenFaaS can be deployed on various cloud providers (AWS, GCP, Azure) or on-premises Kubernetes clusters. This flexibility allows organizations to maintain control over their serverless infrastructure.
- **Event-Driven Architecture**: OpenFaaS supports event triggers from various sources, including HTTP requests, message queues, and custom events, making it easy to create event-driven applications.
- **Scalability and Load Balancing**: OpenFaaS automatically scales functions based on demand and can distribute traffic across multiple function instances, ensuring high availability.

Getting Started with OpenFaaS:

1. **Installation**: OpenFaaS can be installed using Docker, Kubernetes, or Helm. Follow the official documentation for installation instructions.
2. **Creating Functions**: Use the OpenFaaS CLI to create and deploy functions. Developers can specify the runtime, code, and dependencies in the function YAML file.
3. **Triggering Functions**: Functions can be triggered through HTTP requests, scheduled events, or by integrating with external services like message queues.

Knative

Knative is a Kubernetes-native platform designed to build, deploy, and manage serverless applications. It provides a set of components that simplify the process of deploying and scaling applications on Kubernetes.

Key Features of Knative:

- **Built on Kubernetes**: Knative leverages the power of Kubernetes to provide a serverless experience, allowing users to take advantage of existing Kubernetes infrastructure and tools.
- **Serving, Eventing, and Build**: Knative is composed of three main components: Knative Serving (for deploying and managing serverless ap-

plications), Knative Eventing (for managing event-driven architectures), and Knative Build (for building container images from source code).
- **Autoscaling**: Knative automatically scales applications up and down based on traffic, including scaling to zero when no requests are being received, which optimizes resource usage and cost.
- **Supports Multiple Languages**: Knative allows developers to use any language or runtime that can run on Kubernetes, making it versatile for various application needs.

Getting Started with Knative:

1. **Install Kubernetes**: To use Knative, you need a Kubernetes cluster. You can set one up on a cloud provider or use a local development environment like Minikube.
2. **Install Knative**: Follow the official Knative installation guide to set up Knative on your Kubernetes cluster.
3. **Deploying Services**: Use YAML configuration files to define and deploy your Knative services. Knative handles scaling and routing automatically based on incoming requests.
4. **Eventing and Triggers**: Set up event sources and triggers to create event-driven architectures using Knative Eventing.

Summary

Open-source serverless platforms like OpenFaaS and Knative provide flexibility and control that can be appealing for organizations looking to implement serverless architectures. By leveraging these frameworks, developers can build scalable, event-driven applications without being locked into a specific cloud provider. These platforms also facilitate the adoption of serverless computing within existing Kubernetes environments, making them ideal for teams already using container orchestration.

15.5 Migrating Serverless Applications Between Cloud Providers

As organizations evolve, their infrastructure needs may change, leading them to consider migrating their serverless applications from one cloud provider to another. Migration can be driven by various factors, including cost optimization, performance enhancements, feature requirements, or vendor lock-in avoidance. This section will explore the considerations, challenges, and best practices for successfully migrating serverless applications between cloud providers.

Understanding the Migration Process

Migrating serverless applications involves transferring code, data, and configurations from one cloud environment to another. The process generally follows these steps:

1. **Assessment**:

- Evaluate the existing serverless application, including its architecture, dependencies, and integrations.
- Identify the new cloud provider's offerings and determine if they meet the requirements of the application.

1. **Planning**:

- Create a migration plan that outlines the steps, timelines, and resources needed for the migration.
- Assess potential risks and devise strategies to mitigate them.

1. **Code and Configuration Adaptation**:

- Adjust the application code to accommodate the new cloud provider's APIs and services.
- Update configurations, environment variables, and any infrastructure as code (IaC) templates.

1. **Data Migration**:

- Plan the migration of any associated data (e.g., databases, storage) to the

CHAPTER 15: SERVERLESS ON OTHER CLOUD PLATFORMS

new provider's services.
- Ensure data integrity and minimal downtime during the transfer.

1. **Testing**:

- Conduct thorough testing in the new environment to ensure the application functions as expected.
- Validate performance and security configurations.

1. **Deployment**:

- Deploy the migrated application on the new cloud provider.
- Monitor the application closely during the initial launch phase for any issues.

1. **Optimization**:

- After migration, review application performance and cost to identify optimization opportunities.
- Make necessary adjustments based on monitoring feedback.

Key Considerations for Migration

1. **Service Mapping**:

- Identify equivalent services in the new cloud provider that match the functionality of the current services. For example, AWS Lambda can be mapped to Google Cloud Functions or Azure Functions.
- Consider differences in features, limitations, and pricing models between providers.

1. **Data Transfer Costs**:

- Analyze data transfer costs associated with moving large volumes of data between cloud providers.
- Look for strategies to minimize costs, such as bulk transfers or data compression.

1. **Authentication and Authorization**:

- Review and adapt security settings, roles, and permissions in the new environment.
- Ensure that any third-party authentication services are compatible with the new cloud provider.

1. **Vendor Lock-In**:

- Consider adopting multi-cloud strategies or open-source serverless platforms to mitigate vendor lock-in concerns in the future.

1. **Latency and Performance**:

- Evaluate the performance of the migrated application in the new environment, particularly in terms of cold starts and latency.
- Optimize resource configurations and scaling settings to match traffic patterns.

Challenges of Migration

- **Complexity of Dependencies**: Serverless applications often depend on multiple services and APIs, which can complicate the migration process. Ensuring compatibility between services is crucial.
- **Downtime and Service Interruption**: Minimizing downtime during migration is essential. Implementing a phased migration approach or using blue-green deployments can help mitigate service interruptions.
- **Testing and Validation**: Comprehensive testing is vital to ensure that

the migrated application works as expected. Incomplete testing can lead to issues that may affect user experience.

Summary

Migrating serverless applications between cloud providers can be a complex yet rewarding process. With proper assessment, planning, and execution, organizations can leverage the advantages of a new provider, such as better pricing, enhanced features, or improved performance. By following best practices and considering potential challenges, businesses can successfully navigate their migration journey, positioning themselves for future growth and innovation.

15.6 Multi-Cloud Serverless Architectures: Challenges and Solutions

In an era where businesses seek agility and resilience, multi-cloud serverless architectures have emerged as a compelling solution. By leveraging multiple cloud providers for their serverless offerings, organizations can optimize performance, avoid vendor lock-in, and enhance reliability. However, implementing a multi-cloud strategy also comes with its own set of challenges. This section will explore these challenges and propose solutions to effectively manage a multi-cloud serverless environment.

Challenges of Multi-Cloud Serverless Architectures

1. **Complexity of Management**:

- Managing applications across multiple cloud providers can lead to increased complexity, requiring teams to become proficient in different cloud environments and their respective tools and services.

1. **Data Consistency and Synchronization**:

- Ensuring data consistency between various cloud environments can be challenging. Different providers may have unique data storage solutions, leading to potential issues with synchronization and data integrity.

1. **Increased Latency**:

- When serverless functions from different cloud providers need to communicate, there may be increased latency due to network hops between clouds. This can affect application performance, especially for latency-sensitive workloads.

1. **Security and Compliance**:

- Maintaining a consistent security posture across multiple cloud environments can be difficult. Organizations must navigate different security frameworks, compliance requirements, and IAM configurations.

1. **Cost Management**:

- While multi-cloud strategies can optimize costs, they can also complicate billing and budgeting. Different pricing models and services can make it difficult to predict and manage cloud expenditures.

Solutions for Multi-Cloud Serverless Architectures

1. **Unified Management Tools**:

- Utilize multi-cloud management tools that provide a single pane of glass for monitoring, deploying, and managing serverless applications across different providers. These tools can streamline operations and enhance visibility.

1. **Data Synchronization Strategies**:

- Implement data synchronization solutions, such as change data capture (CDC) or event-driven architectures, to ensure data consistency across cloud providers. Using message queues or event streams can help facilitate real-time updates.

1. **Optimizing Network Performance**:

- Deploy applications in regions that minimize latency between services. Consider using cloud interconnect services to enhance performance between cloud providers and facilitate faster communication.

1. **Standardized Security Practices**:

- Develop a standardized security framework that applies to all cloud providers. Leverage automation tools to manage security policies and configurations consistently across environments.

1. **Cost Management Solutions**:

- Implement cloud cost management tools that provide insights into spending across multiple providers. These tools can help identify cost optimization opportunities and ensure budget adherence.

Conclusion

Multi-cloud serverless architectures present an opportunity for organizations to harness the best of various cloud providers while optimizing for performance, flexibility, and resilience. However, the associated challenges, such as complexity, data synchronization, and security management, require careful consideration and planning.

By leveraging unified management tools, implementing effective data synchronization strategies, optimizing network performance, and standardizing security practices, organizations can successfully navigate the complexities of multi-cloud environments. As businesses continue to evolve, adopting a multi-cloud serverless approach can position them to respond swiftly to changing demands and remain competitive in the digital landscape.

16.1 Building Serverless E-commerce Applications

E-commerce has transformed the way businesses operate, offering convenience and accessibility to consumers worldwide. Serverless architecture provides an ideal solution for building scalable and resilient e-commerce applications. By leveraging services like AWS Lambda, Google Cloud Functions, and various managed databases, developers can focus on delivering features without the burden of infrastructure management.

Key Components of a Serverless E-commerce Architecture:

1. **Front-End Framework**:

- Use modern front-end frameworks like React, Angular, or Vue.js to build a responsive user interface. These frameworks can communicate with serverless back-end services via APIs.

1. **Serverless Back-End**:

- Implement the back-end logic using serverless functions. For example, AWS Lambda can handle user authentication, product listings, shopping cart operations, and order processing.

1. **Database Services**:

16.1 BUILDING SERVERLESS E-COMMERCE APPLICATIONS

- Choose appropriate database solutions based on your application needs:
- **NoSQL Databases**: AWS DynamoDB or Google Firestore can handle high traffic and provide flexible data storage for product catalogs and user sessions.
- **SQL Databases**: For structured data, AWS RDS or Google Cloud SQL can be used to store transactional data like orders and inventory.

1. **Payment Processing**:

- Integrate third-party payment gateways (like Stripe or PayPal) through serverless APIs. This ensures secure payment transactions without the need to manage sensitive data directly.

1. **API Gateway**:

- Use AWS API Gateway or Google Cloud Endpoints to expose the serverless functions as RESTful APIs, enabling communication between the front end and back end.

1. **Content Delivery**:

- Implement a Content Delivery Network (CDN) like AWS CloudFront or Google Cloud CDN to deliver static assets (images, stylesheets, scripts) quickly and efficiently to users.

Benefits of Using Serverless for E-commerce:

- **Scalability**: Serverless architecture can handle sudden spikes in traffic during sales events or promotions without requiring manual intervention.
- **Cost Efficiency**: Pay-as-you-go pricing models allow businesses to only pay for the resources they consume, reducing overhead costs.
- **Rapid Development**: Developers can focus on writing code for business

logic rather than managing servers, accelerating the development cycle.
- **Maintenance**: With managed services, the burden of server maintenance, updates, and scaling is offloaded to cloud providers.

Real-World Example: Several leading e-commerce platforms have successfully adopted serverless architecture. For instance, **Trello**, a popular project management tool, utilized AWS Lambda to process webhooks, enabling efficient handling of real-time updates without over-provisioning resources.

As we explore further in this chapter, we will examine additional real-world use cases, showcasing how various industries leverage serverless architecture to enhance their applications and drive innovation.

16.2 Serverless Chatbots and Voice Assistants

In recent years, chatbots and voice assistants have become integral components of customer service and user interaction. Leveraging serverless architecture to build these intelligent systems offers numerous advantages, including scalability, cost efficiency, and reduced management overhead. By using cloud functions, developers can create responsive and adaptive solutions that seamlessly integrate with various communication platforms.

Key Components of Serverless Chatbots and Voice Assistants:

1. **Natural Language Processing (NLP)**:

- Utilize NLP services like AWS Lex or Google Dialogflow to handle user input and generate responses. These services can interpret user intent, making conversations more natural and engaging.

1. **Serverless Functions**:

- Implement the business logic in serverless functions (e.g., AWS Lambda or Google Cloud Functions). These functions can process user requests, integrate with APIs, and perform actions based on user interactions.

1. **Integration with Messaging Platforms**:

- Deploy chatbots on various platforms (such as Facebook Messenger, Slack, or WhatsApp) using APIs provided by these platforms. This allows for widespread reach and accessibility.

1. **Voice Assistant Capabilities**:

- For voice assistants, integrate with services like Amazon Alexa Skills Kit or Google Assistant SDK. These platforms allow developers to create custom skills that users can invoke through voice commands.

1. **Database for Contextual Data**:

- Use a serverless database (like AWS DynamoDB or Google Firestore) to store user data, conversation history, and preferences. This information can help personalize interactions and improve user experience.

1. **Monitoring and Analytics**:

- Implement monitoring and analytics tools to track user interactions, response times, and satisfaction levels. Services like AWS CloudWatch or Google Stackdriver can help gather insights into chatbot performance.

Benefits of Serverless Architecture for Chatbots and Voice Assistants:

- **Scalability**: Serverless functions can automatically scale based on user demand, ensuring that the chatbot can handle sudden spikes in usage without performance degradation.
- **Cost Efficiency**: Pay-as-you-go pricing models allow businesses to minimize costs, as they only pay for the compute resources used during user interactions.
- **Rapid Development and Deployment**: Developers can quickly iterate on features and deploy updates without worrying about server infrastructure, enabling faster time-to-market.

- **Reduced Management Overhead**: By utilizing managed services, teams can focus on improving the chatbot's intelligence and user experience rather than managing servers.

Real-World Example: A notable example of serverless chatbots is **Coca-Cola's** deployment of a chatbot on Facebook Messenger. By leveraging AWS Lambda and Amazon Lex, Coca-Cola was able to create an interactive platform for users to learn about their products, engage with promotional content, and receive personalized recommendations.

16.3 Real-Time Data Processing with Serverless

In an increasingly data-driven world, real-time data processing has become essential for businesses to remain competitive. Serverless architecture provides a robust framework for handling data streams, enabling organizations to process, analyze, and respond to data in real time without the complexities of managing infrastructure. This section will explore how serverless solutions facilitate real-time data processing, the key components involved, and the benefits of adopting such an approach.

Key Components of Real-Time Data Processing in Serverless Architecture

1. **Data Ingestion**:

- **Streaming Data Sources**: Utilize services like **Amazon Kinesis** or **Google Cloud Pub/Sub** to ingest streaming data from various sources such as IoT devices, web applications, and third-party APIs. These services can handle high-throughput data ingestion seamlessly.
- **Event Triggers**: Serverless functions (AWS Lambda or Google Cloud Functions) can be automatically triggered by new data events, allowing for immediate processing as data flows in.

1. **Processing and Transformation**:

- **Real-Time Processing Functions**: Implement serverless functions to transform, filter, and aggregate incoming data. This allows for immediate analysis and manipulation, enabling timely insights.
- **Use of Frameworks**: Leverage frameworks like **Apache Flink** or **Apache Beam** for more complex data processing tasks. These can be integrated with serverless platforms to handle sophisticated data workflows.

1. **Data Storage**:

- **Serverless Databases**: Use serverless databases (such as **Amazon DynamoDB**, **Google Firestore**, or **Azure Cosmos DB**) for storing processed data. These databases can scale automatically to accommodate fluctuating data volumes, ensuring efficient storage and retrieval.
- **Data Lakes**: For larger datasets, consider using serverless data lake solutions (like **AWS S3** or **Google Cloud Storage**) to store raw data. This allows for cost-effective storage and the flexibility to run batch processes later.

1. **Analytics and Visualization**:

- **Real-Time Analytics**: Integrate with services like **AWS QuickSight** or **Google Data Studio** to visualize processed data. This enables stakeholders to monitor key metrics and gain insights in real time.
- **Data Stream Processing Engines**: Implement solutions like **AWS Glue** or **Google Dataflow** to run analytics on streaming data and perform complex event processing.

1. **Monitoring and Alerts**:

- **Monitoring Tools**: Utilize cloud monitoring tools (such as **AWS CloudWatch** or **Google Stackdriver**) to track the performance of data processing functions and identify any anomalies or bottlenecks in real time.
- **Alerting Mechanisms**: Set up alerting mechanisms based on specific thresholds or events to ensure timely responses to data processing issues.

Benefits of Serverless Real-Time Data Processing

- **Scalability**: Serverless architecture allows for automatic scaling in response to fluctuating data loads, ensuring consistent performance without manual intervention.
- **Cost-Effectiveness**: Organizations only pay for the compute resources used during data processing, eliminating the costs associated with idle server capacity.
- **Reduced Latency**: With real-time data processing, organizations can respond quickly to changing conditions, leading to improved decision-making and customer experiences.
- **Simplicity and Focus**: Developers can concentrate on building and optimizing data processing functions without the complexity of managing underlying infrastructure, leading to faster development cycles.

Real-World Example

A notable real-world example of real-time data processing using serverless architecture is **Netflix**. The company utilizes AWS Lambda in conjunction with Kinesis to analyze user behavior in real time. By processing this data as it streams in, Netflix can provide personalized content recommendations, optimize user experience, and make data-driven decisions to enhance its service.

16.4 Implementing IoT with Serverless Computing

The Internet of Things (IoT) is transforming the way we interact with technology, creating vast networks of connected devices that generate continuous streams of data. Serverless computing provides an ideal framework for building IoT applications, enabling organizations to process and analyze this data without the overhead of managing infrastructure. In this section, we'll explore how serverless architecture can enhance IoT implementations, the key components involved, and the benefits of this approach.

Key Components of Serverless IoT Architecture

1. **Device Connectivity**:

- **Protocols**: IoT devices typically use protocols such as MQTT, HTTP, or CoAP to communicate with the cloud. Serverless platforms can seamlessly handle incoming messages from these devices.
- **Gateway Services**: Utilize cloud services like **AWS IoT Core** or **Google Cloud IoT Core** to connect IoT devices securely to the cloud, allowing them to send and receive messages.

1. **Data Ingestion**:

- **Event-Driven Functions**: Serverless functions (e.g., AWS Lambda or Google Cloud Functions) can be triggered by events generated by IoT devices, enabling real-time data processing as events occur.
- **Stream Processing**: Implement data streams using services like **Amazon Kinesis** or **Google Cloud Pub/Sub** to manage incoming data from multiple devices simultaneously.

1. **Data Processing and Analytics**:

- **Real-Time Processing**: Use serverless functions to analyze incoming

data for immediate insights, such as detecting anomalies or triggering alerts based on specific conditions.
- **Batch Processing**: For large datasets collected over time, utilize serverless batch processing tools (e.g., AWS Glue or Google Dataflow) to analyze and derive insights from historical data.

1. **Storage Solutions**:

- **Scalable Storage**: Store IoT data in serverless databases like **Amazon DynamoDB**, **Google Firestore**, or cloud storage solutions such as **AWS S3** or **Google Cloud Storage** for scalable, cost-effective data storage.
- **Time-Series Databases**: Use specialized time-series databases like **Amazon Timestream** or **Google Cloud Bigtable** for storing and querying time-based data efficiently.

1. **Monitoring and Management**:

- **Monitoring Tools**: Leverage cloud monitoring tools (e.g., AWS CloudWatch or Google Stackdriver) to track the health and performance of IoT devices and serverless functions, ensuring operational efficiency.
- **Alerts and Notifications**: Set up alerting mechanisms for device status changes or data thresholds to maintain proactive management of IoT systems.

Benefits of Using Serverless for IoT Applications

- **Scalability**: Serverless architecture automatically scales with the number of connected devices and the volume of data generated, making it suitable for large IoT deployments.
- **Cost Efficiency**: Organizations only pay for the resources consumed during function execution, reducing operational costs compared to traditional server setups.
- **Reduced Complexity**: Developers can focus on building IoT applications and functionalities without worrying about server management, leading to faster development and deployment cycles.
- **Faster Time to Market**: With serverless services, teams can quickly iterate and deploy new features, responding to market demands and user needs more efficiently.

Real-World Example

One example of successful IoT implementation using serverless architecture is **GE Aviation**, which leverages AWS IoT and Lambda to monitor aircraft engines. By collecting and processing data from engines in real time, GE can optimize maintenance schedules, reduce downtime, and improve fuel efficiency, ultimately enhancing operational safety and performance.

16.5 Serverless Machine Learning Workflows

Serverless architecture is increasingly being adopted for machine learning (ML) workflows due to its scalability, cost-effectiveness, and ease of deployment. By leveraging serverless computing, organizations can streamline the process of building, training, and deploying machine learning models without the complexity of managing underlying infrastructure. In this section, we'll explore how serverless computing facilitates machine learning workflows, the components involved, and the advantages of this approach.

Key Components of Serverless Machine Learning Workflows

1. **Data Ingestion**:

- **Data Sources**: Collect data from various sources, such as databases, data lakes, or real-time streams. Serverless functions can be triggered to ingest data as it arrives.
- **ETL Processes**: Utilize serverless services (e.g., AWS Glue or Google Cloud Dataflow) to perform Extract, Transform, Load (ETL) operations on incoming data, preparing it for analysis.

1. **Model Training**:

- **Serverless Training**: Leverage serverless platforms for training ML models. Services like **AWS SageMaker** and **Google AI Platform** allow you to spin up compute resources on demand for training, automatically scaling based on the dataset size and algorithm complexity.
- **Batch Training**: For large datasets, you can use serverless batch processing jobs to handle the training workload without provisioning dedicated servers.

1. **Model Deployment**:

- **API Endpoints**: Deploy trained models as serverless APIs using services like **AWS Lambda** or **Google Cloud Functions**. This enables applications to invoke the model for predictions on demand.
- **Versioning**: Implement version control for models to manage updates and ensure consistency across different deployments.

1. **Inference and Predictions**:

- **Real-Time Predictions**: Use serverless functions to handle real-time inference requests. This can be particularly useful for applications that require immediate predictions based on incoming data, such as fraud detection or personalized recommendations.
- **Batch Predictions**: For large volumes of data, set up serverless batch prediction jobs that process and analyze data in bulk.

1. **Monitoring and Evaluation**:

- **Performance Monitoring**: Utilize monitoring tools (e.g., AWS CloudWatch or Google Stackdriver) to track the performance of deployed models and serverless functions, ensuring they meet required accuracy and response time.
- **A/B Testing**: Implement A/B testing to compare different models or configurations, enabling continuous improvement based on performance metrics.

Benefits of Using Serverless for Machine Learning Workflows

- **Scalability**: Serverless architectures automatically scale to accommodate varying workloads, ensuring that ML workflows can handle spikes in data without requiring manual intervention.
- **Cost Efficiency**: Organizations only pay for the resources used during training and inference, making it an economically viable option, especially for startups and small businesses.
- **Flexibility**: Developers can easily experiment with different algorithms and models, quickly deploying and testing new ideas without the burden of infrastructure management.
- **Faster Development Cycles**: With a focus on code and functionality rather than infrastructure, teams can reduce the time required to build, train, and deploy machine learning models.

Real-World Example

A notable example of serverless machine learning in action is **Netflix**, which uses AWS Lambda to enhance its recommendation engine. By processing vast amounts of user interaction data and preferences, Netflix leverages serverless functions to continuously update and refine its recommendation algorithms. This enables real-time personalization for its users, significantly enhancing the viewing experience.

16.6 Case Studies: Companies Using Serverless at Scale

As serverless architecture continues to gain traction, several companies have successfully implemented it to enhance their applications, streamline operations, and improve overall efficiency. This section highlights a few notable case studies of organizations leveraging serverless technology at scale.

1. Coca-Cola

Coca-Cola implemented serverless architecture to optimize its beverage vending machine operation. By using AWS Lambda and Amazon DynamoDB, Coca-Cola was able to process real-time data from vending machines to monitor inventory levels, track sales, and manage maintenance issues. This real-time processing capability allowed Coca-Cola to enhance customer experience and streamline its supply chain, ultimately leading to better decision-making and resource allocation.

2. Spotify

Spotify adopted serverless architecture to manage its data processing workflows. By utilizing AWS Lambda and Amazon S3, Spotify can analyze millions of user-generated playlists and music tracks to deliver personalized recommendations. The serverless approach allows Spotify to automatically scale its processing power to accommodate the high volume of data, ensuring efficient handling of user requests while minimizing operational costs.

3. iRobot

iRobot, the company behind the Roomba vacuum cleaner, utilizes serverless computing to enhance its product features and improve user experience. By using AWS Lambda for its backend services, iRobot can process data from its connected devices, enabling features like mapping and navigation. This serverless architecture has allowed iRobot to quickly deploy updates and enhancements without the overhead of managing infrastructure.

4. The BBC

The BBC has transitioned several of its applications to a serverless model using AWS Lambda. By adopting serverless architecture, the BBC has improved the performance of its content delivery systems, allowing for faster loading times and a better user experience for viewers. This shift has also helped the organization reduce infrastructure costs and streamline development processes.

5. Nordstrom

Nordstrom, a leading fashion retailer, has integrated serverless technology into its e-commerce platform. By utilizing AWS Lambda, Nordstrom can efficiently handle traffic spikes during peak shopping seasons. This allows the company to provide a seamless shopping experience while minimizing downtime and managing costs effectively.

Conclusion

In this chapter, we explored a diverse array of real-world applications and use cases for serverless architecture, demonstrating its versatility and effectiveness across various industries. We discussed how serverless computing can power e-commerce applications, chatbots, real-time data processing, IoT solutions, and machine learning workflows.

The case studies highlighted significant advantages, such as improved scalability, cost efficiency, and accelerated development cycles, showcasing how organizations like Coca-Cola, Spotify, iRobot, the BBC, and Nordstrom have successfully adopted serverless architecture to innovate and optimize their operations.

By leveraging serverless solutions, these companies not only streamline their processes but also enhance user experiences, proving that serverless architecture is not just a trend but a robust and scalable approach for modern application development. As we move forward, it will be essential for more organizations to consider serverless as a viable option in their digital transformation journeys.

17.1 The Growing Popularity of Serverless

As businesses increasingly seek agile and cost-effective solutions for application development and deployment, serverless architecture has gained significant traction. The growing popularity of serverless is attributed to several factors, which include:

1. **Cost Efficiency**: One of the primary drivers behind the adoption of serverless computing is its cost model. Serverless platforms allow organizations to pay only for the actual compute resources consumed during function execution, eliminating the need for upfront infrastructure investments. This pay-as-you-go model is especially appealing for startups and small businesses, as it enables them to launch applications without incurring hefty operational costs.
2. **Focus on Core Business**: With serverless architecture, developers can focus on writing code and delivering business value without the overhead of managing servers and infrastructure. This leads to faster development cycles and allows organizations to innovate more rapidly, responding to market demands and customer needs more effectively.
3. **Scalability**: Serverless platforms automatically handle scaling based on demand, allowing applications to accommodate fluctuations in traffic seamlessly. This built-in scalability is essential for businesses that experience varying workloads, such as e-commerce sites during holiday seasons or news outlets during major events.
4. **Simplified Operations**: Serverless architecture abstracts away much of the operational complexity associated with traditional application

deployment. This simplification enables development teams to concentrate on writing functions, integrating with APIs, and utilizing cloud services without worrying about underlying infrastructure maintenance.

5. **Increased Adoption of Microservices**: The rise of microservices architecture aligns well with serverless computing. As organizations seek to break monolithic applications into smaller, more manageable services, serverless provides an ideal framework for deploying and managing these microservices. Each service can be deployed independently, allowing teams to work concurrently and deliver updates more frequently.

6. **Advancements in Tooling and Ecosystem**: The serverless ecosystem has expanded rapidly, with various tools, frameworks, and services emerging to support serverless development. Platforms like AWS Lambda, Google Cloud Functions, Azure Functions, and numerous open-source solutions have made it easier for developers to build, deploy, and manage serverless applications. This robust tooling enhances developer productivity and encourages further adoption.

7. **Community and Educational Resources**: The growth of serverless architecture has been bolstered by an active community and an abundance of educational resources. Developers can access tutorials, documentation, and forums to learn best practices, share experiences, and troubleshoot challenges, fostering a collaborative environment for innovation.

8. **Integration with Emerging Technologies**: Serverless architecture is increasingly being integrated with cutting-edge technologies such as artificial intelligence (AI), machine learning (ML), and the Internet of Things (IoT). This integration enables organizations to leverage the benefits of serverless while harnessing the power of these transformative technologies, leading to new opportunities and enhanced functionality.

In summary, the growing popularity of serverless computing is driven by its cost efficiency, focus on core business objectives, scalability, simplified operations, alignment with microservices, and a flourishing ecosystem of tools and resources. As more organizations recognize the benefits of serverless architecture, we can expect to see its continued adoption across various industries.

17.2 Serverless AI and Machine Learning

The convergence of serverless architecture with artificial intelligence (AI) and machine learning (ML) is transforming the way organizations develop and deploy intelligent applications. By leveraging serverless computing, businesses can unlock several benefits for their AI and ML workflows:

1. **Scalability for Machine Learning Workloads**: Serverless platforms automatically scale resources based on demand, making them well-suited for handling fluctuating workloads often associated with AI and ML tasks. During peak processing times, such as model training or batch predictions, serverless architecture can seamlessly allocate more resources, ensuring that applications remain responsive and efficient.
2. **Cost-Effective Model Training and Inference**: Traditional machine learning workflows often require substantial infrastructure investments to support the computational demands of training models. With serverless architecture, organizations can pay only for the actual compute time used, significantly reducing costs. This is particularly advantageous for startups and smaller companies that may not have the budget for dedicated hardware.
3. **Rapid Experimentation and Prototyping**: Serverless environments facilitate rapid experimentation by allowing data scientists and ML engineers to quickly deploy and test models without the need for extensive setup. Developers can focus on iterating their algorithms and features, enabling a more agile approach to model development.

4. **Event-Driven Data Processing**: Serverless architecture excels in event-driven environments, making it ideal for AI applications that rely on real-time data processing. For instance, organizations can set up event triggers that automatically invoke functions for processing incoming data streams, enabling timely insights and predictions. This is particularly useful for applications in fields such as finance, healthcare, and IoT, where timely responses are critical.
5. **Integration with Pre-Trained Models and APIs**: Serverless architecture allows easy integration with cloud-based AI services, such as those offered by AWS, Google Cloud, and Azure. These platforms provide pre-trained models and APIs for tasks like image recognition, natural language processing, and sentiment analysis. By leveraging these services within a serverless framework, developers can quickly enhance their applications with advanced AI capabilities without needing to build everything from scratch.
6. **Simplified Deployment of AI Models**: Deploying machine learning models can be a complex process, often involving multiple environments and configurations. Serverless architecture simplifies this by allowing developers to package their models and associated code into functions that can be easily deployed to the cloud. This streamlines the deployment process and reduces the risk of errors associated with environment configurations.
7. **Collaboration and Interoperability**: The serverless ecosystem encourages collaboration among data scientists, developers, and IT teams. With a shared focus on building and deploying AI solutions, these stakeholders can work together more effectively, leveraging each other's expertise. Additionally, serverless functions can be designed to work alongside various programming languages and frameworks, enhancing interoperability.
8. **Enhanced Security and Compliance**: Security is a critical concern for AI and ML applications, particularly when dealing with sensitive data. Serverless architecture offers built-in security features, such as automated updates, encryption, and IAM roles, which help organizations

17.2 SERVERLESS AI AND MACHINE LEARNING

manage compliance and protect their data. This reduces the burden on teams to maintain secure environments, allowing them to focus on innovation.

In conclusion, serverless architecture is paving the way for more efficient, scalable, and cost-effective AI and machine learning solutions. By leveraging the benefits of serverless computing, organizations can enhance their AI capabilities, drive innovation, and respond more effectively to changing market demands.

17.3 Edge Computing and the Future of Serverless

Edge computing and serverless architecture are two trends that are reshaping the landscape of cloud computing, offering new possibilities for application development and deployment. By bringing computation closer to the data source, edge computing enhances the performance and responsiveness of applications, particularly those that require real-time processing. The integration of serverless principles with edge computing creates a powerful paradigm that can address various challenges in today's digital landscape.

1. Improved Latency and Performance

One of the primary benefits of edge computing is the reduction in latency. By processing data closer to the end-user, applications can deliver faster responses, leading to an improved user experience. When combined with serverless architecture, which allows for automatic scaling and resource allocation, developers can create applications that are both responsive and efficient, regardless of user location. This is particularly beneficial for applications like gaming, streaming, and IoT, where low latency is crucial.

2. Scalability at the Edge

Serverless architecture inherently provides scalability, allowing applications to handle varying workloads without manual intervention. When applied to edge computing, serverless functions can dynamically scale based on local demand, ensuring that resources are utilized efficiently. This scalability is essential for applications that experience sudden spikes in traffic or require rapid adjustments to resource allocation based on real-time conditions.

3. Cost Efficiency

Running serverless functions at the edge can lead to cost savings by minimizing data transfer costs and reducing the need for centralized cloud resources. Since edge computing enables local data processing, less data needs to be sent to the cloud for processing, resulting in lower bandwidth costs. Additionally, serverless models typically follow a pay-per-use pricing structure, allowing organizations to pay only for the compute resources consumed, further optimizing costs.

4. Enhanced Security and Privacy

Processing data at the edge can enhance security and privacy by keeping sensitive information closer to the source. With serverless functions deployed at the edge, organizations can implement security measures that protect data before it is transmitted to the cloud. This is particularly important for industries like healthcare and finance, where compliance with data protection regulations is paramount. Edge computing can help mitigate risks associated with data breaches and unauthorized access.

5. Real-Time Data Processing for IoT

The proliferation of IoT devices generates vast amounts of data that require real-time processing for actionable insights. Combining serverless architecture with edge computing enables organizations to process this data locally, triggering serverless functions based on specific events or conditions. This real-time processing capability is essential for applications such as smart cities, industrial automation, and predictive maintenance.

6. Flexibility and Agility

Serverless edge computing offers increased flexibility and agility in application development. Developers can deploy functions at the edge without worrying about managing the underlying infrastructure, enabling them to focus on building and iterating on their applications. This flexibility fosters innovation, allowing organizations to experiment with new ideas and rapidly deploy solutions to meet evolving customer demands.

7. Integration with 5G Technology

The rollout of 5G networks is set to further accelerate the adoption of edge computing and serverless architecture. With its high-speed connectivity and low latency, 5G provides the ideal environment for edge computing solutions. Serverless functions can be deployed at edge locations with 5G support, enabling new use cases such as real-time analytics, augmented reality, and autonomous vehicles. This synergy will unlock new possibilities for businesses looking to harness the power of edge computing.

Summary

As the digital landscape continues to evolve, the integration of edge computing and serverless architecture presents a compelling opportunity for organizations to enhance their applications and services. By leveraging the benefits of both technologies, businesses can improve performance, scalability, and cost-effectiveness while addressing the growing demand for real-time processing and responsiveness. The future of serverless will likely be intertwined with edge computing, enabling organizations to build innovative solutions that meet the challenges of an increasingly connected world.

17.4 Innovations in Serverless Databases

The rise of serverless architecture has led to significant advancements in database technologies, fundamentally changing how developers interact with and manage databases. Serverless databases offer scalability, flexibility, and cost efficiency, making them an attractive option for modern application development. Here, we explore some of the key innovations in serverless databases and how they enhance the development and deployment of serverless applications.

1. On-Demand Scaling

One of the most notable innovations in serverless databases is the ability to automatically scale resources up or down based on demand. This on-demand scaling means that developers no longer have to provision a fixed amount of database resources. Instead, the database can dynamically adjust its capacity to handle varying workloads, allowing applications to maintain performance during traffic spikes while minimizing costs during low-usage periods.

2. Consumption-Based Pricing Models

Serverless databases often utilize consumption-based pricing models, where users are billed based on actual usage rather than a fixed monthly fee. This pricing structure allows businesses to pay only for the resources they consume, making it a cost-effective solution for unpredictable workloads. Developers can experiment and innovate without worrying about high operational costs, as they only incur charges for the database operations they perform.

3. Automated Management and Maintenance

Serverless databases come with built-in management and maintenance features, such as automated backups, patching, and monitoring. This automation reduces the operational burden on developers and allows them to focus on building applications instead of managing infrastructure. With serverless databases, routine tasks that traditionally required manual intervention are now handled automatically, improving efficiency and reliability.

4. Global Distribution and Low Latency

Many serverless databases are designed to support global distribution, allowing data to be stored closer to end users. This capability reduces latency and enhances application performance, especially for globally distributed applications. Innovations such as multi-region replication ensure that data is accessible from multiple locations, providing resilience and improving user experience.

5. Event-Driven Architecture

Serverless databases are often designed to work seamlessly within event-driven architectures. This means that changes in data can trigger serverless functions or workflows automatically. For example, when a new record is added to a database, an event can be generated that activates a Lambda function to process the data. This integration enables real-time data processing and enhances the responsiveness of applications.

6. Enhanced Security Features

Security is a critical concern for any database, and serverless databases are increasingly incorporating advanced security features. Innovations such as encryption at rest and in transit, built-in access controls, and integration with identity and access management (IAM) systems enhance the security posture of serverless databases. Additionally, serverless databases often support compliance with industry regulations, making them suitable for sensitive applications.

7. Integration with Serverless Frameworks

Many serverless databases are designed to integrate seamlessly with popular serverless frameworks and platforms, such as AWS Lambda and Google Cloud Functions. This integration simplifies the development process, allowing developers to connect their applications to databases with minimal configuration. Pre-built connectors and libraries make it easy to interact with serverless databases from serverless functions, streamlining the development workflow.

8. Support for Multiple Data Models

Innovations in serverless databases are also evident in their support for multiple data models, including relational, document, key-value, and graph databases. This flexibility allows developers to choose the best data model for their specific use case without being locked into a single approach. The ability to work with various data types and structures empowers developers to build more sophisticated applications that can meet diverse requirements.

Summary

The innovations in serverless databases are transforming how developers build and manage applications in the cloud. With features such as on-demand scaling, consumption-based pricing, automated management, and seamless integration with serverless frameworks, these databases offer the flexibility and efficiency needed to meet the demands of modern applications. As serverless architecture continues to evolve, the role of serverless databases will be crucial in enabling organizations to harness the full potential of cloud computing.

17.5 The Role of Containers in Serverless

As serverless architecture continues to gain traction in the development landscape, containers have emerged as a powerful complement to serverless computing. By providing an efficient and consistent deployment model, containers play a significant role in enhancing the flexibility, scalability, and management of serverless applications. In this section, we'll explore how containers integrate with serverless architecture and the benefits they bring to developers.

1. Consistency Across Environments

Containers encapsulate an application and its dependencies, ensuring that it runs consistently across different environments, from development to production. This consistency is crucial in serverless applications, where functions may be deployed across various cloud environments. By using containers, developers can package their serverless functions along with all necessary libraries and runtime environments, eliminating the "it works on my machine" problem.

2. Enhanced Portability

One of the significant advantages of containers is their portability. Applications packaged in containers can run on any infrastructure that supports container orchestration, whether it be on-premises, in a public cloud, or in a hybrid cloud setup. This portability allows developers to move serverless applications seamlessly between different cloud providers or environments, avoiding vendor lock-in.

3. Improved Cold Start Times

Cold starts—when a serverless function is invoked after being idle for some time—can lead to latency issues. By pre-warming containers and keeping them in a ready state, developers can significantly reduce cold start times. Containers allow for the management of function instances in a way that can mitigate the impact of cold starts, ensuring faster response times for serverless applications.

4. Support for Stateful Applications

Traditional serverless functions are stateless, meaning they do not retain any state between invocations. However, some applications require stateful interactions. Containers can manage state more effectively by allowing stateful services to run alongside stateless serverless functions. For example, a serverless function can interact with a containerized application that maintains user sessions or caching, providing the benefits of both paradigms.

5. Seamless Integration with Microservices

Containers naturally align with microservices architecture, where applications are divided into smaller, independently deployable services. Serverless functions can act as microservices, triggering specific containerized services when needed. This synergy allows developers to build complex applications with a combination of serverless functions and containerized microservices, leveraging the strengths of both architectures.

6. Flexibility in Runtime Environments

With containers, developers can choose the runtime environment that best suits their application needs. Unlike traditional serverless environments that may limit choices to specific runtimes, containers enable the use of any programming language or framework. This flexibility empowers developers to leverage existing codebases or preferred languages without having to adapt to the constraints of a serverless platform.

7. Simplified Deployment and CI/CD

Containers streamline the deployment process for serverless applications by allowing for the use of container orchestration tools like Kubernetes or Docker Swarm. These tools can automate the deployment and scaling of both serverless functions and containerized applications, simplifying continuous integration and continuous delivery (CI/CD) processes. This synergy allows teams to deploy updates and new features more efficiently.

8. Resource Optimization

Using containers in serverless architecture can lead to better resource utilization. Containers can be spun up or down as needed, ensuring that resources are only consumed when necessary. This optimization can help reduce operational costs, especially for applications with variable workloads.

Summary

Containers play a pivotal role in the evolution of serverless architecture, providing consistency, portability, and improved performance. By enabling stateful interactions, reducing cold start times, and simplifying deployment, containers enhance the capabilities of serverless applications. As organizations continue to adopt serverless computing, the integration of containers will likely become increasingly prevalent, allowing developers to build robust, scalable, and efficient applications that meet the demands of modern business environments.

17.6 Final Thoughts: What's Next for Serverless Architecture?

As we look ahead to the future of serverless architecture, it's clear that this paradigm is set to evolve significantly. With ongoing advancements in technology, the following trends and considerations will shape the landscape of serverless computing in the coming years:

1. Increased Adoption Across Industries

As more organizations recognize the benefits of serverless architecture—such as reduced operational overhead, faster time to market, and scalability—we can expect broader adoption across various industries. From startups to large enterprises, serverless solutions will continue to be a strategic choice for building innovative applications.

2. Enhanced Tooling and Ecosystem Maturity

The serverless ecosystem is rapidly maturing, with the development of better tools, frameworks, and best practices. We can anticipate improvements in serverless frameworks (like Serverless Framework, AWS SAM, and Google Cloud Functions), which will simplify development, deployment, and management of serverless applications. Enhanced tooling will empower developers to leverage serverless more effectively.

3. Integration with AI and Machine Learning

As AI and machine learning technologies advance, serverless architecture will play a crucial role in enabling scalable and cost-effective deployment of AI-driven applications. Serverless solutions will allow developers to build machine learning workflows that dynamically scale based on demand, making it easier to integrate AI capabilities into applications.

4. Emphasis on Security and Compliance

With the growing popularity of serverless architecture, security will remain a top priority. Organizations will focus on implementing best practices for securing serverless applications, managing access controls, and ensuring compliance with regulations. The development of advanced security tools tailored for serverless environments will also be essential.

5. Edge Computing and Serverless

The convergence of edge computing and serverless architecture will enable applications to process data closer to the source, reducing latency and improving performance. This integration will empower developers to build real-time applications that leverage the benefits of both edge computing and serverless computing, providing a seamless user experience.

6. Support for Hybrid and Multi-Cloud Architectures

As organizations seek flexibility and resilience, hybrid and multi-cloud strategies will become more prevalent in serverless architecture. By combining services from different cloud providers, organizations can optimize costs, avoid vendor lock-in, and ensure high availability. Serverless solutions will evolve to support these architectures, enabling seamless interactions between services across clouds.

7. Focus on Observability and Monitoring

As serverless applications become more complex, the need for robust observability and monitoring solutions will grow. Developers will require tools that provide deep insights into performance, usage patterns, and potential issues. The development of advanced monitoring solutions tailored for serverless will enhance the ability to troubleshoot and optimize applications effectively.

8. Community and Knowledge Sharing

The serverless community will continue to grow, fostering collaboration and knowledge sharing. Open-source contributions, meetups, and online forums will play a crucial role in advancing the understanding and adoption of serverless architecture. Organizations that actively engage with the community will benefit from shared experiences and collective insights.

Conclusion for the Book

In this book, we have explored the multifaceted world of serverless architecture, delving into its core principles, benefits, challenges, and real-world applications. From the fundamental concepts of serverless computing to advanced topics such as security, scalability, and multi-cloud strategies, we aimed to provide a comprehensive understanding of how serverless can transform application development and deployment.

As serverless technology continues to evolve, it offers a promising path for developers and organizations seeking agility, scalability, and cost efficiency. By embracing serverless architecture, teams can focus more on innovation and less on infrastructure management, ultimately leading to faster delivery of high-quality applications.

The future of serverless is bright, with ongoing advancements paving the way for new opportunities and possibilities. Whether you are an experienced developer, a cloud architect, or a business leader, understanding serverless architecture will be crucial in navigating the digital landscape of tomorrow.

Thank you for joining us on this journey through serverless architecture. We hope this book has equipped you with the knowledge and insights needed to leverage serverless computing in your projects and initiatives. As you embark on your serverless journey, remember that the landscape is ever-changing, and continuous learning and adaptation will be key to harnessing the full potential of this transformative technology.

Appendix A: Glossary of Serverless Terminology

1. **Serverless Architecture**: A cloud computing model where the cloud provider dynamically manages the allocation and provisioning of servers, allowing developers to focus on code instead of infrastructure.
2. **Function as a Service (FaaS)**: A cloud computing service that allows developers to run code in response to events without managing servers.
3. **Cold Start**: The latency experienced when a serverless function is invoked after being idle, requiring the cloud provider to allocate resources.
4. **Event-Driven Architecture**: A software architecture pattern that promotes the production, detection, consumption of, and reaction to events.
5. **Microservices**: An architectural style that structures an application as a collection of small, loosely coupled services.
6. **API Gateway**: A service that acts as an entry point for API requests, managing traffic, authentication, and routing to backend services.
7. **IAM (Identity and Access Management)**: A framework of policies and technologies that ensures proper access controls are enforced for resources in a cloud environment.
8. **Deployment**: The process of making a software application available for use, typically involving uploading code and configuring settings.
9. **Monitoring**: The continuous observation of application performance

and resource usage to ensure proper operation.
10. **Cost Optimization**: Strategies and practices aimed at reducing operational costs while maintaining performance and reliability.

Appendix B: JavaScript and Node.js Cheat Sheet

JavaScript Basics:

- **Variables**: let, const, var
- **Data Types**: String, Number, Boolean, Object, Array, Null, Undefined
- **Functions**:

javascript

```javascript
function name(params) {
  // code
}
// Arrow functions
const func = (params) => { /* code */ };
```

Node.js Basics:

- **Modules**:

javascript

```javascript
const moduleName = require('module');
```

- **Package Management**:

bash

npm init -y
  npm install package-name

- **Server Creation**:

javascript

```
const http = require('http');
  const server = http.createServer((req, res) => {
  res.writeHead(200, {'Content-Type': 'text/plain'});
  res.end('Hello World\n');
  });
  server.listen(3000, () => {
  console.log('Server running at http://localhost:3000/');
  });
```

Appendix C: AWS Lambda Pricing Model

AWS Lambda pricing is based on the number of requests and the duration of execution:

1. **Requests**: The first 1 million requests per month are free; thereafter, $0.20 per million requests.
2. **Duration**: The duration is calculated from the time your code begins executing until it returns or otherwise terminates, rounded up to the nearest 1 millisecond. Pricing starts at $0.00001667 per GB-second.

Appendix D: Google Cloud Functions Pricing Model

Google Cloud Functions pricing is also based on requests and execution time:

1. **Requests**: The first 2 million invocations per month are free; thereafter, $0.40 per million requests.
2. **Compute Time**: Charged based on the number of GB-seconds used. Pricing starts at $0.0000025 per GB-second.
3. **Outbound Data Transfer**: Charged based on the amount of data sent out from Cloud Functions.

Appendix E: Additional Resources and Reading List

1. **Books**:

- "Serverless Architectures on AWS" by Peter Sbarski
- "Learning AWS Lambda" by Venkatesh-Prasad Ranganath

1. **Online Courses**:

- Coursera: Serverless Architecture with AWS Lambda
- Udemy: Serverless Applications with Node.js and AWS

1. **Documentation**:

- AWS Lambda Documentation
- Google Cloud Functions Documentation

1. **Communities**:

- Stack Overflow (for serverless-related queries)
- Serverless Forum (for discussions and best practices)

1. **Blogs and Articles**:

- AWS and Google Cloud blogs for updates and use cases.
- Medium articles on serverless best practices and architecture.

www.ingramcontent.com/pod-product-compliance
Lightning Source LLC
Chambersburg PA
CBHW060409220526
45465CB00008B/2813